THE PROJECT MANAGER'S DESK REFERENCE

THE PROJECT MANAGER'S DESK REFERENCE

A Comprehensive Guide to Project Planning, Scheduling, Evaluation, and Systems

JAMES P. LEWIS

McGraw-Hill

Boston, Massachusetts   Burr Ridge, Illinois
Dubuque, Iowa   Madison, Wisconsin   New York, New York
San Francisco, California   St. Louis, Missouri

Library of Congress Cataloging-in-Publication Data

Lewis, James P.
 The project manager's desk reference / by James P. Lewis. -- 2d
ed.
   p. cm.
 Includes bibliographical references.
 ISBN 0-07-134750-X
 1. Industrial project management. 2. Industrial development
projects--Management. 3. Scheduling (Management) I. Title.
HD69.P75L49 1999
658.4'04--dc21   99-32834
                      CIP

McGraw-Hill

*A Division of The **McGraw-Hill** Companies*

5 6 7 8 9 BKM BKM 9 0 9 8 7 6 5 4 3 2 1

ISBN 0-07-134750-X

The sponsoring editor for this book was *Catherine Schwent*, the editing supervisor
was *John M. Morriss*, and the production supervisor was *Tina Cameron*. It was set in
Palatino by *Judy Brown*.

McGraw-Hill books are available at special quantity discounts to use as premiums
and sales promotions, or for use in corporate training programs. For more
information, please write to the Director of Special Sales, McGraw-Hill, 11 West 19th
Street, New York, NY 10011. Or contact your local bookstore.

This publication is designed to provide accurate and authoritative information in
regard to the subject matter covered. It is sold with the understanding that neither
the author nor the publisher is engaged in rendering legal, accounting, or other
professional service. If legal advice or other expert assistance is required, the
services of a competent professional should be sought.
—*From a Declaration of Principles jointly adopted by a Committee of the American Bar
Association and a Committee of Publishers.*

This book is dedicated

to

Eleanor Greek

Teacher, Counselor, Friend

and to the memory of my mother

Hazel Inez McDaniel

April 30, 1919–August 6, 1999

CONTENTS

Chapter 21

Managing Business-to-Business Marketing and Communication Projects Successfully   387

Chapter 22

The Need for Systems Thinking in Project Management   409

Chapter 23

Understanding Systems Thinking   423

Chapter 24

How to Apply Systems Thinking in Managing Projects   437

LIST OF FIGURES

PREFACE

As I wrote in the first edition of this book, I have always liked handbooks. Even if they just sit on the shelf and I never read them, there is the knowledge that I could find almost anything I need to know in one of those great, massive books, which should probably be sold by weight more than by content. So when I was asked to compile the first version of this book, I jumped at the chance. I had visions of incorporating everything—including the kitchen sink—in my book. I quickly realized that if I did so, I wouldn't have a handbook, but a multivolume encyclopedia. The subject of project management is simply too broad to include everything in one book. So this is of necessity an eclectic choice of content. I believe it covers the core knowledge that you must have to be successful as a project manager.

I have been very gratified to hear from readers of the first edition of the handbook. I appreciate the letters and e-mails that people have sent me from all over the world. In addition, although I did not write the book to be used as a textbook, I have found that a number of universities have used it for that purpose. It is definitely written for the practitioner, so I would hope that college students have gained some practical insight into project management, which will be useful to them immediately upon graduation.

This revision has left some material more or less intact, but most content has been updated to make it clearer, to add my current thinking on the topic, or to simply add new aspects of project management. I dropped the big bibliography from the end, simply because very few people have time to read all that much, and feedback from readers suggested that it was a waste of pages. I have added some material on systems thinking, and have tried to arrange all of the material in categories that are more logical than was the case in the first edition.

Three of my colleagues have contributed chapters to the book. One chapter was in the original edition—the material on progress payments written by Quentin Fleming. Another chapter was contributed by my friend Julian Stubbs, a marketing expert from Great Britain, who lives in Sweden. His chapter addresses an area that is currently neglected by most project management books. The only real pain I felt in doing the book was in changing Julian's British English to American English (though the British would argue that American *English* is an oxymoron). Finally, there is the chapter on developing the world class project management organization, contributed by Bob Wysocki. Bob and I are doing research on what makes a good project manager, as well as what makes an organization successful, so this chapter is an early offering that will no doubt evolve over time. I want to thank each of these authors for sharing their expertise in this work.

I have worked with John Morriss, the production editor for this project, on previous books, and John is a professional project manager. I want to thank him for his understanding, patience, and excellent work in making my books as polished as they can be.

Many of the other people involved, I don't know, but my acquisitions editors, Jeffery Krames and Catherine Schwent, were very supportive throughout this project.

As usual, my wife, Lea Ann, has contributed greatly to the quality of this book. As usual, she was at the back end of this project, trying to work to the deadline even though I was late with some of my material.

I hope *The Project Manager's Desk Reference* is just what you have been looking for. Feel free to contact me at my website and give me feedback. The url is www.lewisinstitute.com, and you can send me mail at jlewis@lewisinstitute.com. You can also contact me by phone or through snail mail at the address below. Thanks for buying the book, and good luck with your projects.

Jim Lewis

302 Chestnut Mountain Drive
Vinton, Virginia 24179
Tel. 540-345-7850

September 1999

THE PROJECT MANAGER'S DESK REFERENCE

INTRODUCTION AND OVERVIEW

1

CHAPTER

Overview of Project Management

CONCEPTS OF PROJECT MANAGEMENT

Until everyone in an organization has a shared understanding of what is meant by projects and project management, misunderstandings, conflicts, and miscommunication are bound to exist. One of my associates conducted training for a government agency and found that administrators were using the term "program management" to mean what most people would call department management. This chapter will establish definitions of some terms and introduce general concepts about project management.

WHAT IS A PROJECT?

In recent years writers like Tom Peters have suggested that in typical organizations as much as 50 percent of the work is done in a project format.[1] This makes project management

---

[1] Liberation Management.

an important discipline and one that is receiving increasing attention. Yet many senior managers have had no formal training in project management, and do not understand how the discipline differs from general management. For many years business schools did not recognize project management as a specialized discipline,

> **pro • ject:** A one-time, multitask job that has clearly defined starting and ending dates, a specific scope of work to be performed, a budget, and a specified level of performance to be achieved.

and now that they do, we are experiencing a mad rush for everyone to get on board.

The text box provides a crisp definition of what a project is, but if you ever come across one that conforms to the textbook definition, please contact me. I'd like to write a case study on it! Many projects do not have clear starting points. They just "ooze up out of the mud," so to speak. They certainly don't have clear ending points. Like that famous pink bunny in the battery commercial, they just "keep on going, and going, and going." If you are the unfortunate manager of such a project, you begin to think you are going to make a career of it.

Note also that, to qualify as a project, a job must have multiple tasks. Performing a single task over and over does not qualify as a project. I say this because when people tell me they are working on 43 different projects, I often find that what they really mean are tasks.

Following are some examples and counterexamples of projects.

Examples

- ◆ Developing a new product or service

♦ Building a bridge, house, road, runway, or other structure

♦ Writing software

♦ Installing a new manufacturing process, cell, or assembly line

♦ Writing a book

♦ Developing a new marketing plan

Counterexamples

♦ Processing claims, orders, or invoices

♦ Manufacturing something

♦ Cooking in a restaurant

♦ Driving a delivery truck over the same route every day

♦ In short, anything of a purely repetitive nature

Another definition of projects that I like is the one offered by J. M. Juran (1989), the quality expert. He says that a project is a problem scheduled for solution. This definition makes us realize that project management is problem solving on a large scale. However, the word "problem" invariably means some-

> A project is a problem scheduled for solution.
> — J. M. Juran

thing bad. When people tell you that they have a problem, you know bad news will follow.

However, I am using the word "problem" in this context to have a much broader meaning. Developing a new product or software program is a problem, but a very positive one to have. So problem does not always mean something negative, although it will sometimes have that meaning, such as in an environmental cleanup project.

One of the common difficulties in running a project is that insufficient time is spent at the beginning of the job defining exactly what problem is to be solved. This can have the unfortunate consequence of developing the right solution for the wrong problem. Guidelines will be presented in the planning chapters of this book on how to avoid such an error.

PROJECT STAKEHOLDERS

Before we go any further, it might be useful to examine the stakeholders involved in any project. First of all, note the definition of *stakeholder*—anyone who has a vested interest in the project. This includes customers, suppliers, contributors, project sponsors, managers, and sometimes local citizens when the project involves public works.

> **stake • hold • er:** Anyone who has a vested interest in the project.

A *customer* is the user of the project deliverables. In some cases the customer is the person who ordered and will pay for the project, as in the case of construction of a building, home, or road. In other cases, the customer is the person who buys products developed by the project and later manufactured by the company. The quality improvement movement stressed the importance of meeting customer needs as a condition for success in business, and I would contend that this is still an issue for many projects—not truly meeting customer needs. More on this in the chapter on project planning in Section Two.

> **cus • to • mer:** The user of the project deliverables.

The project *sponsor* is the person who actually orders the project to be done in the first place. This person could be the customer, but in many cases it will be a third party, such as a marketing director who orders that a new product be developed. The sponsor is responsible for ensuring that the project is properly budgeted, that the schedule is accept-

> **spon • sor:** The person who orders that a project be done.

able, and that the team has the resources needed to achieve the desired results.

The *project manager* is the person with overall responsibility for making sure that the project is completed on time, within budget, within scope, and at the desired level of performance. In too many cases, the project manager is given too weak a

> **pro • ject man • a • ger:** The person who has total responsibility for ensuring that the project is completed on time, within budget, within scope, and at the desired performance level.

role to fully control these outcomes.

DEFINITION OF PROJECT MANAGEMENT

Project management involves three major categories of activities aimed at achieving project objectives. These are planning, scheduling, and controlling. Each of these activities is treated in a major section of this book. For now, we will examine the four primary objectives

> **pro • ject man • age • ment:** The planning, scheduling, and controlling of those activities that must be performed to achieve project objectives.

that exist in all projects. Specifically, project work must be completed:

P → At the desired *performance* level

C → Within *cost* or budget constraints

T → On *time*

S → For a given magnitude or *scope* of work

The first three of these are referred to as the **P, C,** and **T** aspects of project management. Some people call them good, fast, and cheap (P = good; C = cheap; T = fast). The **S** aspect, or scope, defines the magnitude. Note that there are several cost components to a project. These are labor, capital equipment, and supplies or materials. If we consider only labor costs, then all four of the variables are interdependent, as illustrated by the following mathematical relationship:

$$C = f(P, T, S)$$

In words, the equation says, "Cost is a *function* of performance, time, and scope." (This does not mean that we can forget about capital equipment or materials; rather, these costs do not have a direct relationship to the other variables. They are generally tracked separately from labor costs.) Ideally, the functional relationship could be expressed as a specific mathematical equation, such as:

$$C = 2P + 3T + 4S$$

However, the exact relationship is almost never known. The values for all four are being estimated. Nevertheless, we know that they are related, because if you try to change one of them, at least one of the others will change. For example, if you increase the scope of the project while holding P and T constant, you will certainly increase the cost to do the job.

Figure 1.1. illustrates the concept. Note that performance, cost, and time are the sides of the triangle, while scope is the area. From geometry, we know that if the lengths of the sides are given, we can determine the area or scope of the triangle. Alternatively, if we know the lengths of two

F I G U R E 1.1

Relationship between P, C, T, and S

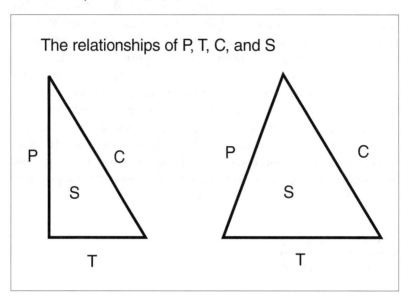

The relationships of P, T, C, and S

sides and the area, we can determine the length of the third side. This leads to a very important practical aspect of managing projects: Values for any three of the variables can be dictated, but the value of the fourth one will be determined by the relationships among them—the constraints of the area equation.

I like to say it this way: Whoever assigns the project to me (usually the project sponsor) can specify three of the variables, but I get to pick the fourth one. For example, if the sponsor tells me that the job must be completed by a certain date, at a specific performance level, and within a defined scope, then I should be allowed to tell the sponsor what I need (cost) in order to achieve those results. If the sponsor replies that this is more than he can afford, then a trade-off must be made in one of the other variables—usually scope. If we reduce scope, we can do the project for a lower cost. It is only when the sponsor insists that the job be done for a cost less than the project manager specifies that we are headed for possible failure. We can certainly *try* to find ways to do the project for less money, and that is always a challenge for a project manager, but to have all four targets dictated arbitrarily is a recipe for disaster—for everyone involved.

Generally speaking, the cost of the project will increase as P, T, and S increase, except in the case of trying to crash the project. To crash a project means to try to complete it in the absolutely minimum time possible. Naturally the usual approach to getting projects done really fast is to apply more resources. New people can be added or, if no more people are available, existing staff can work more hours per day

F I G U R E 1.2

Time-Cost Trade-off Curve

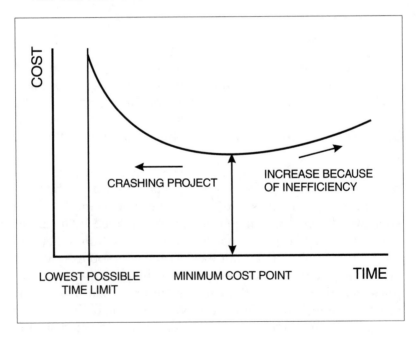

(overtime). Doing so then leads to a time-cost trade-off curve like the one shown in Figure 1.2.

Notice that crashing a project results in a curve that rises very sharply. This is because you quickly reach a point of diminishing returns as you add more people to the project—people get in each other's way, the work can be subdivided only so much, you need more communication as you add people, and so on. Furthermore, there is a lower boundary below which you can't go, no matter how many people you add. I call this the "forbidden zone."

There's more. If you add people to an already late project, you are likely to make it later, because the new people must be trained and someone on the project has to do it. The training period causes productivity to drop, which leads to overtime work to keep up, which re-

> **BROOKS' LAW**
>
> Adding people to an already late project may only make it later.
>
> — F. P. Brooks

sults in fatigue, which causes productivity to drop, which . . . As you can see, this is a vicious loop that rapidly spirals out of control. The principle was originally expounded by Brooks (1975) in his book on software development, and I believe it applies to a lot of other projects as well.

One of the most common problems that project managers face is an increase in scope of the project as time passes. People think of things that did not initially occur to them. Or they do not take enough time at the outset to properly define the problem being solved.

Unfortunately, the scope tends to increase in small increments, rather than in large ones, making such changes a bit invisible. Such incremental changes are called *scope creep*. The difficulty is that many people suffer from amnesia at the end of a project, which means that they try to hold the project manager accountable for original targets in spite of the fact that the scope increased. For everyone's protection, scope creep must be controlled—a typic covered in Section Four.

More and more organizations are demanding that project managers find ways to cut the time it takes to do the job, while simultaneously reducing the cost—and while leaving performance and scope alone. In many cases, the cut is by 50 percent or more. As an example, U.S. auto makers have been challenged repeatedly to reduce the time required to design a car. At one time they needed six to eight years. Then some Japanese firms reduced the cycle to about three years, and American companies had to follow suit.

Remember that when you crash a project, you do so by throwing resources at it, which increases costs significantly. Yet here project managers are being challenged to reduce *both* time and cost! Is this an impossible demand?

Not at all.

To see why, consider an old saying from behavioral science: "If you always do what you've always done, you'll always get what you always got." In other words, if what you have been doing does not get the desired result, change the *process*. In fact, that is what formal project management is all about.

No doubt you know managers who have been getting projects completed successfully for years, without using this formal project management stuff. The problem is, you don't know how much better they could have done *with* formal methods. Some managers have estimated that as much as one-third of the labor cost in projects is rework. Under that condition, one of every three individuals on the job is spending full time just redoing what the other two people did wrong in the first place! If you reduce the rework, you have just improved productivity by a corresponding amount.

Formal project management can help you achieve that result.

How? By recognizing that much of the rework is caused by poor project planning. If you do a better job of planning, then you will see a drop in rework.

This is, in fact, one of the fastest ways to show that you are making progress with project management. Unless you have reliable baseline data for previous projects, it is hard to show that you are getting better at managing them. However, if you start measuring rework, you should be able to show a decline over time, which is a good sign that you are making progress.

THE PERFORMANCE OBJECTIVE

The often forgotten objective in project management is the performance target. This target is not just a technical specification. It is a translation of the customer's needs into performance criteria, and that translation may be a technical specification. As I stated previously, failing to meet the customer's needs is a recipe for failure, even if you meet your schedule, budget, and scope requirements.

THE PROJECT LIFE CYCLE

As a rule, the project life cycle consists of four to six phases. For a six-phase model, the phases are concept, definition, design, development or construction, application, and postcompletion. For a four-phase model, the phases are: concept, planning, execution, and close-out. The character of the program changes in each life-cycle phase. See Figure 1.3.

There are two major pitfalls in the life cycle of a project. The first is that the concept for the project is accepted as the definition, leading to the outcome mentioned previously—namely, the right solution is developed for the wrong problem.

The second pitfall is at postcompletion. Note that a final review should be conducted for the project. The aim is to learn what was done well in the job and what might need to be improved. However, this stage is often aborted. At the 1998 Frontiers Conference on project management, the keynote speaker asked an audience of 400, "How many of you

The Project Life Cycle

Project Life Cycle

Concept	Definition	Design	Development	Application	Post-Completion
• Marketing Input	• Specify objectives	• Architectural, engineering	• First units	• Install and field test	• Final de-staffing
• Feasibility Studies	• Establish PCTS targets	• Design reviews	• Begin sales campaigns	• Begin de-staffing	• Final "les-sons-learned" review
• Survey of Competition	• Quality Assurance procedures	• Assessment reports	• Quality control procedures	• Advertising begins	• Final reports
	• Set up control system	• Revise cost & perform-ance targets		• De-bug and redesign	• Closeout
	• Establish project organization				
	• Set up project notebook				

Level of Planning Required Over Time

have a mandate that you must do a lessons-learned review at the end of your projects?"

About 10 or 12 people raised their hands.

He then asked a very poignant question: "How many of you are required to show management how you will avoid making the same mistakes on your next project that you made on your last one?"

Only two hands went up.

This is tremendously important! As the adage goes, "People who do not know history are doomed to make the same mistakes again."

I think there are a couple of reasons that people don't conduct lessons-learned reviews. First, by the time they finish the project, they are anxious to get on with the next job (or maybe they already have). Second, they may be reluctant to face the fact that some areas need improvement. In our win-at-all-costs, take-no-prisoners culture, admitting that you need to do better is almost unthinkable. Perhaps, too, failure to face such issues may be caused by not wanting to embarrass anyone. Nevertheless, no matter how well a job has been done, there is always room for improvement, and a lessons-learned review should be conducted in that spirit. Naturally, any climate of blame or punishment simply increases the likelihood that no one will conduct an "honest" evaluation of a project.

THE PROJECT MANAGEMENT SYSTEM

The project management system consists of seven components, as shown in Figure 1.4. If any one of these is defective, then the management of projects will suffer.

The Human System

The human system is placed at the bottom of the pyramid because it forms the foundation for everything else. A project manager must deal with all the "people issues." These

F I G U R E   1.4

The Project Management System

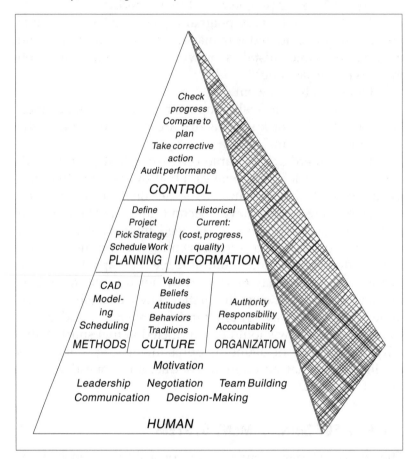

include communication, team building, conflict management and resolution, motivation, and, yes, that "dirty word" *politics!* The list covers only a handful of the issues that must be handled.

Dealing with people is a major function that a project manager must perform. This is partly because project managers have a lot of responsibility and (usually) very little authority (or none at all). That is almost a given in project management. So the only way to get anything done is through using people skills. These include persuasion, influence, negotiating, and sometimes just plain begging.

I can almost hear the groaning now from the techies. As a former engineer, I know that the human element is not typically one of our strong suits. In fact, some techies complain bitterly that they hate the people problems they have to deal with. To them, I suggest that they rethink their careers. They don't want to be project managers. Or any other kind for that matter. You are not likely to be good at something you hate, and in my view, life is too short to spend doing something you hate. Also, you can't get around it.

So if you hate dealing with people, have a heart-to-heart talk with your boss and state up-front that you don't want to be a project manager. You would rather be a techie for the rest of your life. If that doesn't work, change jobs! I'm serious. But then it's your life, and your career, and you have to make your own choices.

If you are one of those individuals who don't actually hate dealing with people, but feel that you need to improve your skills, then hang in there. Everything listed in the box in Figure 1.4 can be learned—even leadership. That is, it can all be learned if you really want to. So set yourself a career objective to develop those skills, and read Chapter 19, by my colleague Bob Wysocki, on how to go about it.

Culture

Related to people issues is culture. Every organization has a culture, which is the sum total of values, beliefs, attitudes, behaviors, and traditions. In fact, one way you can tell when people are talking about culture is that they say, "We don't do it that way around here."

Broadly speaking, there is nothing right or wrong, good or bad about cultures. But when people from different cultures interact, it often results in misunderstanding, conflict, and downright fighting. Perhaps a few examples will help.

My wife and I have hosted exchange students from several different countries, for 10 months at a time, partly because we are interested in cultures. Our first guest was a Japanese student named Yukiko. When she arrived, I asked her how to say things in Japanese. "Well, yes is *hai,* and no is *e-a*," she said, "but we don't like to say no very much."

At the time, I didn't fully appreciate what she was telling me. Later I learned that the Japanese consider saying no directly to be fairly rude. For instance, I was in a Japanese restaurant one evening when a fellow customer ordered a beer by name. The waitress, who was Japanese, said, "Maybe we don't have that kind. Maybe you'd prefer a different kind." Now she knew very well that she did not have the beer he asked for, but she could not say so directly. She had to soften it a bit.

The "roundabout no" is very mystifying to Americans, who are used to being direct. So we sometimes get into trouble with Japanese business deals. "I thought we agreed on this," says the American negotiator, after finding an apparent violation of what she thought was agreed to. "Oh, we agreed on *this*," says her Japanese colleague. Such misunderstandings can be a serious source of conflict.

My favorite experience with culture shock occurred in Malaysia. After I completed a day of teaching at Petronas, the oil company, a company driver pulled up in a van to take me to the airport. I started to get into the back seat, which is common in the United States. He looked back at me and said, "Sir, you're kind of fat. You'd be more comfortable up here in the front."

It was all I could do to keep from laughing. Fortunately, I had done my homework and I knew that to many people from Asian cultures being fat is not a stigma, as it is in our American "twiggy" society. It is actually a sign of affluence, because over several thousand years, only the wealthy could afford a diet that would allow them to be fat.

What I found funny was to imagine my driver taking a job with a U.S. limo company and doing to some unwary person what he did to me. The person complains and the driver gets fired for insulting the customer. He is totally bewildered. "What happened?" he says. "I was only trying to be helpful." Which he was.

Organization

Every organization must define the authority, accountability, and responsibility conferred on each member of that organization. As I mentioned previously, project managers always

Every organization must define authority, responsibility, and accountability.

have a lot of responsibility and little authority. It has almost always been that way, and probably will continue.

However, there are two kinds of authority. One is to tell people what to do and expect them to do it. That one a project manager will never have. And it doesn't matter very much in the first place. Ask any CEO of any company, "You have a lot of authority, don't you?" The reply will be yes. Then ask, "Does your authority guarantee that people do what you want done?" The response turns to no. Then what does persuade people to do what a CEO wants? Every CEO I have asked has said, "In the end analysis, people have to want to do it, and my job is to get them to want to do it."

I call that influence.

If a CEO has to use influence to get things done, you and I can hope to do no better. That's why you need those people skills listed at the bottom of the pyramid.

The second kind of authority is decision-making authority. This one I consider a major problem for many project managers, especially when it comes to decisions to spend money. Some project managers can spend no more than $100 without approvals. Yet they have project budgets of hundreds of thousands of dollars.

They are being given mixed messages by their companies. The first message tells them, "We trust you, because we've put you in charge of a project that will spend a lot of our money." The second message, however, is, "If you want to spend any of it, you have to get it approved first." To me, this message says, "We don't trust you."

Now when two messages differ, the negative one takes priority over the positive one. In other words, these managers are being told that the company doesn't trust them.

If you follow my process for managing projects, you will find that the implementation plan must be approved, and this plan will include a budget for the project. After that, so long as the project manager is spending in accordance with the already approved plan, why should any more approvals be needed? Doing so is a total waste of everyone's time.

Methods

Methods are the "tools of the trade." For project managers, the only issue that usually comes up here is scheduling software. I fully understand the need for some standardization in organizations, because information systems (IS) departments can support only so many software programs. However, one size does not always fit all—in clothing *or* in software—and insisting that everyone use a low-end package will cause major problems for managers of very large construction projects. Alternatively, insisting that everyone use a high-end package because a few people manage large projects is to provide everyone with a sledgehammer when only a mallet is needed.

One solution to this problem, adopted by a few companies, is to have one person do all scheduling for a group of project managers. That way the scheduler can become intimately familiar with the high-end package, and all that the project managers have to know is its capability. The approach works very well and saves a lot of money. Furthermore, it frees project managers from the drudgery of long hours at a computer trying to massage a schedule, and it allows them to concentrate on the important things that they should be doing, such as dealing with political issues.

Control

For the moment, we will skip to the top of the pyramid and then backtrack. When you get right down to it, the reason for managing is always to maintain control. You are expected to control the application of scarce resources to achieve desired objectives.

> **con • trol:** Control is exercised by comparing where you are to where you are supposed to be, then taking corrective action when discrepancies are found.

The question is, how is this done?

The answer is partly provided by the definition of control. Control is exercised by comparing where you are to where you are supposed to be, and taking corrective action when discrepancies are found. It is clear that this is a feedback systems definition of control, as opposed to a power or authority definition.

This means that the two boxes under "**control**" in Figure 1.4 play a vital role in allowing a project manager to exercise control over a project.

Planning

It is the plan that tells you where you are supposed to be in the first place. Without a plan, you have no idea if you are doing okay or not. Thus, if you have no plan, you have no control. I consider this to be one of the most important principles of project management, because it clearly explains why planning is not an option—it is a necessity.

> **PRINCIPLE:** If you have no plan, you can not have control—by definition!

Information

If you don't know where you are, you certainly can't exercise control. This is a problem for most organizations. They have excellent information systems for inventory control, order tracking, and so on, but no system for tracking projects. The reason is simple—they didn't know they needed one. For the time being, you will most likely have to track each project manually. That isn't too big a problem for most project managers.

You will also need to estimate how long a task will take. Organizations don't have history databases. If you want to estimate how long a task will take, your best starting point is data on how long it took previously. All too often, this information exists only in the memories of individuals, and these are notoriously faulty. I can hardly remember what I did yesterday, much less what I did three months ago. So historical data really *must* be captured and recorded. We will discuss this issue more in the Control chapters of the book.

2

CHAPTER

A Model for Managing Projects

DOES ONE SIZE FIT ALL?

It is fair to ask whether one approach to managing projects will work for *all* jobs, regardless of content. Can the same approach be used in construction, research and development, marketing, and product development? The answer, I believe, is a resounding yes! The reason is that project management is a disciplined way of thinking about a job, and that thinking process should be followed in any project, regardless of the content, size, or complexity.

> **PRINCIPLE:** Project management is a disciplined way of thinking about a job, and this way of thinking should be followed in all projects, regardless of content, size, or complexity.

F I G U R E 2.1

The Lewis Method of Project Management

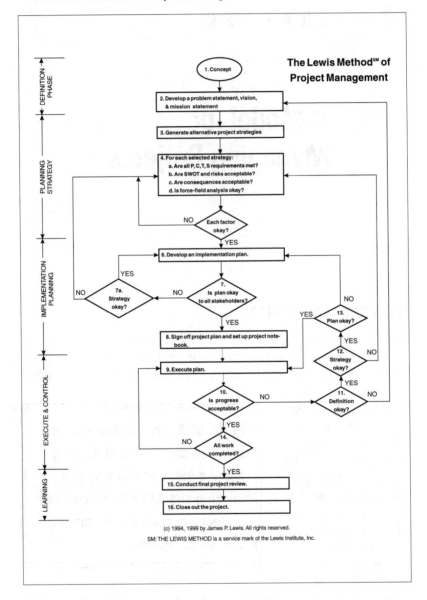

Over the past 20 years, after looking at projects of all kinds, I have developed an approach that I call the Lewis Method^{SM} of project management. It is represented by the flowchart in Figure 2.1.

Before discussing the flowchart, I think it is useful to differentiate between my method and a project management *methodology*. My method represents the overall *process* used to manage a project. It is robust, because it specifies or includes the principles that guide the project manager in his or her practice. A *methodology*, however, spells out the nitty-gritty procedures to be followed in carrying out the overall process. It tells what forms are to be filled out, who must sign approvals, what meetings must be held, and so on. This means that the methodology will differ from organization to organization, while the overall process remains the same.

People are often confused by the fact that many projects contain projects within projects. One way to relieve the confusion is to call these smaller jobs *subprojects*. Alternatively, you can think of the total job as a program and all the components as individual projects. This terminology is clarified in the section on work breakdown structures in Chapter 6.

Consider a research and development (R&D) project. You could actually deal with this as two projects—the first being a research project with its own goals, deliverables, project team, and so on, and the second being a development project with different goals and deliverables, and perhaps even a different team.

You will notice that the first real action to be taken by a project team is to develop a definition of the problem to be solved (see step 2 in Figure 2.1). This can be a project in itself! The mission is to define the problem. In a case like this, the definition might be stated as, "We don't know the problem that we are dealing with at this point," and the mission may be, "To define the problem to be solved." The deliverable would then be a crisp definition of the problem that everyone could agree with.

OVERVIEW OF THE MODEL

Because the model in Figure 2.1 represents the complete process of managing a project, to explain the steps in detail would be to write the entire book as a single chapter. Therefore, this chapter will offer only a general overview of the steps, and subsequent chapters will flesh them out in detail.

Steps 1–8 constitute the planning process, including project scheduling. Steps 9–16 specify the steps involved in monitoring and controlling progress. The model is designed to prevent the more common problems that seem to occur in projects, but cannot capture the complexity of the entire process without becoming unwieldy.

Step 1: A Concept Is Developed

As shown in the project life-cycle model in Chapter 1, a project begins with a concept. Someone identifies a need for something. The problem is that a concept can be very vague. The identified need has not been thought through very thoroughly. For that reason, the concept stage is followed by the definition stage.

Step 2: Develop a Problem, Vision, and Mission Statement

The next step is to develop a good definition of the problem that is intended to be solved by execution of the project. This is probably the single greatest hurdle that must be overcome in the entire process. Insistence on writing a problem statement is usually met with skepticism, the reaction being, "We all know what the problem is. Let's get on with it. This is a waste of time!"

> ☞ A project is a problem scheduled for solution.

Many examples described in the literature show that this is often not the case. I will cite only one. In their book *Breakthrough Thinking,* Nadler and Hibino (1990) tell about a company whose distributors complained that it was sending them damaged goods. The company hired an efficiency expert to investigate, and she accepted the definition of the problem as offered—to reduce damage to goods. To solve the problem, the expert designed a computer-controlled conveyor to load trucks. She estimated that the conveyor system would cost $60,000 per warehouse location, with savings yielding a payback of about eight months. Since the company owned 24 warehouses, the total investment was to be $1.44 million.

The vice president was inclined to accept the expert's recommendation, but decided (perhaps for political reasons) to ask the internal industrial engineering group for a second opinion. The assignment was given to a staff engineer fresh out of college. He studied the situation. However, rather than accept the definition of the problem as given, he asked a new question: "What are we really trying to achieve?" His answer was, "We are trying to find the best way of distributing our products to the marketplace." From that problem statement, he completed the study and prepared a presentation for management.

When time came for the presentation, the vice president asked, "Well, do we go ahead and spend the $1.44 million?"

The young engineer responded, "No, sir. I think you should sell all the warehouses."

It turned out that he did not mean selling *all* the warehouses—just most of them. The company ultimately followed his recommendation and sold all but a few regional warehouses, each stocked by air shipments directly from the company's manufacturing plants. Eliminating local warehouses simplified freight transfers so there were fewer physical handling points for each shipment, and consequently less likelihood of damaging goods. The solution saved the company hundreds of millions of dollars each year, and eventually forced its competitors to restructure along the same lines.

This example drives home a most important point about problem solving: *The way a problem is defined determines the solution possibilities.* It is this fact that makes it so important to define the problem correctly before any planning is done.

> **PRINCIPLE:** The way a problem is defined determines the solution possibilities.

Chapters 25–27 present more complete approaches to problem-solving methods that should be applied at this step.

Step 3: Generate Alternative Project Strategies

As the saying goes, "There is more than one way to skin a cat." With most projects, there will be more than one approach that can be applied to achieve the desired result. For example, a house can be built from the ground up by constructing every single element at the site, or it can be assembled from prefabricated parts. Further, it can be built entirely by one contractor, or various parts can be subcontracted (e.g., plumbing, wiring, roofing).

In technological projects, proven technology may be applied to reduce risk. Or "cutting edge" technology may be used to achieve a competitive advantage, in spite of the fact that risk is increased.

The common approach to be used here is to brainstorm a list of available strategies and then select one. Creativity-enhancing methods can be employed to increase the likelihood of developing a good strategy. Edward de Bono is considered by many to be the world's leading expert on creativity, and his 1992 book, *Serious Creativity*, presents his approach in detail. The interested reader should consult that book.

Step 4: Select and Evaluate the Strategy

After a list of strategies has been developed, one must be selected. A strategy will be considered suitable only if it passes four tests summarized in the questions below. These questions cannot always be answered in a quantitative way, but the analysis is important in identifying potential problem areas before time is wasted developing a detailed plan.

Step 4a: Are P, C, T, S Requirements Met?

This test determines whether the approach meets all performance, cost, time, and scope requirements. In other words, will it do the job?

Naturally, this is a judgment call, but experience can usually serve as a guide to answer the question. However, it may be necessary to do some broad-brush implementation planning before the question can be answered definitively. For that reason, if the implementation plan is not okay at step 7, the strategy must be examined to determine if it is acceptable. If it is not, a new one must be developed and the process repeated.

Step 4b: Are Identified Risks Acceptable?

This step is intended to identify any risks that might cause the approach to fail. Some managers are opposed to doing a risk analysis because it causes people to begin *thinking negatively*, and they fear that morale problems will result. That might be the case if such an analysis is not done correctly. To simply ask, "What could go wrong?" and leave it at that would very likely cause people to consider the approach unviable. However, I do not conduct a risk analysis in that manner. For those risks that are considered serious, I ask, "What might we do if it happens?" In other words, we must identify *contingencies* for every risk, if at all possible. Using this approach, risks are being *managed*, rather than just being identified. The procedure is covered in detail in Chapter 17.

Step 4c: Are the Consequences Acceptable?

Whenever action is taken to solve a problem, peripheral effects may occur. These are *unintended consequences* of the steps taken. Such unintended consequences result in new problems being created. The question is, then, whether we can live with those consequences. If not, we must consider a different approach to the project.

As an example of unintended consequences, consider the enactment of legislation some years ago to make streets more accessible to handicapped Americans. The law required that ramps be placed at street corners so that people in wheelchairs could cross the street without having to negotiate difficult curbs.

This solved the problem for wheelchair-bound individuals, but created problems for blind people, who use their canes at intersections to feel for the curb—which has now

In taking any action to solve a problem, peripheral effects may occur. These can be called *unintended consequences.*

been removed! It also makes sidewalks more hazardous for sighted individuals who do not always spot sudden drops in pavement level.

Another example of unintended consequences is a sale to reduce inventory levels. When the sale ends, some customers perceive the product to be of lower value than it was before the sale.

In a project context, we know that projects may have environmental impacts that are undesirable. Or in a product development situation, pursuing "safe" technology may achieve a speedy time-to-market, but result in a competitive disadvantage. In addition, it may cause the organization to fall behind in the development of its technological capability.

As was mentioned previously, if such consequences are not acceptable, then a different approach (strategy) for the project should be considered.

Step 4d: Does the Strategy Pass a Force-Field Analysis?

Of the four tests that a strategy must pass, the force-field analysis is probably the hardest to quantify. Nevertheless, it is well worth doing. As shown in Figure 2.2, a force-field analysis looks a little like a risk analysis, but it is very different. On the right side of the figure are those forces in the environment that can be expected to *assist* in the implementation of the project, while on the left side are those forces that might *hinder* or *resist* its implementation.

Notice that these are mostly social forces. They result from the attitudes that people have toward certain approaches. For example, we sometimes hear people say in organizations, "We don't do things that way around here." If a project manager is attempting to run a project using an approach that a powerful member of management considers out of line with "how things are done around here," then it is likely that the manager's resistance will cause the approach to fail.

The factor labeled NIH means "not invented here." Sometimes people resist a particular approach simply because

Force-Field Analysis

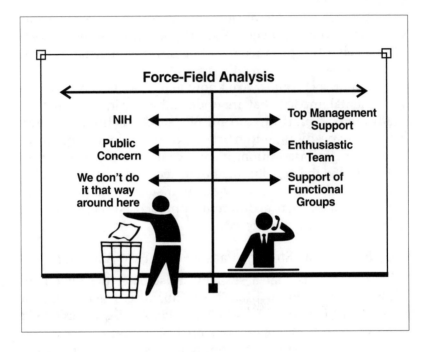

they did not think of it. Although such resistance may be petty, it can sabotage a project, and should not be underestimated.

Once both positive and negative forces have been identified, force-field analysis calls for the strengths of all forces to be estimated and tallied up, with the understanding that the sum of the positive forces must be greater than the sum of the negatives—or the approach will not work. The usual procedure for measuring the forces is to rate them on a 10-point scale, then multiply by a weighting factor (assuming that they are not all of equal importance), and sum them.

In my opinion, this is an exercise in futility. It appears to give a measurement to something that I believe usually is unmeasurable. For that reason, I do not advocate the practice.

Rather, I suggest simply trying to deal with the negative forces.

There are three approaches that can be used to deal with forces identified in the analysis. They are:

1. Strengthen the positive forces so they are definitely stronger than the negatives.
2. Find ways to get around the negatives.
3. Find some way to weaken or eliminate the negatives (called "neutralizing them").

What people do in case after case is to choose option 1. They try to overcome the negative forces with stronger positive forces. This is in spite of the lesson taught by countless experiences: *The harder you try to overcome a negative force, the stronger it becomes!* The principle has been understood by systems theorists for years, yet it seems to elude the rest of us. The "push-resist" interaction typifies all conflict and competitive situations, and the stronger one side pushes, the more the other side resists. All you have is escalation.

The most helpful way to deal with forces is to try to neutralize them. Find some way to make them go away. For example, if someone thinks the selected strategy is bad, ask that person, "What would I have to do to convince you that this is a good approach?"

There are two possible responses. The person can tell you to "forget it." You will never be able to convince that person that the approach is sound. If so, you may have to forget trying to be persuasive and decide whether to proceed or choose a different option.

However, I will always ask the person, "Are you sure there is *nothing* I can do? That's pretty heavy." Usually this gets the second response, which is for the person to say, "Well, I suppose if you can do this (explaining what it will take) I would be convinced." The nice thing about this approach is that you now know what it takes to "make the sale." You no longer have to hunt for the selling proposition. If you can do what the person suggests, you are "home free."

Step 5: Are the Above Factors All Okay?

If your selected strategy has passed each of the four tests, you can consider it to be tentatively acceptable. It is still possible for problems to arise during implementation planning that force you to reject the approach, but this is not highly likely. There is one caution: Very analytical individuals sometimes go into "analysis paralysis" at this step in planning a project. The purpose of these steps is not to identify every single risk or consequence that may exist, but to assess some of the more likely ones. Project managers may have to state their limits a number of times with skeptical or negatively oriented members of the proposed project team.

Step 6: Develop an Implementation Plan

Up to this point, the planning process has answered the broad question of what strategy will be employed to manage the project. Now the strategy must be translated into specific steps to be taken to get the job done. These steps will define *what* is done, by *whom,* for *how long,* at *what cost,* and so forth. An overriding concern will be deciding how to translate customer needs into solutions. During this stage a work breakdown structure will be developed, a schedule using CPM or PERT will be formulated, resources will be allocated, responsibilities assigned, control systems developed, and so on. How this is done is the subject of Chapters 3–10.

Step 7: Is the Plan Okay to All Stakeholders?

A stakeholder is defined as anyone who has a vested interest in the project. Stakeholders include suppliers, contributors, customers, senior management, financial contributors, members of the community, and so on. In the case of contributors, we need to ensure that they can make their contributions when required at the desired level of quality. In the case of customers, we want to be sure the work done will meet their needs. If the answer is no, then we must reexamine our strategy (**step 7a**). If the approach is deemed unacceptable at this point, the model routes us back to step 4, where a new strategy is selected and tested, and plans are revised.

If only the implementation plan is at fault, the loop routes us back to step 6, meaning that we must fix the working plan to the satisfaction of all stakeholders.

Step 8: Sign Off Project Plan and Set Up a Project Notebook

Stakeholders indicate their approval by signing the plan. It is their okay for the execution phase to begin. I recommend a looseleaf notebook to hold all project documentation.

Step 9: Execute the Plan

At this point work begins. The detailed implementation plan is the guide to the steps taken during the execution phase. All too often, the plan is not followed during execution of the work. This is especially true when problems are encountered. It is tempting to forget the plan and just start trying to correct the problems. Note, however, that steps 10–13 are designed to overcome this pitfall.

Step 10: Is Progress Okay?

As work is performed, it is monitored. One of the principal tools of monitoring is earned-value analysis, which is discussed in Chapter 13. However, it is important to remember that earned value analysis can be properly used only if the *performance* objective is being met. That is, work can be deemed on target only if it meets customer requirements. The fact that what has been done functions correctly according to a technical specification does not mean that the project is on target. The Edsel may have functioned correctly according to its engineering specs, but it was not accepted by the market. If the answer at this step is no, the model routes into control steps.

Step 11: Is the Definition Okay?

This checkpoint ensures that we are still trying to solve the correct problem, rather than the wrong one. If the answer is no, the model routes all the way back to step 2, meaning the project must be totally replanned. This won't happen very often, but it must be considered as a possibility.

Step 12: Is the Strategy Okay?

As in step 7, it is important to ask whether an implementation difficulty is caused by a defective strategy. If it is, the model routes back to step 4, so another strategy can be selected.

Step 13: Is the Plan Okay?

If the answer to this question is no, then we have to change the implementation plan. However, if the answer is yes—and we are still asking the question—then the plan is not being followed. In many cases, the reason is that insufficient resources have been provided. If so, new resources must be forthcoming or the project will have to be replanned. Note that resources can be increased by adding people or overtime.

Step 14: Is All Work Complete?

This just keeps looping back to the execution step, meaning that during execution we monitor progress, take corrective action when necessary, and so on. Once the answer is yes, we are ready for step 15.

Step 15: Conduct a Final Lessons-Learned Review

Before the project can be considered actually complete, a lessons-learned review should be conducted. The purpose of the review is to learn what was done well and what could be improved, so that progress can be made in future projects. More on this in Chapter 11.

Step 16: Close Out the Project

Final reports are written, the project notebook containing all documentation is placed in a central file, and the project is considered complete.

SECTION TWO

PROJECT PLANNING

3

CHAPTER

General Aspects
of Project Planning

This chapter introduces project planning and establishes guidelines for what should be contained in a formal project plan.

PROJECT PLANNING AND CUSTOMER NEEDS

As the quality movement emphasized, the first order of business in today's world must be meeting the needs of customers. In project management, the customer must be identified and his or her needs defined.

This is often easier said than done. There is, first of all, identifying just who the customer is. In customer-funded projects, the answer is clear, but in product development projects, it is not. For example, in software system development projects, group leaders are often regarded as customers when it might be more appropriate to consider their direct reports to be the real customers, since they are the people who will

The first order of business in today's world must be meeting the needs of customers.

ultimately use the system. More than one project has been turned over to users who complained that the system did not meet their needs.

The information systems (IS) person is bewildered. "We talked to your boss," he says. "She told us this was what you needed."

To which the user replies, "Why did you talk to her? She doesn't know what we do!"

And this is often true. Group leaders can be so busy that they do not really know what their people are up to. So you really need to talk to that user to get a clear understanding of his needs.

This, too, can be a significant problem. Often, customers have an "itch" that they want scratched. That is the best definition they can offer. They want the product to be "easy to use." They want "convenience." These basic "itches" must be *translated* into product or service features. We can say that *solutions* are developed for customer needs.

One important point is that we want to do more than the bare minimum required to satisfy customer needs—we want to actually *delight* the customer. To do so requires that we actually *exceed* customer expectations. If we can do that, we can build customer loyalty and, in a competitive situation, defend against competition.

One approach used to translate customer needs into product or service features is quality function deployment (QFD). An in-depth discussion of QFD is outside the scope of this book, but a short overview is in order. For those readers interested in learning more, consult *The QFD Book* (Guinta & Praizler, 1993).

Figure 3.1 shows a QFD matrix stripped to its bare essentials. Down the left side is a list of customer requirements. Across the top are some of the features of the product (in this case, a hotel) that are expected to satisfy those customer requirements. In those cells containing a plus sign (+), there is a positive correlation between the feature and the requirement. Where an asterisk (*) is shown, the correlation is still positive and very strong. A zero (0) means no correlation. And, although there can be negative correlations, none are shown in this example. Finally, on the right side of the matrix is a ranking of the customer's requirements, with number 1 being most important. This ranking is obtained through customer surveys, interviews, and so forth.

The idea is to give the customer those features that have positive correlations with high-ranking requirements and to avoid providing those features that have no correlations or that correlate only with very low-ranking requirements. As you can see, the folks who initially set up the hotel matrix have missed the fact that security is the most important customer requirement. They need to go back to the drawing board, as we say.

F I G U R E   3.1

QFD Matrix for a Hotel

+ = CORRELATION * = STRONG CORRELATION 0 = NO CORRELATION	Individual Temp. Control	Lighting	Furnishings	Cable TV	Room Service Menu	Courteous Staff	Airport Courtesy Van	Rank
Comfort	*	+	*	0	*	0	+	2
Service	0	0	0	0	*	*	*	3
Price for Value	*	*	*	*	*	*	*	5
Security	0	0	0	0	0	0	0	1
Able to Read or Work Comfortably	0	*	*	0	0	0	0	4
Access to Telephone / Computer	0	0	+	0	0	0	0	6
Convenience	0	0	0	0	*	0	*	7
In-Hotel Entertainment	0	0	0	*	+	0	0	8

THE PROJECT NOTEBOOK

In steps 1–8 of the model for managing projects, a plan is being developed and ultimately signed off. This plan is usually housed in a looseleaf notebook (or notebooks, in the case of very large projects). Subsequently, as the project is executed, progress reports, revisions, and so on, are placed in the notebook, so that when the job is finally closed out, the notebook provides a complete "track record" of the project from start to finish. The notebook is then placed in a central file so that others can refer to it as an aid in planning subsequent projects.

Following are the items that should be part of every project plan and that should be in the notebook when it is first set up:

- Problem statement.
- Project mission statement—formal for large projects; informal for smaller ones. (See Chapter 5 for developing a formal mission statement.)
- Project strategy, together with a SWOT (strengths, weaknesses, opportunities, threats) analysis supporting it.
- Project objectives.
- Documentation of QFD analysis or other means of translating customer needs into solutions.
- Statement of project *scope.*
- Contractual requirements: a list of all *deliverables*—reports, hardware, software, and so on.
- End-item specifications to be met—building codes, government regulations, and so forth.
- Work breakdown structure.
- Schedules: both milestone and working schedules should be provided.
- Required resources—people, equipment, materials, and facilities. These must be specified in conjunction with the schedule. Loading diagrams are helpful.
- Control system.
- Major contributors: use a linear responsibility chart.
- Risk analysis with contingencies when available.

Statements of work (SOWs) are optional.

SIGNING OFF THE PLAN

Once the plan has been prepared, it should be submitted to *stakeholders* for their signatures.

- If the stakeholder is a contributor, her signature indicates that she is committed to her contribution, agrees with the scope of work to be done, accepts the specs as valid, and so on. However, a commitment is not considered a *guarantee*, since no one has 20/20 foresight or complete control over his or her time. Rather, it is a promise to do everything within reason to meet project objectives.

- If the person is the customer, his signature indicates that he agrees with what the project will accomplish. It will meet his needs.

- If the signer is a financial officer, she is agreeing that the project can be funded at the rate indicated over time.

The plan should be signed in a *project plan review meeting*, not by mail! People should be encouraged to "shoot holes in the plan" during the meeting, rather than waiting until problems develop later on.

Does everyone have to sign? Not necessarily. I would suggest that signatures are required for stakeholders who are taking responsibility for some aspect of the project, but are not required for people who are not taking responsibility for anything. This eliminates the need to obtain 27 signatures to get anything done—a situation that sets up a tremendous organization inertia.

CHANGING THE PLAN

It would be nice to think that a plan, once developed, will never change. However, that is unrealistic. Unforeseen problems are almost certain to arise. The important thing is to

☞ Make changes in an orderly way, following a standard *change procedure.*

make changes in an orderly way, following a standard change-control procedure.

If no change control is exercised, the project may wind up over budget, behind schedule, and hopelessly inadequate, with no warning until it is too late.

> **PRINCIPLE:** The first rule of planning is to be prepared to replan!

- Changes should be made only when a significant deviation occurs. A significant change will usually be specified in terms of percent tolerances relative to the original targets.
- Change control is necessary to protect *everyone* from the effects of scope creep.
- Causes of changes should be documented for reference in planning future projects.

DEFINITION OF PLANNING

Planning is the answering of the following questions:

- What must be done?
- How should it be done?
- Who will do it?
- By when must it be done?
- How much will it cost?
- How good does it have to be?

SUGGESTIONS FOR EFFECTIVE PLANNING

1. Plan to plan. It is always difficult to get people together to develop a plan. The planning session itself should be planned or it may turn into a totally disorganized meeting of the type that plagues many organizations.

Don't plan in more detail than you can manage.

2. Make sure the people who must implement the plan participate in preparing it.
3. Be prepared to replan. Unexpected obstacles will undoubtedly crop up.
4. Conduct a risk analysis to anticipate the more likely obstacles that may occur. Develop Plan B just in case Plan A doesn't work. Why not just use Plan B in the first place? Because Plan A is better, but has a few weaknesses. Plan B has weaknesses also, but they must be different from those in Plan A, or there is no use in considering it a backup.
5. Begin with a definition of the purpose of doing whatever is to be done. Develop a problem statement. All actions in an organization should be taken to "achieve a result," which is another way of saying "solve a problem." If this step is skipped, you may

find yourself developing the right solution to the wrong problem.

6. Use the work breakdown structure to divide the work into smaller "chunks." Then develop accurate estimates for duration, cost, and resource requirements.

PHASED PLANNING

When a project spans a long period of time, or when considerable uncertainty exists about the approach to be taken (as in some research projects), it is impossible to plan far-term activities in much detail. The approach is to plan near-term work in detail, and as each phase is completed, to plan the next phase in detail.

Although this is a valid approach, the politics of your organization may prohibit its application.

4

CHAPTER

Planning: Developing the Project Mission, Vision, Goals, and Objectives

DECIDING WHAT MUST BE DONE: DEFINING YOUR MISSION, VISION, GOALS, AND OBJECTIVES

I have already pointed out that projects do not fail at the end; they fail at the beginning. We are now entering step 2 of the Lewis Method (see Figure 4.1), and this is where it all can go wrong. There are two fairly common recipes for disaster. One is that people are convinced that they know what is supposed to be done, so they don't think there is any reason to take time clarifying problem, mission, and vision. The second is a communications failure. The project manager communicates the mission to the team and thinks people understand when, in fact, they don't.

In the second instance, where people think they understand but don't, there are many possible reasons. One is that they are not good at defining problems. They mistake symptoms for causes, or accept the first definition that someone

F I G U R E 4.1

Step 2 of the Lewis Method

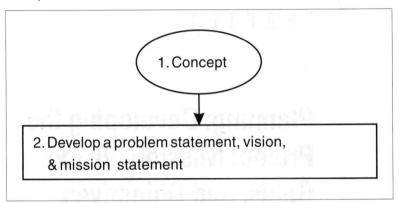

offers without ever questioning whether it is valid. As an example, if I say, "I have a headache," I have just expressed a symptom. I do not know what the problem is. It could be stress, something I ate, or a brain tumor. One thing is certain: If I take painkillers, the headache may go away, but if the problem continues, the pain will return. By taking a painkiller, I have treated the symptom without addressing the underlying cause of the pain.

Or suppose the electrically operated window in my car won't go down. The dealer says the motor is burned out, and replaces it. A few weeks later the window won't go down again. Dealer says motor is burned up. This seems suspicious, doesn't it? Two motors burned up. I challenge the dealer to find the reason why the motor has burned up. It turns out that my voltage regulator is defective and my alternator voltage is going really high. Until the regulator problem is corrected, the motor will continue to burn up. Determining that the regulator is the cause of the problem is called identifying the *root cause.*

The communication problem is often the result of the *Abilene Paradox.* This is a name invented by Jerry Harvey

(1988) to describe the *false consensus effect*. Harvey relates a farmhouse parable to illustrate false consensus. Briefly, several people are sitting around a Texas farmhouse one Sunday morning in 100-degree heat. They have nothing to do, and when someone asks, "What would you like to do today?" another person suggests that they drive to Abilene and have lunch at the cafeteria.

Soon they are on their way, in an old car with no air conditioning, and it is about 90 miles to Abilene. By the time they get there, they are pretty grungy, because of the heat. They have lunch, which turns out to be mediocre, then walk around Abilene for a while. It turns out there is nothing to do in Abilene, so they are bored again. They get back into the car and head home.

"Boy, that was a waste of time," someone says.

Surprised, Pa responds, "I thought you wanted to go!"

"No, I just went because the rest of you did," says the disgruntled Sonny.

So they take a poll. Surprise, surprise—*nobody* really wanted to go to Abilene, not even the person who suggested it. It was just an idle thought!

The essence of the false consensus effect is that silence means consent. But the most important point is this: As Harvey says, it *appears* that this is a failure to manage agreement.

It is not!

It is a failure to manage *disagreement!*

JUST WHAT IS THE DIFFERENCE BETWEEN MISSION AND VISION?

In teaching project management to about 18,000 people over the past 15 years, I have found that many of them do not have a clear idea of what a mission statement—much less a vision—entails. No doubt this is because the terms have been used in so many different ways that no one is sure just what they mean.

The very term "mission statement" induces nausea in many people. One fellow in a seminar said, "You're not going to get into mission statements, are you? Those things have been thoroughly discredited."

I agree with him. Most of what we see—especially on the walls of corporate America—is banal. It could all be cloned and stated as follows: "The mission of company XYZ is to make a lot of money for our stockholders."

Now I don't know about you, but that doesn't do a lot to excite me. How many of you have awakened in the morning with your first thought being, "Let me get to work so I can make a lot of money for the stockholders"? I don't think so.

Still, can you imagine leading a team to a destination when people don't know what that destination is? Well, perhaps if they are a herd—the lead cow runs amok and the rest follow blindly. But I don't want my project team to be a herd; I want it to be a true team, in which each member is helping us all move toward that destination.

A few years ago, I had a call from a project manager at a client company. He said, "I just got off a conference call with key members of my team and realized that we are not all on the same page together."

"I'm not surprised," I said.

"I am," he exclaimed. "We've been on this project for two months, and for me to find they don't understand what we're trying to do is a shock."

A week later we got all 19 people together in a conference room, with me facilitating the session. I told them we would begin by writing a problem statement. "What is the problem being solved by the project?" I began. "If we don't know that, we can't write a proper mission statement."

Someone in the group protested. "We don't need to do that," he said. "We all know what the problem is."

I was unfazed. "If that's true," I said, "it will take only five minutes to write the problem out, and it should be in writing in case junior members of the team are unclear. So let's do it."

Three hours later we finished writing the problem statement.

The project manager was right. They did not agree on the problem, so they couldn't agree on the mission. And this is the vital point: *Without a shared understanding of the problem, vision, and mission, a team cannot possibly be successful!*

We never polled the group to see if there was a disagreement, so we fell into the trap of thinking that silence meant consent.

DEFINING THE PROBLEM

Most teams are not given a problem statement. They are given a mission statement. "Your assignment," says the project sponsor, "is to go forth and conquer." The thing is, the sponsor has identified a problem and has decided that it can be solved by having the team go forth and conquer. If the sponsor has misdefined the problem, however, then achieving the mission will not solve it at all.

For that reason, a team must begin by gaining a clear understanding of the problem to be solved. Only then can it start to polish the mission statement. Furthermore, the only good way to achieve a *shared understanding* of the problem is through participation in developing a formal statement.

Yes, I know this sounds like overkill. You, as project manager, should not have to go through such a laborious process. You should be able just to get people together, explain the problem, and let them go forth and conquer.

Unfortunately, it doesn't work that way.

Project managers are probably more frequent victims of the Abilene Paradox than anyone else on earth.

The problem remains pervasive, even though Jerry Harvey called it to our attention years ago. The reason is that groups are socialized to keep quiet. If you admit you don't understand something, you're labeled stupid. If you raise an objection, you're not a good team player. So rather than be thought stupid or a loose cannon, you remain silent, hoping that sooner or later the issue will be resolved.

The only way around this problem is to work with the group in such a way that every member has an opportunity to test his or her understanding of what is going on. The process is described later in this chapter.

IMPORTANCE OF THE MISSION STATEMENT

Without a clear understanding of its mission, a project team is like an airplane without a rudder. It will go wherever the winds blow, but not necessarily where it is intended to go.

As is true for an organization as a whole, a mission statement gives a project a sense of purpose and direction. It is a broad statement, from which all subsequent planning can proceed. It can be developed using a very formal procedure (presented later in this chapter), or it can be more informally stated.

> **PRINCIPLE:** A mission statement provides the basis for setting goals and objectives and for making decisions, taking actions, hiring employees, and so forth.

The mission statement should be used to set goals and objectives, to make decisions, and to determine what goods and services the project group or overall organization should be providing.

THE MISSION IDENTIFICATION PROCESS

A project is always conducted to achieve a purpose, solve a problem, or meet a need for the organization. Unless the problem, need, or purpose is clearly understood, then the mission itself cannot be clear. One way to arrive at the real purpose of a project is to ask the question "Why?" five times.

Suppose someone suggests that a meeting be held. By asking "Why?" we get the following:

"Why should this meeting be held?"

"Because people in the project team need information on some changes we are going to make."

"Why do they need this information?"

"Because they may do their jobs incorrectly without the information."

"Then the purpose of the meeting is to give people information that they need to prevent them from doing their jobs wrong?"

"Right!"

In this case, we had to ask "Why?" only twice to arrive at the true purpose of having the meeting. In other cases, it may be necessary to go the full distance, but rarely will we have to ask "Why?" more than five times.

Note also that the real meaning of the word "mission" is to identify the *purpose* of the project. This is, to me, the heart of the matter. If you can't state the purpose of a project, then something is wrong. You may, in fact, be doing a project that shouldn't be done.

Consider the following example. I have just taken a job in a distant city. I plan to move there, and the first thing I realize is that I have no place to live. This is a problem to be solved or a need to be met. I might say, then, that my mission is to find a place to live.

True, but will just any place do? I could live under a bridge. Or I could live at the YMCA. Some people do. But as I think about it, neither of these will do. I have in mind some specific requirements for the kind of place I want to live in. So I make a list of the desired characteristics or requirements:

Must Have	Want	Nice to Have
3 bedrooms	Old trees on lot	Deck in back of house
2 bathrooms	No more than 5 miles	
2-car garage	from work	
3/4 acre lot		

I also no doubt have an idea in mind of roughly what the place should look like. I may prefer modern architecture, a more traditional structure, or something very old. I may want a one- or two-story house. Collectively, the must-have, want, and nice-to-have and my mental image of the appearance of the house constitute a *vision* of the place I am looking for. I may not find exactly what I am seeking, or I may find something that I like better than my original concept, but that concept is the starting point. Without it, I could flounder hopelessly.

In addition, if I am hunting for a place to live with my family or significant other, I have an entirely different problem than if I am doing it alone. When I compare my list of musts, wants, and nice-to-haves with my partner's, I find that they are not the same. My must-have features are not even on his or her list! And vice versa. Naturally, until these two lists can be made to agree in the major details, my partner and I will never be able to agree on a selection. This is called achieving a *shared vision*. Every project manager must instill such a vision in the project team, or chaos will be the result.

In addition, I would suggest that for projects, you burn the list of nice-to-haves. The 80/20 principle says that 80 percent of your time will be spent on 20 percent of project requirements. That means you should spend 80 percent on the must-have components, of course. So the safe thing to do is be absolutely unmerciful in tossing out that nice-to-have list. The road to project hell is paved with that list.

Koch (1998) suggests that the way to do so is to give your team an almost impossible deadline. That way, people don't have time to fool with the nice-to-haves. Whenever teams find themselves faced with an impossible deadline—and meet it—I can assure you that they do not include any nice-to-have features in the product! To me, Koch's suggestion is a bit severe and need not be practiced literally but there is merit in the *intent* of the recommendation.

Now, if we combine the statement of need with the vision, we arrive at the mission: My mission is to find a place to live that conforms to my vision. This is shown in Figure 4.2. Note that if I find a place to live that conforms to the vision, I will have met my need or solved my problem. Otherwise, I have not.

Note also that many people will say, "My *problem* is to find a place to live." It is because we use the word

pro • blem: A gap between where you are and where you want to be, confronted by obstacles that prevent easy movement to close the gap.

"problem" in so many ways that we become confused about the meaning of the word. To simplify, if you will confine yourself to the following meaning, it will help in clarifying mission and vision: A problem is a gap between where you

F I G U R E 4.2

Problem, Vision, and Mission

Problem: I have no place to live.		
MUSTS	WANTS	NICE
3 bedrooms 2500 sq. ft. 2-car garage 1 acre lot large family room	room for home office basement	fireplace in family room

Mission:
To find a place that meets all musts and as many of the others as possible.

are and where you want to be, confronted by obstacles that prevent easy movement to close the gap.

It is the *obstacles* that actually create the problem. If you had no obstacles, you would have no problem. As an example, if I am at one end of a long hallway and I want to be at the other end, than all I have to do is walk. I have no problem, just a goal. On the other hand, if I cannot walk, or if someone has placed a hungry alligator in the hall that plans to bite my leg off as I try to go by, then I have a problem. Solving problems always involves overcoming obstacles.

THE FORMAL MISSION STATEMENT

A mission statement should answer two questions:

1. What are we going to do?
2. For whom are we going to do it?

Some people suggest that a third question be answered: How do we go about it? To me, this is asking the team to decide on a *strategy* at the same time that it tries to decide on a mission. It is wise to reserve this question for step 3 in the Lewis Method of project management.

In the case of finding a place to live, it is not even necessary to answer the second question, since I am the "for whom." In most cases, however, it is important to identify who the customer is.

The process outlined in Figure 4.3 can aid the team in answering these questions.

Working through the process gets the team actively involved in drafting a mission statement, so that the Abilene Paradox is avoided.

Another reason for following this approach is that teams seldom are told that there is a problem to be solved. They are usually *given* a mission to achieve. The difficulty is that the manager or sponsor who gave them that mission may not have fully thought through all the issues involved, and may have misdefined the problem being solved. (Yes, I know this is insubordination or heresy, but that's the way it is.) By having the team take a fresh look at the situation, you avoid the misstep of solving the wrong problem.

F I G U R E 4.3

Steps in Writing a Mission Statement

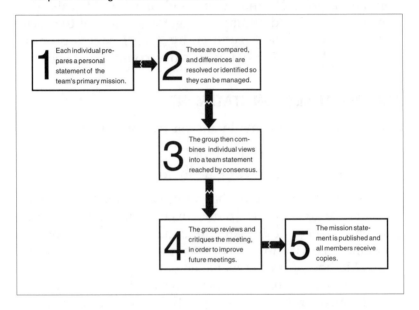

If you are working on a very important, long-duration project, you may also want to take your team through the steps in Table 4.1. By doing so, you will collectively address issues that the team must deal with over the long run. At the same time, you will achieve a greater shared understanding of the team's situation than might be possible by any other means.

Once you have written your mission statement, make sure that it is distributed to everyone and that it is *used!* How? Every time a step must be taken, you should ask how to take that step in such a way that it supports the achievement of your mission. These actions include solving problems, making decisions, recruiting team members, and so on. By following this procedure, you make the mission statement operational. Otherwise, you will have the mission-statement-in-the-drawer effect: A statement is written, filed neatly in someone's desk drawer, and forgotten. Subsequent steps lose their meaning as the plan goes out of focus.

T A B L E 4.1

Developing a Mission Statement

STEP TO FOLLOW	COMMENTS
1. List all the team's *stakeholders.*	A stakeholder is *anyone* who has a vested interest in what the team is doing—customers, suppliers, senior management, and so on.
2. Highlight the team's *customers* from within the list of stakeholders just generated.	A customer is a *user* of the team's output.
3. Check the three most important stakeholders—at least one of them should be the team's major customer.	This step will generate much discussion and debate. Do not cut it off prematurely.
4. Make a list of those things your three most important stakeholders want from the team.	The objective is to ensure that you satisfy the customer's **needs!** Don't *guess*—find out!
5. When the team has finished its job, how will members know they were successful? List those *criteria for success* that will be used to judge the team's performance.	Criteria can be hard or soft. Budgets, schedule, and quality are often hard. Learning, satisfaction, and other criteria are soft. They can be as important as the hard measures.
6. Determine what critical events might occur that could affect the team's success either positively or negatively.	Examples include a merger, hostile takeover, recession, technology breakthrough, and population change.
7. Write the mission and purpose statement.	Follow the steps in the model presented in Figure 4.1.

GUIDELINES FOR DEVELOPING GOOD OBJECTIVES

Before detailed planning can be carried out, specific objectives must be established. Those objectives *should be written out*—for at least three reasons.

First, the discipline of writing out your objectives will force you to clarify them in your own mind. I have found that when I start to write out my objectives, I am sometimes not too clear on them myself.

Objectives may be to:

- Develop expertise in some area
- Become competitive
- Improve productivity
- Improve quality
- Reduce costs
- Modify an existing facility
- Develop a new sales strategy
- Develop a new product

Second, when objectives are in writing, everyone in the team has access to them and can refer to them periodically.

Third, being able to refer to objectives in written form should help members of the team resolve differences of opinion about what is supposed to be done.

Clearly defined objectives meet the following conditions:

- They are **specific**—that is, not fuzzy, vague statements, such as "I want to be the best." What does that mean?
- They are **achievable.** That is, they contribute to the team's overall purpose.
- They are **measurable** insofar as possible. This can be very difficult to achieve. How do you measure performance improvement of knowledge workers, for

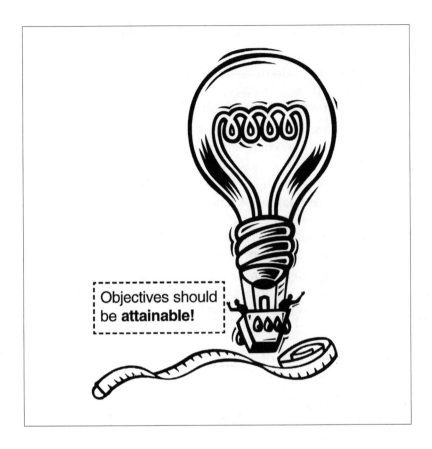

example? See the following section for ideas on units to use in quantifying targets.

- They fit **higher-level** organization objectives.
- They are stated in terms of **deliverables** whenever possible. Deliverable items include assessment reports, written recommendations, and so on.
- They are **comprehensible**—that is, *understandable*. Objectives must be stated in such a way that other people will know what you are trying to achieve. Have you ever left a meeting and wondered what everyone was supposed to do? Chances are the

objectives were not stated clearly or in understand-able language.

- They are **realistic**—something that you should be doing. If the objective is not in line with the overall project mission, then it should be challenged.
- They are **time-limited** to the extent possible. Remember this rule when setting performance improvement objectives for employees. If such targets are not time-limited, they will never happen!
- They are **attainable.** That means that they are both realistic and achievable. When appropriate, objectives should be **assigned a risk factor** so others in the organization become aware of such risk.
- They specify a **single** end result. When multiple objectives are combined into one statement, it becomes difficult to sort out what is being said.

A POINT ABOUT DEFINITIONS

People tend to confuse *tasks* and *objectives.* An objective is a desired end state: You are presently at point A and want to get to point B. Tasks are those actions you take to arrive at the final destination.

Determining what tasks or actions must be taken to reach an objective is part of problem solving and/or planning. Note that no statement should specify *how* an objective will be achieved, since this may lock you into a method that is not the best to pursue. Keep the problem-solving process separate from setting objectives.

ESTABLISHING PRIORITIES

In a project, many objectives will be sequenced strictly by *logical* considerations. However, some objectives may have priorities that are a function of other factors of importance. Such importance may be determined by **need, economics,** or **social**

desirability. Care must be exercised that less important objectives do not sidetrack progress toward more important ones.

Objectives that must be accomplished before some other target can be reached are called **feeder objectives.**

To prioritize your objectives, it may be enough simply to group them into categories A, B, and C—with A being most important. On the other hand, you may need to actually rank-order your list. If you try to rank more than 10 objectives, the task becomes very

> Doing the right things is more important than doing things right.
> — Peter Drucker

difficult. To make the job easier, try using paired comparisons.

Suppose I have four objectives that I want to rank-order. They are listed below:

1. Replace roof on house.
2. Enter the MBA program at local college.
3. Learn to play golf.
4. Take a trip to Europe.

Rather than trying to rank these by "brute force," I compare all possible pairs, and put a check beside the one in each pair that is more important to me. The number pairs are as follows:

1 ✓	2
1 ✓	3
1 ✓	4
2 ✓	3
2	4 ✓
3	4 ✓

As can be seen, objective 1 is the most important, with three votes, followed by objective 4, then 2, and finally 3.

THE PRIORITY MATRIX

Because there are so many comparisons to make for a large
number of objectives, the method of paired comparisons can
be greatly simplified by using a priority matrix, as shown in
Figure 4.4. Consider six alternatives, which must be ranked:

1. Install new grinder.
2. Develop standard test procedure for product X.
3. Recruit person for position Y.
4. Do performance appraisal for Charlie.
5. Find second source for part Z.
6. Review standards document for quality department.

The matrix makes the comparison very straightforward.
If two or more rows are tied (add to the same total), you need
only look inside the matrix to see which row ranks highest.

FIGURE 4.4

Priority Matrix

	1	2	3	4	5	6	Total	Rank
1		1	0	0	1	1	3	3
2	0		0	0	0	0	0	6
3	1	1		0	1	1	4	2
4	1	1	1		1	1	5	1
5	0	1	0	0		1	2	4
6	0	1	0	0	0		1	5

The vertical axis is more
important than the horizontal axis.

For example, if rows 3 and 4 were tied, you look on row 3 to see if 3 is more important than 4. If it is, then option 3 is a step above 4.

The matrix is most useful for ranking things that cannot be quantified. When some measure can be assigned to an item, it can be ranked using the measure itself.

5
CHAPTER

Planning Project Strategy

PLANNING PROJECT STRATEGY AND STRATEGIC PLANNING

Strategic planning is an attempt to define where an organization would like to be several years in the future. Planning project strategy is trying to figure out the best way to achieve a project mission. Strategic planning is the responsibility of senior managers, while planning project strategy is the job of the project manager and key team members.

WE NEED A GOOD GAME PLAN!

The word *strategy* has military origins. The *Oxford English Dictionary,* considered to be the authoritative source of definitions, offers the following :

> *tactics:* the art of handling forces in battle or in the immediate presence of the enemy.

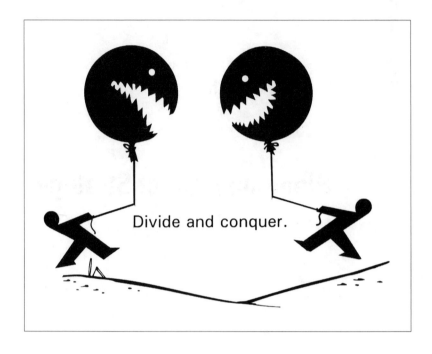

strategy: the art of projecting and directing the larger military movements and operations of a campaign. The mode of executing tactics.

During World War II, it was imperative that ships and planes be built at an accelerated rate, so manufacturers devised a number of approaches to speed up the process. One of these builders was Avondale Shipyards, which devised a new way of constructing ships. For centuries, shipbuilders had followed the "logical" approach of building a ship in the position that it ultimately occupies in the water. That is, the keel was set on the ground and the decks were built above it.

Avondale decided to build the ship upside down. The reason—it was far easier to weld steel when the ship was upside down. When a ship is in its normal position, workers have to stand on their heads to weld the keel. By building the ship upside down, the workers could stand upright. Naturally, Avondale had to devise a way of turning the ship over once the assembly was complete up to the decks—and they did. This strategy was so much more efficient than the traditional approach that Avondale had a significant competitive advantage over shipyards that employed the old method.

Just how important were these building strategies? Liberty ships were built at the rate of one every 10 to 12 days at the height of the war! They were put to sea with the painters on board, and painted on the voyage across the Atlantic. And B-24 bombers were built at the rate of one every 55 minutes. Pilots were waiting to test-fly the planes as soon as they came off the assembly line.

In colloquial terms, strategy is a "game plan," an overall approach to achieving our major objectives. The important point here is that strategy can be decided upon only after an organization's mission and objectives have been determined. All planning is done to meet objectives, and strategy is only the broad outline of the plan.

To give examples of organizational strategy, we have JIT (just in time) inventories, concurrent or simultaneous engineering, and self-directed work teams as ways of achieving business objectives. We also have downsizing as many organizations reduce their number of employees and contract out work previously done by staff. By doing so, they avoid the problem of seasonal downturns in the economy that might force them to lay off excess employees, only to have to rehire them when the economy comes back up.

In developing a strategy, the project team must answer two fundamental questions:

- What are we going to do?
- How are we going to do it?

As we saw in Chapter 2, the first major step in the project management model is to define the problem to be solved. That is, we must understand what the project is intended to do for the organization and the end user. Since the need to clearly define the problem is stressed in that chapter, it will not be emphasized here.

Activities Involved in Planning Strategy

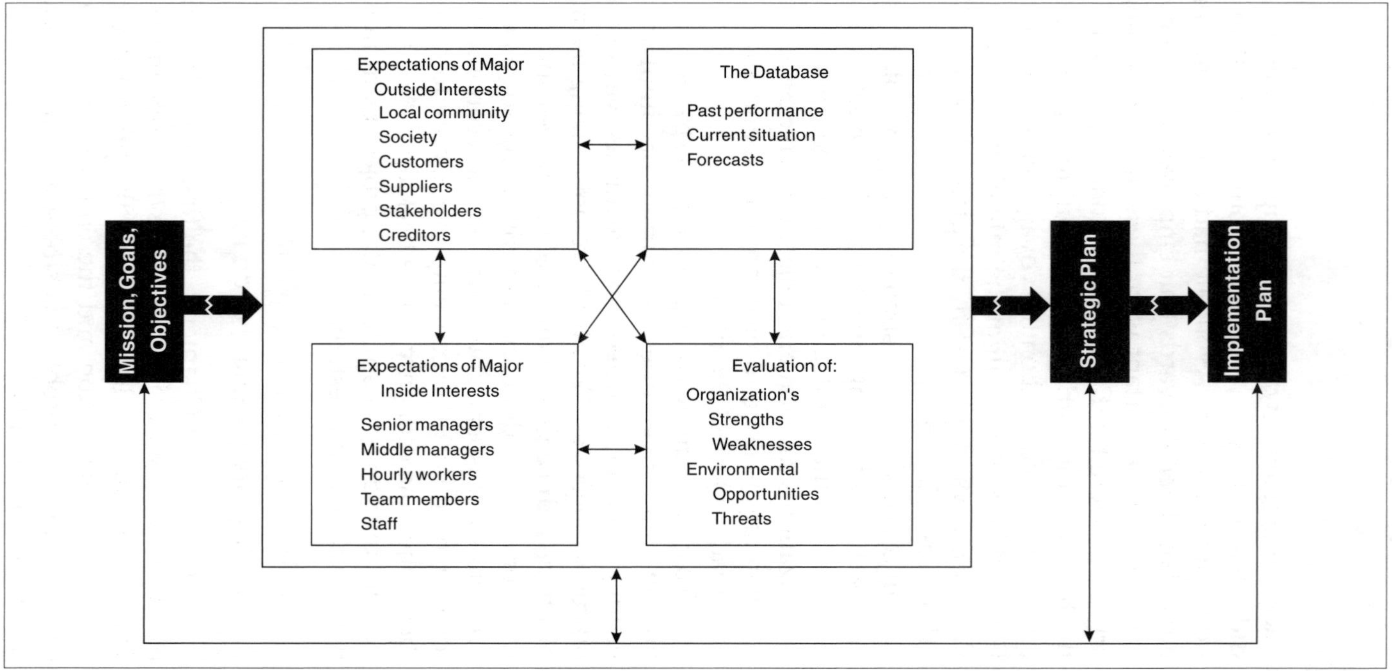

Mission, Goals, Objectives

Expectations of Major Outside Interests
Local community
Society
Customers
Suppliers
Stakeholders
Creditors

Expectations of Major Inside Interests
Senior managers
Middle managers
Hourly workers
Team members
Staff

The Database
Past performance
Current situation
Forecasts

Evaluation of:
Organization's
Strengths
Weaknesses
Environmental
Opportunities
Threats

Strategic Plan

Implementation Plan

Once we are clear on what the project is supposed to achieve (problem, mission, and vision), we can proceed with the how-to (strategy) phase. Strategy planning must be a distinct part of the process. Implementation planning must be deferred until a clear strategy has been devised. Timing is very important. If strategy planning is done too soon, it may be so vague (because of lack of sufficient definition) as to be useless. If it is done too late, decisions may have been made that limit possible alternatives.

The strategy planning phase, defined as steps 3 and 4 of the overall project management model. (Figure 2.1), actually consists of a number of substeps. These activities are shown in Figure 5.1.

THE STRATEGY PLANNING MODEL

The activities in the strategy planning model are not in any particular sequence. In fact, they are to some degree interactive, since the information derived from one analysis may require going back to another step and digging out more information. Note that two of the components in the strategy planning model are contained in the model for developing a mission statement, presented in Chapter 4. These are the identification of the expectations of major inside and outside interests, which are called stakeholders in the mission development model (Figure 4.1). This means that, if a mission statement has been developed in accordance with the model, stakeholder expectations have already been identified. Also, for a project team, some of those stakeholders listed in the strategy planning model may be relevant while others may not. However, the team should be careful not to dismiss a party as irrelevant without considering whether that conclusion is correct. Stakeholders are identified by whether the project may *impact them* in some way or whether they may have an impact on the project. If either is true, they should be considered important to the analysis.

Conducting the database analysis is limited in some organizations by a lack of good historical data. In that case, the analysis depends on the memories of individuals, and is subject to all the biases and inaccuracies to which human beings are prone. Those limitations should be noted in making use of remembered data.

Analysis of the current situation should be easier, assuming that the project team members have access to vital information on the business, its competitors, and so on.

Forecasts are based on environmental scanning. They should include examination of technological developments, economic trends, pending government regulations, social trends, and so on. Naturally, forecasting is very difficult and is limited by what information is available on competitors and other key entities.

Finally, we have the evaluation of environment and company for some specific variables. This evaluation is generally called a SWOT analysis. It prescribes that the team examine the company's *Strengths* and *Weaknesses* as well as the *Opportunities* and *Threats* presented by the environment.

These factors are clearly not independent. For example, forecasting is based on evaluations of the external environment and on understanding the expectations of stakeholders. The current situation is also influenced by the environment and the expectations of stakeholders. For that reason, the model is drawn to indicate that interdependence.

CONDUCTING THE ANALYSES

Environmental Factors

The major environmental factors that may affect a project are economic, technological, government or legal, geographic (including weather or terrain), and social. The economic variables can affect a project in many ways. During a recession companies tend to run "leaner" than in more prosperous times, making resources more scarce and conflicts among projects almost inevitable. When the project spans national borders, currency fluctuations can be a significant factor. In addition, the economies of the host country and home country will be considerations. For those projects that have long time frames, inflation becomes a factor: Will inflation affect the project and, if so, what parts?

Technological changes can be the most difficult to forecast and deal with. One of my own projects, for example, called for designing a new 1000-watt linear amplifier with totally solid-state devices (no vacuum tubes). However, a feasibility study showed that current devices were not capable of meeting all the technical requirements, so a conventional vacuum tube design had to be implemented.

Projects are increasingly affected by government regulations and legal issues. Product liability suits in the United States have grown to such an extent that companies are very cautious in their handling of new products and services. No one wants to make sports helmets, for example, because of the possibility of being sued if a player is injured. Environmental regulations have forced many businesses to change their way of running projects. According to one test engineer at the NASA facility near Las Cruces, NM, rocket components were once tested with minimal concern for the effluents. However, because of population growth near the test facility, NASA has had to take measures to contain toxic gases so that no danger is posed to nearby residents.

Geographic factors certainly play a part in how some projects are run. Many companies are now global, and colocation of project participants is impossible. Fortunately, with modern communications technology, they are able to achieve what is called *virtual colocation,* whereby members of the team "meet" as often as necessary through teleconferencing. Naturally, geography also affects strategy in construction projects in terms of terrain, material resources available, and so on. Human resource availability plays a role as well. I recently saw the construction of a large Shell refinery in Bintulu, Sarawak. Ten years ago, Bintulu was a small fishing village of about 6000. Now almost 60,000 people live there—naturally most of them imported.

It may be, of course, that key members of a project team will not want to spend long periods in very inhospitable locations, so local personnel may have to be recruited and trained for the duration of the job.

Social factors are sometimes overlooked, especially by technical people, in planning project strategy. The social dimension includes an assessment of the values, beliefs, traditions, and attitudes of people—in short, the culture of the people who are stakeholders in the project. Religious and other significant holidays must be factored into project scheduling. In January in the Far East, Chinese new year is celebrated with much more fanfare than new year in the West. Everything may come to a halt for a few days while people take part in this important event.

By the same token, ignorance of the social *taboos* of a culture can lead to embarrassment and even project failure. As an example, an engineer from Germany was visiting a company in the United States. He went to the men's restroom and saw a sign at the entrance saying it was being cleaned. Inside he found a woman cleaning the facility. In Germany, men go about their business even when women come into the restrooms to clean. So he did.

The woman cleaning the restroom was horrified. It simply is not done in the United States. She filed a complaint alleging that he had deliberately used the facility to harass her. The president of the German company had to write a formal letter of apology to the U.S. company in order to resolve the issue!

Given the scope of these environmental factors, we may wonder whether they represent an *opportunity* or a *threat* to the success of the project. Technological developments, for example, can be either, depending on circumstances. If a design is frozen with a certain technology and a new development cannot be integrated with the design, then that change represents a threat to the success of the project, since acceptance by customers is likely to be low. Stereo manufacturers must certainly have been alerted by the development of CD players that there was a limited market for conventional record players. If they were really on their toes, they took steps to enter the CD market. Otherwise, they might have experienced the same decline that manufacturers of buggy whips did when the automobile displaced the need for their product.

Organizational Factors

Assessing an organization's strengths and weaknesses is a key element in strategy planning. Unfortunately, biases too often discredit the analysis. Managers are inclined to be optimistic

Assessing an organization's strengths and weaknesses is a key element in strategic planning.

about the strengths and a bit blind to the weaknesses of the organization. Nevertheless, the analysis must be done.

Factors to examine include expertise of personnel; labor
relations; physical resources; experience with the kind of project being planned; company image; senior management attitudes; morale of employees; market position of the
organization; tendencies to overdesign or miss target dates;
and commitment of the organization to supply resources to
the project as promised. Naturally, you want to capitalize on
strengths and minimize the impact of weaknesses. Further,
those identified environmental threats must be capable of being offset by the team's strengths, and a conscious effort
should be made to take advantage of opportunities presented
by the environment.

Expectations of Stakeholders

Expectations of senior managers can be a major influence on
the success or failure of a project. When those expectations
for project performance are unrealistic, the impact is almost
always negative. One of the more common expectations is
that *all* target dates will be met. Such expectations lead to
conflict.

The expectations of other stakeholders can also make or
break a project. As an example, members of the community
hear about the project and believe that it will create job opportunities for them. The project manager considers the skills
needed for project success to be missing from the local community and recruits outsiders. There is public outrage, followed by unpleasant altercations, and senior management is
pressured to abandon the project. Numerous examples exist
of public pressures to abandon construction of hazard-
ous-waste facilities, nuclear power plants, and other projects
that considered communities to be a threat to their security.

On the other hand, construction of the Saturn plant in
Tennessee was undoubtedly aided by positive public reaction.

FORMULATING PROJECT STRATEGY

Once all of these factors have been identified and examined, the project team is ready to develop a number of alternative methods for project implementation. These methods must meet external threats and take advantage of opportunities. Usually strategy will be a combination of several elements, such as contracting out part of the work, developing a creative financial plan, and partnering with another organization.

Coxon (1983) lists 12 possible strategies for projects:

1. **Construction-oriented.** An example is the Avondale Shipyards approach to building ships.
2. **Finance-based.** Some creative way may be found to fund a project, perhaps through the use of bonds or grants; or special attention may be paid to cash flow and cost of capital.
3. **Governmental.** Always take government requirements into account and work closely with appropriate agencies to ensure that no pitfalls will block progress.
4. **Design.** When certain design techniques have an advantage over others, this strategy may serve well.
5. **Client/contractor.** A partnership may be formed between client and contractor.
6. **Technology.** Employing a cutting-edge technology may present certain risks, but it also offers greater competitive advantages. As mentioned previously, choosing the right level of technology can be important in developing countries.
7. **Commissioning.** If the commissioning aspects of the project are considered to be especially difficult or complex, this strategy might be in order.
8. **Cost, quality, or time.** Because these factors are interrelated, emphasizing one will be at the expense of another. For example, when speed is of the utmost

importance, and quality standards must be simultaneously maintained, then cost must increase. Nevertheless, if there is a significant market advantage to
be gained through speed, the cost may well be offset
by the profits made.

9. Resource. A resource strategy may be called for
    when a particular resource is limited or abundant.
    For example, in Indonesia, Thailand, and other East-
    ern countries, labor costs are so low that many con-
    struction projects are labor-intensive by Western
    standards.

10. Size. For certain kinds of projects, economies of scale
    may be obtained only if the size of the job exceeds a
    certain level.

11. Contingency. This strategy goes only so far as plan-
    ning what to do if certain things happen.

12. Passive. Here the project manager decides (con-
    sciously or unconsciously) to have no strategy at all
    (a paradoxical approach, since this is in itself a strat-
    egy). It might be appropriate when the future is be-
    lieved to be very stable or, conversely, when the
    future seems so chaotic that developing a strategy is
    virtually impossible. This is also called "flying by
    the seat of the pants."

CONDUCTING A SWOT ANALYSIS

Following are the questions asked in conducting a SWOT
analysis. The accompanying form should help simplify the
process. The questions that must be answered are:

- What **Strengths** do we have? How can we take advantage of them?
- What **Weaknesses** do we have? How can we minimize their impact?

- ◆ What **O**pportunities are there? How can we capitalize on them?

- ◆ What **T**hreats might prevent us from getting there? (Consider technical obstacles, competitive responses, values of people within your organization, and so on. Note that threats are not necessarily the same as *risks*.)

- ◆ What can we do to overcome or get around every obstacle identified? (This helps you develop contingency plans.)

See SWOT analysis form on page 86.

SWOT Analysis Form

Project:	Prepared by:
Date:	Strategy, goal, or objective being considered:

List strengths of your team	How can you best take advantage of these?	List weaknesses of your team	How can you minimize the impact of these?

What opportunities does this project/strategy/goal present?	How can you best take advantage of them?	List those threats that might keep you from succeeding	How can you deal with each identified threat?

6
CHAPTER

Implementation Planning

Once a suitable strategy has been chosen for a project, details on how to execute the strategy must be developed. Strategy answers the broad question, "How are we going to go about this job?" while implementation planning dots all the *i*'s and

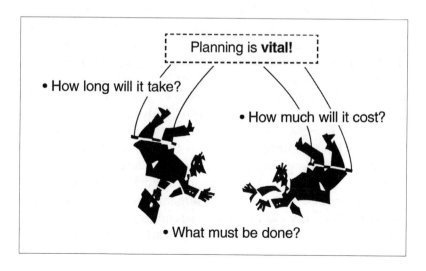

crosses all the *t's*. In other words, implementation planning deals with nitty-gritty details about how the job will be done.

One of the mistakes that people make in planning projects is to begin implementation planning before they have really developed a solid strategy. Of course, a strategy is implied by an implementation plan, but if you don't have the strategy clearly in mind, your detailed execution plan will almost certainly contain "holes."

In any case, once implementation planning starts, the most important tool of project management is the work breakdown structure (WBS). The WBS lists all the tasks that must be done in the project to achieve desired results. The first part of this chapter outlines how the WBS is created and used.

DEVELOPING AND USING THE WORK BREAKDOWN STRUCTURE

In a previous chapter, I said that planning involves answering questions, about what, who, when, where, how long, and how much. The work breakdown structure provides a tool for identifying *what* must be done, *who* will do it, *how long* it will take, and *how much* it will cost. In doing so, the WBS ties the entire project together.

I would say that there are some projects that do not need a critical path or Gantt schedule, perhaps because the job is so small, but there is no project that won't benefit from doing a WBS. One reason is that forgetting something critical is one of the major causes of project failure. The WBS identifies all tasks and can be reviewed for completeness by all stakeholders—before other planning is done.

Another major cause of project failure is that ballpark estimates become targets. These estimates are made by taking, as a starting point, figures for a previous project that is similar to the one in question, adding a little on for differences, then inserting some contingency for unknowns. For the benefit of my non-American readers, we use the term "ballpark" to mean that the number is approximately correct.

These ballpark estimates are often extremely inaccurate, varying by as much as several hundred percent. Yet they are accepted by senior managers, who then expect the project manager to achieve them. As a result, they become targets.

If a complex project is broken down into small units of work, more accurate estimates can be made than those achieved by ballpark estimates. We will come back to how the actual estimating is done later in this chapter.

Format of the Work Breakdown Structure

There are two popular formats for the work breakdown structure. One looks similar to an organization chart (Figure 6.1), and may even be thought of as such, except that the boxes represent work activities rather than reporting structures. The second WBS format is line-indented (Figure 6.2). It is a straightforward listing of project activities, with each new indentation being a lower level of detail (smaller unit of work to be performed). This is a convenient format to use, in that it can be produced entirely in text format on a computer, complete with line numbering. However, it does not visually show the scope of the project as well as the graphic form.

F I G U R E   6.1

Standard Work Breakdown Structure

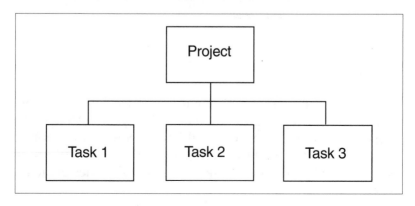

F I G U R E 6.2

Line-Indented Work Breakdown Structure

Write Project Management Book

1. Develop Proposal
   1.1 Survey competition
   1.2 Estimate market potential
   1.3 Identify publishers

2. Do Research
   2.1 Review literature
   2.2 Interview experts
   2.3 Interview project managers

3. Write Text
   3.1 Develop first draft
   3.2 Revise
   3.3 Submit to publisher
   3.4 Approve edited copy

4. Develop Illustrations
   4.1 Roughs
   4.2 Final drafts
   4.3 Camera-ready copy

5. Index
   5.1 Make word list
   5.2 Master document
   5.3 Generate

A typical work breakdown structure has six levels, named as shown in Figure 6.3. It is perfectly acceptable to use more than six levels, but you will find it almost impossible to devise names for the lower ones. After the sixth level, most people just use the word "task" or "activity" to designate the work.

F I G U R E 6.3

WBS-Level Names

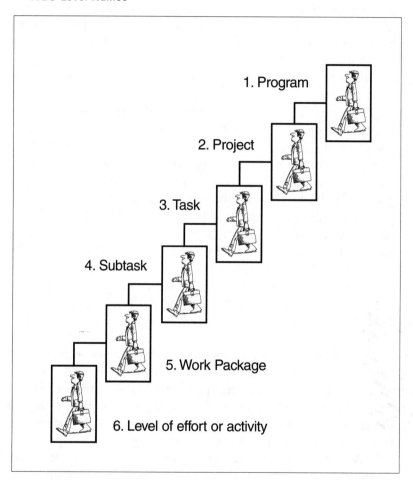

The main reason for using names is for communication purposes. If everyone uses common terminology, then you can inquire about a work package, and everyone will know that you are referring to level 5 of the structure.

Note that level 1 is called a program and level 2 is called a project. This will clarify the difference between program and project management. A program is a very large job that consists of a number of projects. An example is the design of an airplane (Figure 6.4). Designing an engine, avionics, or a fuselage are large enough components to be called projects. In fact, engine and avionics design are usually carried out by companies other than the aircraft manufacturer. This means that the program manager is responsible for managing those subcontractors.

One of the traps that people fall into when they are learning to develop the WBS is to turn it into a grocery list. For example, suppose that I have taken off a week to do a number of projects around my home, such as landscaping, the yard, repairing the roof, and restocking the pantry. I make a WBS like the one shown in Figure 6.5.

You will notice that on the major task labeled Shop for Groceries, I have listed buy eggs, buy bread, buy potatoes, and so on. I have actually put my grocery list on my WBS. This is not what I should do.

What I should be listing are those activities that must be performed in order to buy groceries. These include drive to store, load cart, pay, drive home, and so on, as shown in Figure 6.6.

Now here is how you test it. When all the activities in Figure 6.6 have been completed, the task Shop for Groceries will have been done. In the previous WBS, however, after I have bought bread, eggs, and potatoes, I am still standing in the store, and I don't know how I got there. Furthermore, the task of shopping for groceries is not complete!

Another trap in developing the WBS is to try to think sequentially and place underneath one box something that must be done before the box above can be done. This is a predecessor arrangement, and is actually confusing the WBS with critical path scheduling. Again, the test is whether the box above is completed in the process of doing the tasks below. When a predecessor is placed below another task, completing that predecessor will not result in completing the task above.

F I G U R E 6.4

Tiny Portion of a WBS for an Airplane

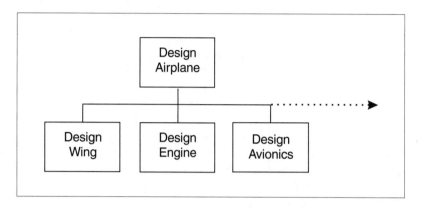

F I G U R E 6.5

WBS for a Home Project

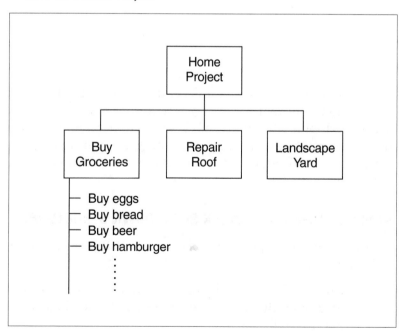

Corrected WBS for the Home Project

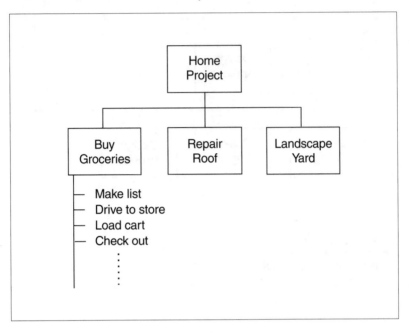

It is very hard not to think sequentially when doing the WBS. I don't know if we are born with that mindset or if we learn to adopt it later in life, but it seems to beset almost all of us. You simply have to keep reminding yourself that at this step you are not worrying about the order in which things get done.

GENERAL ASPECTS OF WORK BREAKDOWN STRUCTURES

Following are some general aspects of the WBS that you need to keep in mind:

- Up to 20 levels can be used. More than 20 is considered overkill. For smaller projects, four to six levels will generally be adequate.

- All paths on a WBS do not have to go down to the same level. That is, you don't have to force the structure to be symmetrical. On any given branch, when you arrive at a level that will produce an estimate of the required accuracy, you stop.

- The WBS does not show sequencing of work except in the sense that all level 5 work packages hanging below a given subtask must be complete for the subtask to be complete, and so on. However, work packages below that subtask might be performed in series or parallel. Sequencing is determined when schedules are developed.

- A WBS should be developed before tasks are scheduled and resources allocated. The objective is to identify all the work to be done first, then think about who will do it, how long it will take, and how much it will cost.

> ☞ A work breakdown structure *does not show the sequence in which work is performed.* Such sequencing is determined when a schedule is developed.

- The WBS should be developed by individuals knowledgeable about the work. This rule applies to projects that involve a lot of disciplines, such as designing an airplane, as we saw in Figure 6.4. Typically, the engine and avionics designs are developed by subcontractors who put together a WBS for their projects. The subcontracted work is then consolidated with the rest to provide an overall structure.

Break down a project only to a level sufficient to produce an estimate of the required accuracy. This needs elaboration. While there is a danger that ballpark estimates will become targets, they need to be developed so that decisions

> ☞ Don't plan in more detail than
> you can manage.

can be made on whether to do a project. In such cases, it is helpful to break the work down a couple of levels. For detailed working estimates, however, the question is when to stop.

The basic guideline is that you stop when you have identified work that you can manage. For example, if the task involves maintenance work, such as overhauling a big power generator, they often have enough history to allow scheduling to the nearest hour. Such a level of detail is far too fine for most activities. In many cases, you can't control work to better than the nearest day—or even the nearest week—so when you reach a level where tasks have durations of a day, you stop.

> ☞ No task should have a
> duration greater than four
> to six weeks.
> ☞ Engineering and
> programming tasks should
> have durations no greater
> than one to three weeks.

The opposite side of this is planning in too little detail. Generally speaking, tasks should have durations no greater than four to six weeks. In the case of engineering or software programming, the duration should not exceed one to three weeks. In other words, there must be balance between too much and too little detail.

ESTIMATING TIME, COST, AND RESOURCE REQUIREMENTS

Every project manager is faced with the same problem: How do you estimate what it will take to do something? After you have done something once, estimating what it will take to do the next job is easier, but that does not mean that an exact determination of time, cost, and resources can be given. It will still be an *estimate*, and an estimate is *not exact!*

Estimating is never simple, and the higher the stakes become, the more anxiety-provoking the job is. However, unless

PRINCIPLE: An *exact estimate* is an oxymoron!

the estimating problem can be managed, projects will never come in on time or on budget.

The question is: How do you know how long it will take to do a project, even given that you know how many human resources are available to do the work? The answer is, *from experience!* That is the standard answer that everyone gives. However, it is not at all clear exactly what that means.

Let us examine what we mean by experience and its relationship to estimating activity durations. As an example, if you have been driving to the same workplace from the same home for several years, using the same route each time, you know about how long it takes to get to work. In large metropolitan areas, people report times like those shown below:

DRIVING TIMES IN URBAN AREAS	
Typical	45 min.
Best	30 min.
Worst	90 min.

When asked, "What is your best estimate of how long it will take you to get to work tomorrow?" people usually respond, "Forty-five minutes." That is, they give the typical driving time. When the driving time follows a normal distribution curve, the typical time is an average, and the probability of achieving that time or less is 50 percent. If the distribution is skewed, then the probability may be greater or less than 50 percent. Assume for now that it is almost normal,

F I G U R E 6.7

Normal Distribution Curve

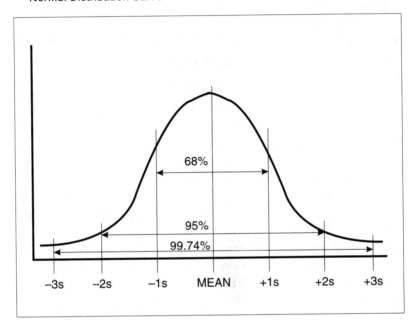

as shown in Figure 6.7. If you are unfamiliar with statistics, you can consult a basic text, such as the one by Walpole (1974), to see why this is true.

People are generally not too concerned that their typical time for driving to work has a 50/50 likelihood of success. But ask them the same question for a project activity, and they don't like to give numbers that have such low probability. The reason is that there are penalties for taking longer than you say it will take. (You get yelled at, if nothing else!)

Note that, even in the case of driving to work, people like to improve their chances. Just ask: "How long would you allow yourself to get to work if you had to meet with the president of your company and being late would be career suicide?" The response: "One hour." That is, people allow themselves the upper limit, just in case they are faced with a wreck or whatever causes their time to go to the upper limit.

That way, they will be sure to get to work on time, unless the situation is extreme and the time exceeds the one-hour upper limit. What they are doing, of course, is increasing their probability of success from 50 percent to 99.9 percent.

In a project, much the same process is involved. If a task has been performed a large number of times, the average duration is known, given a certain level of human resources to do the work, and this average can be used as the basis for an estimate. However, if people are punished for taking longer to do a task than they say, they will not give average durations. As in driving to work, they will allow more time. This is called padding the estimate, and it is an attempt to increase the probability of success to guard against being punished.

As the normal distribution curve in Figure 6.7 shows, there is a probability of 84 percent that a duration one standard deviation above the mean can be met, 98 percent for two standard deviations, and 99.9 percent for three standard deviations. Thus, by padding, the individual can greatly increase the probability that the work will be completed in the estimated time.

Unfortunately, safety carries a price. Although padding the allowed time increases the probability of a successful scheduled completion, it also increases the budgeted cost of the project, and it is likely that such an increase will raise the total estimated project costs to the point that the job will not be funded.

For this reason, one of the assumptions behind project estimating

> **PRINCIPLE:** As the probability of success approaches 100 percent, the probability of getting the project funded approaches zero.

is that *average durations are used, unless specified otherwise.* The idea is that, for a project consisting of a large number of activities, some of the work will take longer than the average estimated duration, while other tasks will take less than the average. Thus the total project completion time will gravitate toward the average expected time for the critical path! The exception is the activities actually on the critical path. In this case, if any task takes longer than estimated, the project end date will slip, so on the critical path, effort must be adjusted to make sure that estimated durations are met.

Some organizations exert pressures on people to keep them from completing work sooner than specified. That is, even though you would expect some tasks to be completed early, they aren't. There is one common reason: If you complete a task early, you are expected to do so next time. This is insane! It is the same as saying that if a person who averages 45 minutes driving to work gets there in 30 minutes one day, he should *always* get there in 30 minutes. A "sample of one" has set an expectation.

Nonsense! When this happens, it means that either people do not understand statistical variation or they are ignoring it. *All processes vary!* This is a law of nature, and it cannot be set aside. You can reduce variation. This is what much of technological progress is aimed at doing. But you can never

> # PARKINSON'S LAW
> Work expands to take the time allowed.
>
> —C. Northcote Parkinson

reduce it to zero. Until this is understood, people will follow Parkinson's Law and take as long as or longer than allowed to complete their work—meaning that those projects end up costing more than necessary.

Now does this mean that estimates should never be padded? Absolutely not! There are situations in which failure to allow for uncontrollable events would be poor project management practice. Construction is one example. We know how long various activities will take because we have good history. However, the *calendar* time taken will be a function of how many days we have bad weather and can't work. By consulting weather history for the area, we can estimate how many weather delays we will probably encounter and pad the schedule accordingly. This is called *risk management*, a subject discussed in more detail in Chapter 17.

Padding is certainly justified to reduce risk, but in my opinion it must be done aboveboard, on a task-by-task basis. Otherwise, the project manager might assume that every member of the team has provided average-duration estimates and then put some padding into the project at the top level, thus adding "fat" to that which individuals have already put into their estimates. The project is sure to be too expensive then.

This is one reason for not getting into game-playing in an organization. Sometimes after obtaining an estimate, the top-level manager cuts it by 10 or 15 percent, on the belief that the estimate contains at least that much "fat." Note that the probability of achieving a time one standard deviation below the mean is only 16 percent, so cutting an estimate that was an average expected duration severely reduces the probability that the time can be met.

If the project manager gets burned because her estimates were averages and they were cut, then the next time she is asked for an estimate, she will indeed pad, since she expects the estimate to be cut. This time, however, the top manager cuts 20 percent, so the next time the project manager pads 25 percent, and so on. Such "games" are hardly productive.

The objective of all project planning should be to develop a plan that is *realistic*, so that managers can make decisions as to whether to do the work. The objective should not be to try to "get" the project manager when he is unable to meet unrealistic deadlines.

OTHER FACTORS IN ESTIMATING

An average expected duration for an activity can be developed only by assuming that the work will be nearly identical

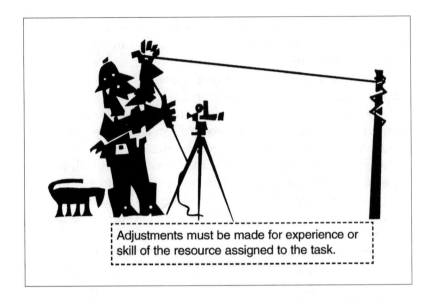

Adjustments must be made for experience or skill of the resource assigned to the task.

to work previously done and that the person(s) being assigned to the task will have a certain skill level. A less skilled person can be expected to take longer at the task; conversely, a more skilled person can probably do the job faster. Thus, adjustments must be made for the experience or skill of the resource assigned to the task.

However, we also know that there is no direct correlation between experience and speed of doing work. It may not actually be true that the more experienced person can do the job faster than the person with less experience. And putting pressure on the individual will pay dividends only up to a point. On one project, I once insisted that a team member get the job done faster, and he got fed up with the pressure. Finally, he said, "Putting two jockeys on one horse won't make it run any faster." He was right.

Then there was a project manager who told me that when his boss doesn't like an estimate of how long a task will take, he tells him to *use a more productive person!* That was the boss's solution to all scheduling problems. See Figure 6.8.

F I G U R E 6.8

More Productive Person

Another factor is how much productive time the person will apply to the task each day. It is not uncommon for people in organizations to spend 25 percent of each day in meetings, on the phone, waiting for supplies, and other activities, all of which reduce the time available to spend on project work. Allowances must be made for such nonproject time.

In addition, if experience with a task is minimal, the expected duration might be adjusted upward, using the closest task for which experience exists for comparison. If virtually no experience can be used as a basis for estimating, then PERT techniques may be appropriate (see Chapter 10). Another possibility is to use the Delphi technique or some other method, such as consensual estimating.

Consensual Estimating

In consensual estimating, several people who know something about the work to be done are asked to estimate task durations independently of each other. They then meet and reveal their estimates. When these estimates are clustered very closely together, the group may agree to use an average. However, when a significant discrepancy exists, the differences are discussed and the group tries to determine what each person was thinking that accounts for the spread. An example of such a spread is shown in Figure 6.9.

In this discussion, the group decides whether to agree with the person who had the significantly different number or whether to ask that person to modify her estimate to be in line with the others. This should not be a strongarming session, but an open discussion with mutual respect for differing points of view. The objective is to reach a consensus on what the number should be.

In this case, consensus means that each person must be able to say, "Although I don't entirely agree with the rest of you, I am fully willing to support the majority position." Notice that the approach does not rely on majority voting alone, since doing so gains compliance but not necessarily

F I G U R E 6.9

Estimates with Significant Disparity

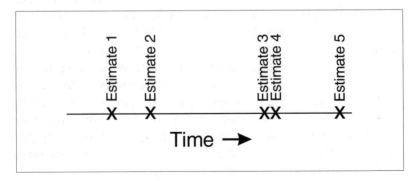

support for the majority position. If any member of the group has strong objections to the majority position, then the group can continue the discussion until a consensus has been reached. As a last resort, the group can overrule the minority member.

There are several advantages to this approach. First, various points of view are brought into the discussion, so that the probability is reduced that something will be overlooked. Second, no one person is on the hook for the estimate, so no one gets "blamed" if the time actually required misses the target. Finally, everyone learns more about estimating through this process.

Means Tables

For construction projects, there are books available containing *means tables*, which list the average expected durations for typical construction activities, together with "fudge factors" to be used in adjusting those times to compensate for geographic location, weather, and so on. A source of means tables is listed in the Resources section at the end of the book.

For other types of projects, unfortunately, there are no means tables available, so historical data must be developed by keeping records on previous project work. This is, perhaps, one of the most important benefits of developing a standardized project management methodology. By doing the work in specified ways and by keeping records on actual working times, an organization can develop a database that can be used to greatly improve future project estimates.

USING CHARTS OF ACCOUNTS FOR WBS NUMBERING

Ultimately, it will be necessary to compare actual progress on the project against the plan. In particular, labor costs will be charged back to the project, and accomplishment of work will be compared with the plan. The device for tracking costs is the chart of accounts, as shown in Figure 6.10.

F I G U R E   6.10

Chart of Accounts

Account Number	Activity Description	Account Number	Activity Description
000 *		032	Camera work
001	Development of concepts	033	Office layout
002	Preliminary design	034	Reserved
003	Computer analysis	035	Reserved
004	Environmental tests	036	Contract administration
005	Alternative selection	037	Contractor payroll
006	Delphi technique		certification
007	Systems analysis	038	Reserved
008	Reserved	039	Reserved
009	Field investigation	070 *	
010 *		071	Project management
011	Final design	072	Project planning &
012	Draft specifications		scheduling
013	Drafting/graphics	073	Project coordination
014	Checking drawings	074	Reserved
015	Specifications review	075	Client meetings &
016	Maintenance work		conferences
017	Technical writing	076	Public meetings & hearings
018	Cost estimating	077	Reserved
019	Bid preparation	078	Reserved
020 *		079	Project review meetings
021	Quality control checks	080 *	
022	Reserved	081	Administrative services
023	Reserved	082	Clerical support
024	Computer data preparation	083	Composing & editing
025	Computer analysis	084	Typing
026	Computer keypunching	085	Reproductions/printing
027	Reserved	086	Training
028	Shop drawing review	087	Marketing & sales
029	Reserved	088	Reserved
030 *		089	Reserved
031	Prepare visual aids	090 *	

Each scheduled task in the project is assigned a chart-of-accounts number, and as people work on that task, they fill out a time report that tells how many hours they spent as well as how much of the task they completed. The report allows for good project control as well as for building a history database over time.

THE LINEAR RESPONSIBILITY CHART

Once the WBS has been completed, a linear responsibility chart can be filled out to show who has responsibility for which tasks. The standard organizational chart is of the pyramidal variety. It portrays the organization as it is "supposed" to exist at a given point in time. However, the pyramidal organization chart is insufficient for projects, because it does not display the nonvertical relations among members of the team. Although not normally defined, the interaction between people in a working environment affects the success of the effort and cannot be overlooked.

One of the common problems of interaction in a project is that someone makes a unilateral decision that affects one or more other team members. For example, capital equipment may be purchased without consulting other users to determine their needs, and the purchased equipment may be lacking. Or one designer may do her work without consulting another designer about aspects of the project that concern both of them.

Linear responsibility charts (LRCs) help by showing such requirements as *must be consulted* or *must be notified*. An example of a linear responsibility chart follows. The empty form can be copied and used in your own projects.

See pages 108 and 109 for the linear responsibility charts.

F I G U R E 6.11

Linear Responsibility Chart (Sample)

| Project: Notebook for Proj. Mgrs. | Date Issued: | 01-Dec-90 | Sheet | 1 | of | 1 |
| Manager: Jim Lewis | Date Revised: | 13-Dec-92 | Filename: | | | LRCSAMP |

PROJECT CONTRIBUTORS

TASK DESCRIPTIONS	Lea Ann	Susi	Jim	Norm S.	Carolyn				
Design forms	2		1						
Final layout of forms	1	2							
Write guidelines for use			1	2					
Design package	1		2	2					
Develop sales plan			1	2					
Production coordination	1	2	2		2				

Codes: 1 = Actual Responsibility || 2 = Support || 3 = Must be notified || Blank = Not involved

Linear Responsibility Chart

| Project: _____ | Date Issued: 13-Dec-92 | Sheet _____ of _____ |
| Manager: _____ | Date Revised: 13-Dec-92 | Filename: LRCSAMP |

PROJECT CONTRIBUTORS

TASK DESCRIPTIONS										

Codes: 1 = Actual Responsibility || 2 = Support || 3 = Must be notified || Blank = Not involved

SECTION THREE

PROJECT SCHEDULING

7

Developing a Project Schedule

Project scheduling is both art and science. The science comes from determining where in a network the critical path is and how much slack or float exists on the noncritical paths. It also involves determining calendar dates, by dropping out nonworking days, such as holidays, weekends, and individual contributor vaca-

> The real emphasis on scheduling is in finding ways to parallel as many activities as possible to complete projects in minimum times.

tion periods. When used, the science also involves leveling the application of resources so that large peaks and valleys do not occur. Finally, there are programs such as @Risk™ that can do Markov process analysis of various paths through the project to determine worst-case scenarios, so that managers can plan for the uncontrollable things that can wreck a project.

The *art* is in constructing a workable schedule. Although we talk about critical path method (CPM) and performance evaluation and review technique (PERT), which is a variation on CPM that uses statistics to determine probabilities of completion times, the real emphasis on scheduling is in finding ways to parallel as many activities as possible to complete projects in minimum times.

In my experience, the real struggle with scheduling is in the art, not the science. For most projects there will be a lot of schedule networks that will get the job done. However, some are better than others (depending on the criteria used to determine *best*), and you can never be certain that you have realized the *one best network* for your project.

I said above that the science of project management involves resource leveling. This is done by a computer algorithm, and many of these exist. However, the result is only as good as the art applied in assigning people to

> No one is available to work on *anything* 100 percent of the time!

the project in the first place. As an example, novice schedulers sometimes assign personnel to projects on a 100% basis, and this is bound to fail. No one is available to work on anything 100 percent of the time. We know that the maximum is usually around 80 percent, because people must have breaks (a *personal* factor), they get tired and productivity drops (called *fatigue*), and they are held up while waiting for other people (*delays*). These are called the PF&D factors that reduce worker availability.

In most instances, the 80% figure is too high, especially for knowledge workers. They have to attend meetings, which don't contribute directly to getting work done. They must talk with customers, do nonproject work, and so on. For these people, availability is seldom better than 50 percent.

Unless the project manager knows the actual availability of personnel, the schedule is likely to be very optimistic. For example, during a refueling operation at a nuclear power plant, workers must go down into the cavity that normally contains the fuel. It is still hot down there, and they have to wear shielded suits. The outside temperature may be 85 to 90 degrees, and inside the suit it is

> Unless you know the actual availability of your personnel, your schedule is likely to be optimistic.

much higher. Because of the temperature and the cramped space, they can work for only a few minutes at a time, thereby stretching out the total time to do the work.

This is one industry that has made major gains in scheduling. Only a few years ago a refueling job took about six months to complete. Through skillful scheduling, the time has been reduced to as little as 90 days.

Another example. In 1983 the San Diego building industry sponsored a contest to see how fast a 2000-square-foot, single-story house could be built. Normally a builder needs several months for a job like this. The winners spent several months planning the job (developing the schedule) and were able to build

> In 1983 a 2000-square-foot house was built in 2 hours and 45 minutes to set a world record! It could be done only by using a really good schedule!

the house in 2 hours and 45 minutes! They had 350 workers on the job. They poured the cement slab, using chemicals to make the concrete cure in only 45 minutes, and while that was being done, crews were building the wall structures, the roof, and other parts of the house. Once the foundation was cured, the wall structures were moved into place and nailed down, then the roof was lifted with a crane and lowered onto the walls. Finally, the interior and exterior were completed, the lawn was landscaped, the wiring and plumbing were installed, and the house was ready to move into. All in 2 hours and 45 minutes! The film is available from the Building Industry Association of San Diego County (call 619-450-1221).

SO HOW IS IT DONE?

Suppose you have made a to-do list for yourself for the week. There are 10 fairly big tasks that you need to do before the end of the week. It might be that they can be done in any order, or it could be that one task must be done before you can do another. This sets up a *logical dependency*, with the second task depending on completion of the first one.

> A logical dependency occurs when a task cannot start until a preceding one is completed.

It is also possible that your boss has said she wants a certain job completed by Monday afternoon, so you must do it before you do the other things. This establishes a *priority relationship* between the task your boss wants done and the other tasks that are on your list.

> A priority relationship exists when your boss wants one task done before something else, but no logical dependency exists.

If there is no priority or logical sequence relating tasks to each other, then they could all be done at the same time—except that you have only two hands and happen not to be ambidextrous, so you can do only one at a time. A *resource dependency* exists between the tasks. The nice thing about resource dependencies is that they can be resolved by getting someone to help you. This can't be done with logical dependencies—until the first task is done, you can't do the second. Of course, the first task might be done faster with help and might even speed up the overall project, as was done in building the house.

If you wanted to determine the absolute minimum amount of time required to do a project, you would parallel all tasks that can be logically done that way and logically sequence the others. So assume your to-do list containing 10 tasks has only 2 that are logically sequenced. You have estimated that one will take two days to complete and the other will take one day. In series, they will need three days to complete.

> A resource dependency exists when one task cannot be done before another one is completed by a certain individual.

If none of the remaining tasks will take more than three days, and they could all be done in parallel with the other two tasks, you would have the situation diagramed in Figure 7.1. In this arrangement, all 10 tasks would be finished by the end of three days.

The only problem is that you would need at least 9 people to do all 10 tasks! Nevertheless, this is the quickest way the tasks could be done. When tasks that can be done in parallel are drawn in that way, regardless of whether the resources are available to do them, you have created a schedule under the assumption of *unlimited resources*. Naturally, no organization has unlimited resources, so what is the value of creating an unworkable schedule? Simply that it tells you the best time that can be achieved for the project.

If no one helps you, how long will it take to do everything on your to-do list? Well, the tasks will clearly have to be done one after the other, so that you have the result shown in Figure 7.2. With unlimited resources, you need three days

F I G U R E 7.1

To-Do List in Order

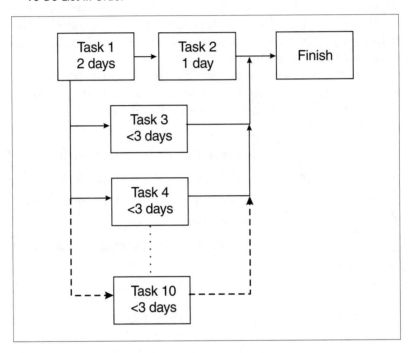

F I G U R E 7.2

The To-Do List in Series

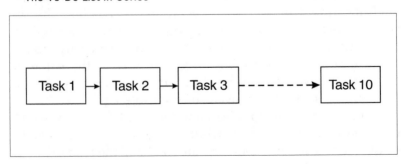

to do the work, but with only one person working on everything, you need five days.

The only thing anyone can question is your estimates of how long each task will take. The problem with any estimate is that the only way you ever know if it is "right" is to do the task and time it. Furthermore, if you do the task this week, it might take 4 hours and next week it might take 4 hours and 15 minutes. All activities vary in duration, from time to time and from person to person, as pointed out in Chapter 6. This normal variation is a law of nature and must be accepted, meaning that the only way you can ever consider project dates as exact is to vary the effort applied in order to finish each task in the specified calendar time. Project schedules are probabilistic and not deterministic!

Overlapping Work

There is one special situation that must sometimes be managed. You don't always need to completely finish one task before you can begin another. You might have to do part of it, but not all. A good example is constructing a pipeline that is several miles long. You start digging the trench, and after you get a sufficient amount done, you begin laying pipe, as shown in Figure 7.3.

F I G U R E 7.3

Pipeline Construction

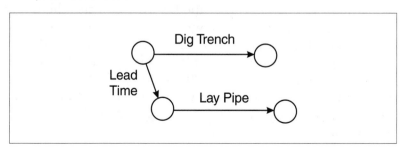

F I G U R E 7.4

Pipeline with Fill Operation Added

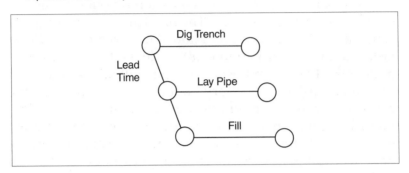

Also, you don't need to wait until all the pipe is in the trench before you begin filling dirt back in, but you definitely want to get a certain amount of pipe laid. Again, a lead time will be needed for the pipe laying, after which you can start the filling operation. This is shown in Figure 7.4.

Now consider the trench-digging operation. Imagine that the operator of the trenching machine gets finished. He looks back and in the distance he sees the pipe-laying crew. It will be some time before the crew is finished, but he can leave this site and go on to another job. In this case, a *lag* exists between the completion of the trenching and completion of the pipe laying. The same is true between the pipe laying and the filling operation. The relationship, called a ladder network, is shown in Figure 7.5.

Some scheduling software won't let you do a full ladder. Note that the relationship at the beginning of trenching and pipe laying is a start-to-start, with a lead time of X days, and the relationship at the end of each task is a finish-to-finish, with a lag of Y days. Microsoft Project 98™ will allow you to do only a start-to-start, or a finish-to-finish, but not both. Generally, a start-to-start will get the job done, but in some special situations you may have to finagle to achieve what you want.

F I G U R E 7.5

Lags Shown for Pipe-Laying Job

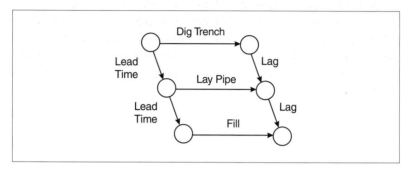

Practical Suggestion

The easiest way to construct a schedule is to use a large whiteboard and Post-it™ note sheets. These can be moved around until the logic you want is achieved, then connected with lines. Once everyone is satisfied that you have the logic you want, and that nothing is mislinked, you can have the diagram entered into your scheduling software. Trying to do this "from scratch" often leads to schedules that don't work, and at best requires that you print the network diagram many times to check it for accuracy. Quite frankly, some scheduling programs don't do a very good job of printing the PERT diagram, so it is very cumbersome to check.

> The best way to construct a schedule is to use a large whiteboard and Post-it notes.

Another thing: If a task has no predecessors, it would have to be a beginning task. If it has no successors, it would have to be an ending task. In completing your diagram, you may occasionally forget to link a task to something else, even though it is neither a beginning nor an ending task. This is called a *dangle*—a task that has been left hanging out "in the air," so to speak. Many software programs won't warn you about dangles, and you cannot see one on a bar chart unless you print links between tasks. Again, it's a good idea to construct the Post-it schedule first, since it is usually easier to spot dangles this way.

8
CHAPTER

Schedule Computations

As a working project manager, you need to know how to perform scheduling computations—only because you need to know what your scheduling software is telling you. If you happen to need an in-depth understanding of how to compute critical path, float, and so on, I highly recommend Moder, Phillips, and Davis (1983). Because the most common form of scheduling used today is activity-on-node (AON) notation, I will show how computations are done for AON networks only. The procedure is exactly the same for activity-on-arrow (AOA) networks, but the notation is different. If you are interested, I again refer you to the Moder et al. book above.

AN EXAMPLE

To illustrate the computation procedure, consider the network shown in Figure 8.1. This is a small project to prepare a meal. However, it is not just a routine family meal. Rather, it

FIGURE 8.1

Network Diagram for a Meal Project

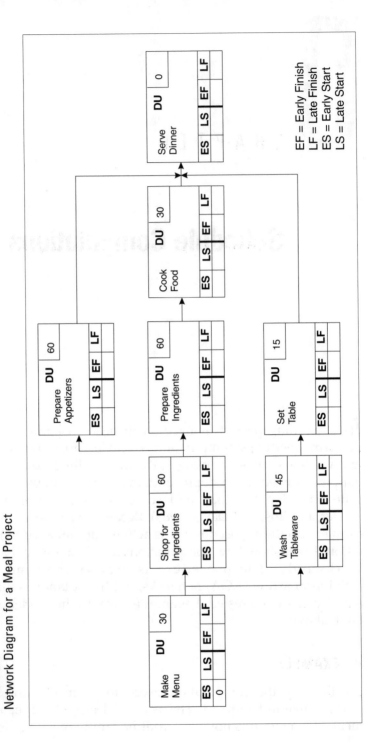

is a dinner party, and our plan is to begin the project at 5:00 P.M. so that we can have the meal on the table by 7:00 P.M. This will give us enough time to eat a leisurely meal, drive to the theater (five minutes away), attend a play that starts at 8:15 P.M.

In my experience, most projects are assigned with a due date. Furthermore, they are often constrained to start on a certain date, because funding, specifications, or resources won't be available. This means that we must fit the work between two fixed dates. Inevitably, this leads to the *10 pounds of trash in a 5-pound bag* problem. Put simply, the schedule just won't fit between those dates. It is too long, and we must try to compress it. Since that is the way scheduling works most of the time, that is how we will cover it in this chapter.

You may notice several apparent discrepancies in the meal project network if you study it closely. First, why does Wash Tableware have to wait until the menu has been set? Because the menu will determine whether we need certain dishes. Next, why do we serve appetizers at the same time that we serve dinner? Simply to keep the network from being overly complicated. In fact, we would serve appetizers and, when everyone has finished, we would serve dinner.

You may also ask why the menu cannot be prepared the day before. It probably could. However, I am operating under the ground rule that the project has a constrained start time, to illustrate later on how the network will be compressed. So let's just assume that some international guests are arriving around noon. We will ask them what they would like for dinner this evening, and that is why we can't make the menu a day ahead of time.

Network Assumptions and Conventions

Under conventional network rules, once Make Menu has been completed, both Shop for Ingredients and Wash Tableware can begin. We assume that there is no handoff time, so the early finish (EF) for Make Menu becomes the early start (ES) for the two following tasks. We also assume that the estimated durations are fixed numbers, so that all tasks will take as long as indicated, and this will yield the upper limit on project time. If anything takes less than shown, then the project might finish early. On the critical path (which we have not yet determined), if anything takes longer than the time shown, then the end time for the project will slip.

The Forward Pass Computation

The first step is to do a forward pass through the network to determine ES and EF times for each task. Note that scheduling software does exactly what we are going to do, but will drop nonworking times out of the schedule and will show resulting calendar times. This is a tremendous benefit gained from the software, since calendar computations can be very messy.

Because Make Menu has a duration of 30 minutes, if we assume it starts at some time = zero (we can convert to clock time later on), then it will finish 30 minutes into the project. This means that Wash Tableware and Shop for Ingredients can start as early as 30 minutes into the project.

Wash Tableware takes 45 minutes to complete, so it will have an EF of 75 minutes into the job, while Shop for Ingredients takes 60 minutes, so it will have an EF of 90 minutes into the project. Proceeding in this manner, we finally reach the box labeled Serve Dinner, which will have an ES of either 90, 150, or 180 minutes. Since the dinner cannot be served until everything preceding it has been completed, it will be 180 minutes into the project. The rule to follow is that, when several tasks converge, the ES for the following task must be the largest of the EF numbers from the preceding tasks. (In terms of times, the early start must be the latest of the early finish times of the preceding tasks.)

We now have a special situation. Serve Dinner has a duration of zero, which means that it is not a task, but an event or *milestone*. It is useful to put milestones at critical points in projects, to force the software to print dates on which these will occur. I could have put a beginning milestone in this project, but since only one task started at time = zero, I chose not to do so. If several tasks had started at zero, it would have been useful to have a beginning milestone. Another reason to place milestones at critical points in projects is that reviews are usually conducted at these points. They will probably represent points at which significant phases of the project should be complete.

For the final milestone, the EF time will be the same as the ES time, since the duration is zero. We now know the answer to our question: If we start the project at 5:00 P.M., can we serve dinner at 7:00 P.M.? No. We will be an hour late, and we now have to decide what to do. See Figure 8.2 for the solution to this point.

We know that we need to shorten the network if we are going to complete the project in two hours. But is that the only option? At this point it should be considered the only one, since we have been given these dates by whoever gave us the project (speaking in terms of most real-world situations). Our job as project managers is not to try to have the times changed until we have first tried everything we can think of to meet them. So what might we do?

Well, the first thing to recognize is that we don't yet know which of the paths through the project is causing us to be late. To find this path, we have to do a backward pass through the network. This will be illustrated next.

The Backward Pass Computation

There are two ways to make a backward pass. One is to impose a late finish (LF) time of 120 minutes on the project. After all, that is the time by which the project needs to be finished. If this is done, we will have negative float (or slack) on the longest path through the project. Float is calculated as shown:

F I G U R E 8.2

Network with Forward Pass Completed

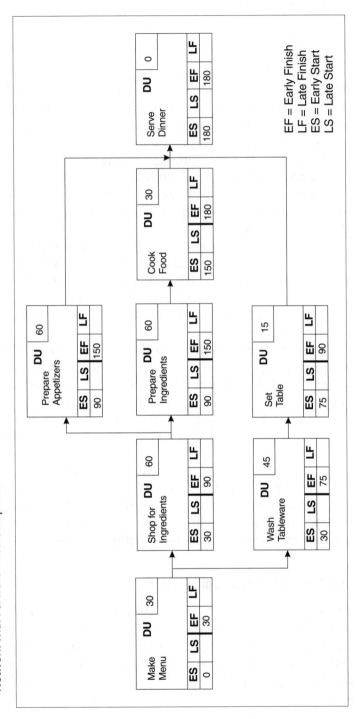

$$Float = LF - EF$$

or

$$Float = LS - ES$$

If we impose a LF time of 120 minutes on this project, we will have negative 60 minutes of float (120 - 180 = -60). When a path or activity has zero float, we call it the critical path, as has been stated previously. However, when the float goes *negative,* the path is considered *supercritical,* and the amount of negative float is the amount of time by which the path needs to be compressed in order to meet the imposed completion time. Since we already knew this, not much is gained by knowing that we have a supercritical path, except that other paths might also have negative float, and this would suggest that they need to be shortened as well. I will show this solution later on.

The second approach to the network is to let the LF time be the same as the EF time, or 120 minutes. This is the default condition that most software programs follow. The assumption is that the project won't finish any earlier than the EF time unless something is changed. Since we don't want to stretch the job out unnecessarily, the LF time should be the same as the EF time. Doing this will force one path to have zero float, and it will be the critical path. Once this path is known, we can concentrate on trying to reduce durations of activities along the path, and this is the procedure that will be shown first.

Since Serve Dinner has a zero duration, if it has a LF of 180 minutes, it will have to start no later than 180 minutes into the project. This 180 minutes will also be the LF for Prepare Appetizers, Cook Food, and Set Table. This is because they must all finish by the LS time for Serve Dinner if it is to be possible to start the task at that time.

Prepare Appetizers has a duration of 60 minutes. If this task must finish no later than 180 minutes, it must start no later than 180 minus 60 or 120 minutes. The Cook Food task has a duration of 30 minutes, so it will have a LS time of 180 minus 30 or 150 minutes. This 150-minute LS time becomes the LF time for Prepare Ingredients, and since this task has a duration of 60 minutes, it will have a LS time of 150 minus 60 or 90 minutes. See Figure 8.3.

Now what should be the LF time for Shop for Ingredients? It must be either the 90-minute LS time for Prepare Ingredients or the 120-minute LS time for Prepare Appetizers. If we study the network, we will see that it has to be the smaller number. If we were to let Shop for Ingredients end at 120 minutes, rather than 90 minutes, then it would slide the critical path out and the project would be even more late than it already is. So the rule on a backward pass is that, at a junction, we let the LF for the preceding task be the smaller of the LS times on succeeding tasks. (In terms of time, the LF must be the earliest of the LS times on succeeding tasks.)

Continuing with the backward pass calculations, we finally achieve the solution shown in Figure 8.4. The path through the middle is the critical path, and the paths through Prepare Appetizers and Wash Tableware have float. We now know the path that must be shortened by 60 minutes if we are to complete the project in 120 minutes.

Reducing Activity Durations

If you are going to reduce durations of activities on the critical path, you will have to do one of the following:

1. Add resources. This can be done by adding people or by working the people you have more hours per day (this is called overtime). You can't use overtime on the meal project, of course.

2. Reduce the scope of the task. In the case of the meal project, you could do this by buying ingredients that have already been cut up (frozen vegetables, for example).

3. Reduce the quality of the work. This is not desirable, but if you put people under enough pressure to finish on time, it may be what they do.

Network with Partially Completed Backward Pass

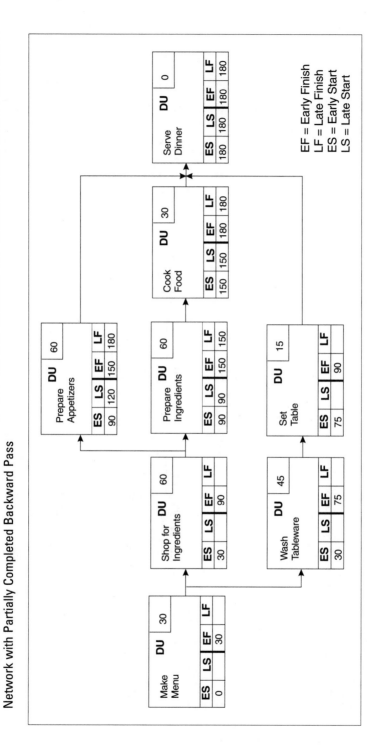

EF = Early Finish
LF = Late Finish
ES = Early Start
LS = Late Start

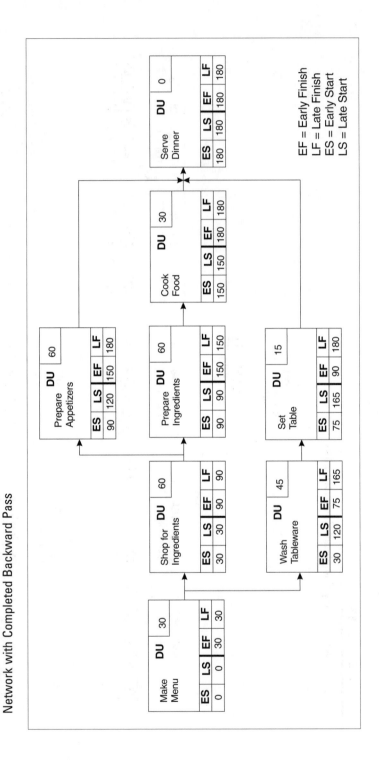

FIGURE 8.4

Network with Completed Backward Pass

4. Change the process by which work is done. For the meal, this might mean microwaving the food instead of cooking it conventionally on a stove.

If none of these things works, then you may be able to change the way the network is drawn so that more things are done in parallel, or work is overlapped.

One caution. As a project manager, you may be tempted to tell everyone that overtime is needed in order to meet the end date for a project. This is very bad practice. If you later encounter problems, you can't use overtime to "bail out" the project, and your chance of missing the end date is increased.

Constrained Finish Computations

When the LF time on our meal project is constrained to 120 minutes, we get the numbers shown in Figure 8.5. As you can see, there is a float of negative 60 minutes on the middle path (which, as we saw above, is the standard critical path). There is also negative 30 minutes of float on the Prepare Appetizers path. This suggests that we will have to take 30 minutes out of the Appetizers path and 60 out of the critical path, unless we do something clever. It turns out that if we can reduce Prepare Ingredients to 30 minutes and Shop for Ingredients to 30 minutes, we will reduce the critical path time by the 60 minutes we need and also avoid having to reduce the time required for Prepare Appetizers. This is shown in Figure 8.6.

Overlapping Work

Another alternative is to use the ladder network idea from the previous chapter. If our meal contains potatoes and broccoli, for example, we know that potatoes need considerably longer to cook than broccoli. So if we get the potatoes on to cook first, we can then continue preparing broccoli and other ingredients. Suppose we can get the potatoes on to cook 30 minutes after we begin preparing ingredients. If we do, we will have the solution shown in Figure 8.7.

FIGURE 8.5

Finish Constrained to 120 Minutes

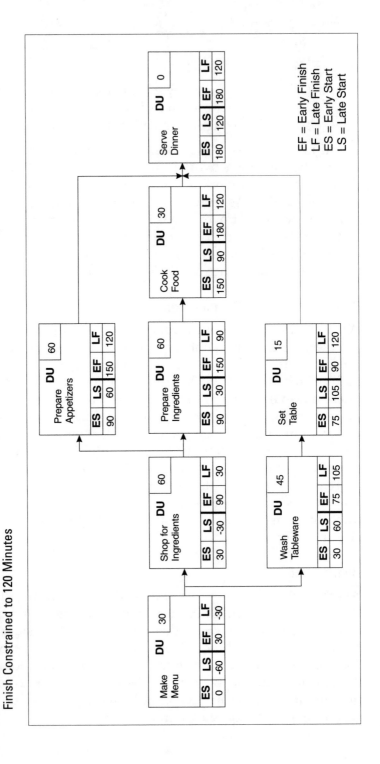

Network with Times Reduced for Shopping and Ingredients

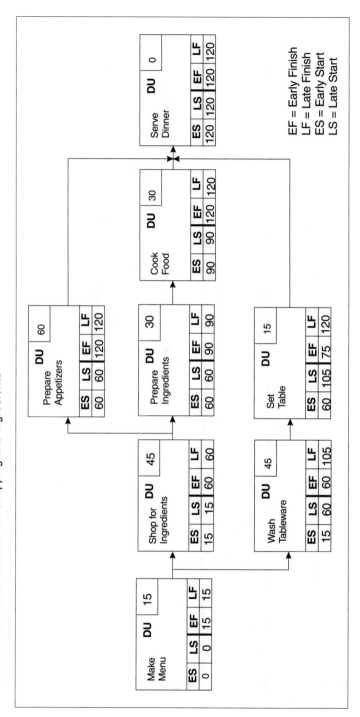

FIGURE 8.7

Network with Overlap on Preparing Ingredients

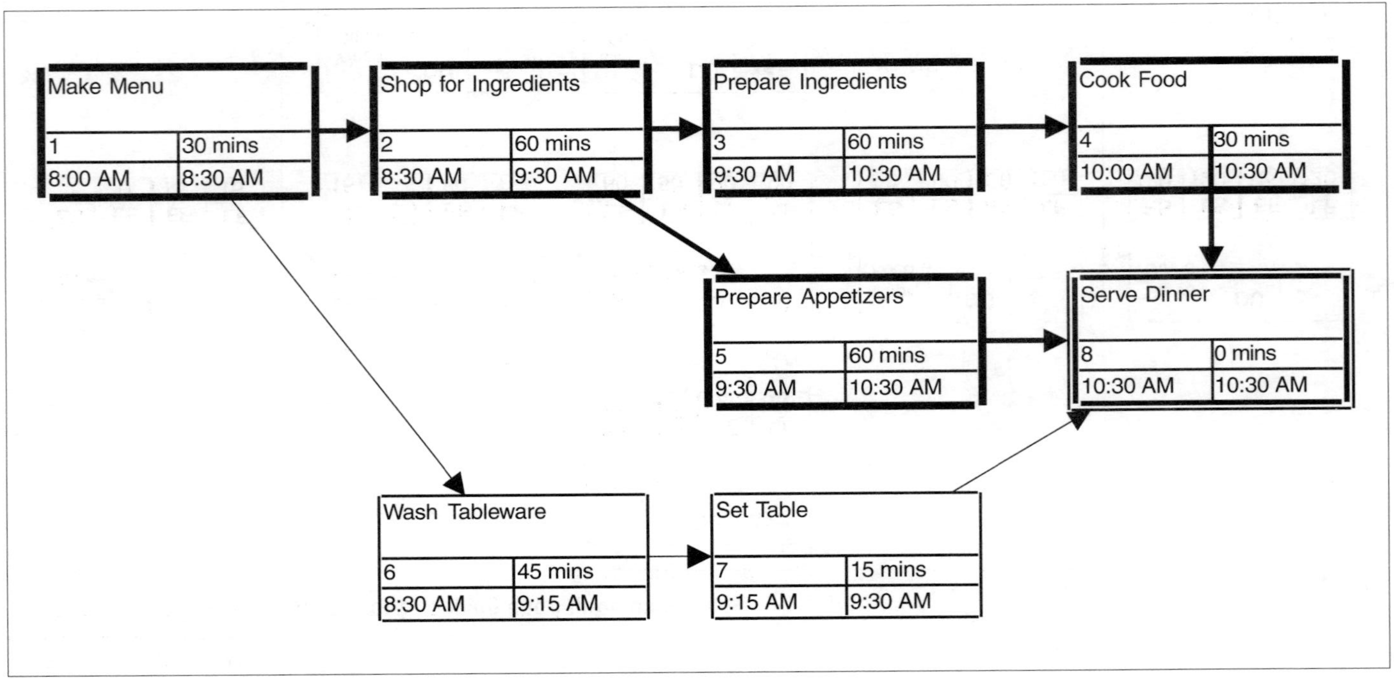

The project now finishes 30 minutes earlier. If we can also reduce the shopping time to 30 minutes, we will be able to complete the entire project in the 120 minutes required.

THE EFFECT OF NONWORKING TIMES ON SCHEDULES

Calendar time and working time will be the same only when a project is run 24 hours a day, seven days a week. In the case of the meal project, the two are equal because we are essentially conforming to this condition. When weekends are not worked, when holidays intervene, or when people are on vacation, then calendar time will always exceed working time.

In most scheduling software programs, you can enter holidays and other periods when no one works on the project into the global calendar. The software will then schedule around these dates and tell you the actual date on which the project will end. You also can enter vacation days into a calendar for each resource, and the software will schedule around these. This feature is one of the most useful offered by current software.

Network Diagrams and Bar Charts

Bar chart schedules were first developed for use in project scheduling by Henry Gantt, and are called Gantt charts for that reason. The beauty of bar charts is simplicity—they are easy to read—and they should always be provided to team members for that reason. However, it is absolutely essential to construct the schedule using network diagrams in order to find the critical path and float. This is done in most software programs by specifying the predecessors or successors for each task. (You specify one or the other but not both.)

You can also tell the software that a task must start by a certain date or must end by a certain date. However, if you do too much of this, the software will simply regurgitate what you have told it, and you have lost the power of the tool, which is to tell you when tasks are going to end, given the task durations you have specified. Then if the procedure does not yield acceptable target dates, you need to massage the activity durations, revise the network, or negotiate a change in target dates.

9

CHAPTER

Scheduling with Resource Constraints

THE ASSUMPTION OF UNLIMITED RESOURCES

All the scheduling computations in the previous chapter were made on the assumption that the activity durations were achievable. However, the time required to complete an activity depends on the resource(s) assigned to it, and if the level of required resources is not available, then the work cannot be completed as planned. Further, if two tasks can be done in parallel, they should be drawn that way, even though this leads to the assumption that we have unlimited resources. Naturally that is not the case, even for the largest organizations.

Project scheduling cannot be successful unless the project manager can solve the resource allocation problem. Every organization has a fixed number of resources, which are shared among all projects. Also, whereas basic schedule computations can be made manually—even for fairly sizable networks—the resource allocation problem quickly grows to

such proportions that it can be solved only with a computer. Therefore, this chapter will illustrate how a schedule is developed to account for the availability of resources, using Microsoft Project 98™. Other PC software may handle the problem differently, but the approach illustrated here will give a general outline that is representative of most of the software available today.

THE EFFECT OF LIMITED RESOURCES ON SCHEDULE FLOAT

When resource limitations exist, the float that was determined through conventional critical path analysis may have to be used to avoid overloading resources. To illustrate the resource allocation approach, we will rely on the network shown in Figure 9.1, with resources assigned to each activity. When a number of people can all do the same work, they are treated as a "pool" of resources. The initial analysis

F I G U R E 9.1

PERT Diagram for Resource Allocation Example

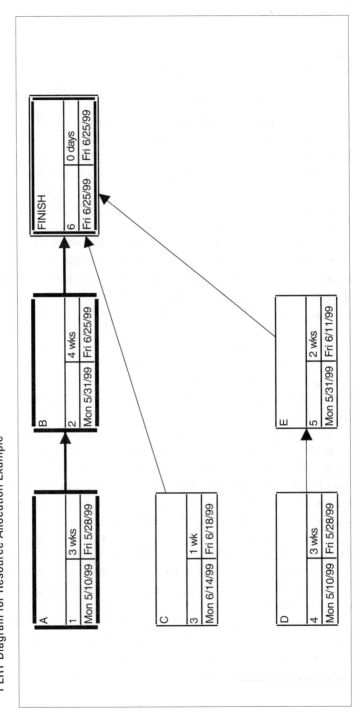

presented here will make use of pooled resources. That analysis will be followed by one in which specific individuals are assigned to the tasks.

As we saw in Chapter 6, estimating an activity duration begins by assuming that a certain kind of resource will be applied. For example, a 10-year-old boy probably cannot mow grass with a push mower as fast as a 16-year-old boy. So if we are going to estimate how long it will take to cut the grass, we must begin by deciding who will do it. Then we know how long it will take.

When this approach is used, there is another assumption involved. It is that the task has a fixed duration. This is the most usual way in which activity durations are handled, so that system will be illustrated first. However, if a task duration depends on how many resources are applied, we may be able to achieve a better schedule if we move resources around, changing activity durations. This is the *variable-duration* approach, and Microsoft Project 98 is defaulted to treat resources as variable-duration. If you want the task to have a fixed duration, you have to force Project 98 to treat it that way.

Another way to think of variable-duration tasks is to consider how many working hours the task will require, then ask what percent of time the person will work on it, and figure out the calendar time from that. For example, if a task will take 10 working hours to complete, but the person plans to work on it only 25 percent of her time, then it will take 40 calendar hours (or one working week) to complete the task. This is the Microsoft default. Going into significant detail on how to use the software is outside the scope of this book, but for this chapter, activities have been treated as fixed-duration.

To allocate resources, the level of resources *available* to the project must be specified, together with the level *required* by each activity. The software then attempts to schedule work so that the available resources are not overloaded.

The resource level available is measured by taking the number of people, multiplying by the total amount of time they are going to work, and specifying the product as the availability. If two individuals are available for 40 hours per week, then 80 person-hours per week are available. If time is measured in days, then for a five-day week, with two people, 10 person-days per week are available. In Project 98, if you have three workers available, you tell the program that the resource called "worker 1" is available 300 percent, which is the same as having three people available.

Note that holidays, vacations, and overtime will affect the amount of labor available during the period in which they occur, so that the schedule will reflect a total *elapsed* time that is different from that obtained if a constant level of labor were available. For the analysis that follows, no vacations or holidays have been entered.

The initial Gantt chart for the project is shown in Figure 9.2. Tasks A and E have two workers assigned (Worker 1 @ 200%), and tasks B, C, and D have one worker assigned. Notice that the project will require four workers during the first week if the work is to be done as scheduled, but only three workers are available. This overload is confirmed by the resource-loading diagram shown in Figure 9.3.

TIME-CRITICAL AND RESOURCE-CRITICAL LEVELING

Once you have developed a schedule to meet a required end date, you don't want it to slip because of resource limitations. So when resources are overloaded, you want the software to level them so that the end date can still be met. This is called *time-critical* leveling. In Project 98, the dialog box asks if you want to level within the available slack. If you check this box, you get time-critical leveling.

Suppose you find that the overloads cannot be resolved with time-critical leveling. This will often be the case. Then you have to find additional resources, work your available

FIGURE 9.2

Gantt Chart for Generic Resource Project

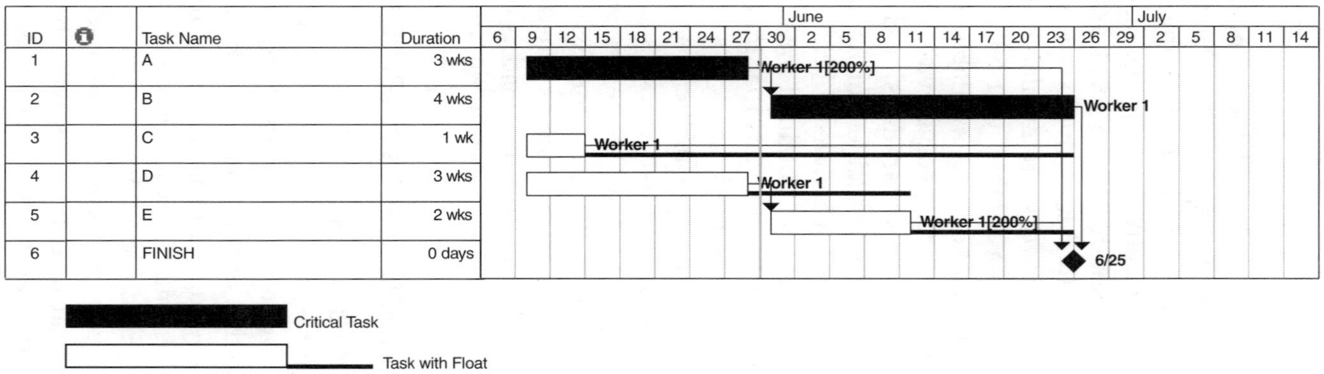

ID	ⓘ	Task Name	Duration
1		A	3 wks
2		B	4 wks
3		C	1 wk
4		D	3 wks
5		E	2 wks
6		FINISH	0 days

Critical Task

Task with Float

Resource-Loading Diagram for Project in Initial Form

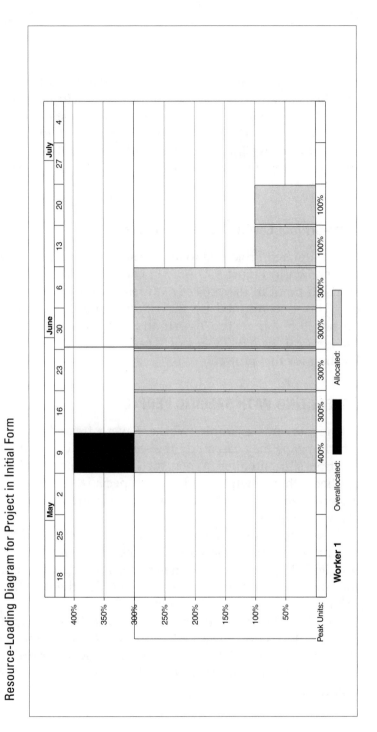

people overtime, reduce scope, reduce quality, or extend the deadline. In many cases, the only options will be applying overtime or slipping the end date. The question is: How much will it slip? The answer can be found through *resource-critical* leveling. To do this with Project 98, be sure that the box asking if you want to level within the available slack is not checked.

Time-Critical Leveling of the Example

If you now tell Project 98 to level resources, you get the solution shown in Figure 9.4. As you can see by a simple visual scan, no point in the project requires more than three workers. This is confirmed by the resource-loading diagram in Figure 9.5. Since the overloads can be resolved with time-critical leveling, you don't need to do resource-critical leveling for this project.

SCHEDULING WITH SPECIFIC PEOPLE

In the previous example, workers were treated as a pool, which means they can all do the same work. This is the simplest possible situation. When such an assumption cannot be applied—that is, when workers are specialized—you have to assign them by name. A project to illustrate this case is shown in Figure 9.6.

As you can see, Tom and Sue are double-scheduled in this project. Mary's tasks are in series, so she is okay. If you now tell Project 98 to do time-critical leveling of resources, the overload for Tom can be resolved, but the one for Sue cannot. The result is shown in Figure 9.7.

This is the best that can be done, unless another person can handle one of Sue's tasks. If not, then the project will slip. To find out what will happen, you level resources under resource-critical conditions. The solution is shown in Figure 9.8.

Schedule with Resources Leveled

ID	ⓘ	Task Name	Duration
1		A	3 wks
2		B	4 wks
3		C	1 wk
4		D	3 wks
5		E	2 wks
6		FINISH	0 days

Critical Task

Task with Float

F I G U R E 9.5

Resource-Loading Diagram with Resources Leveled

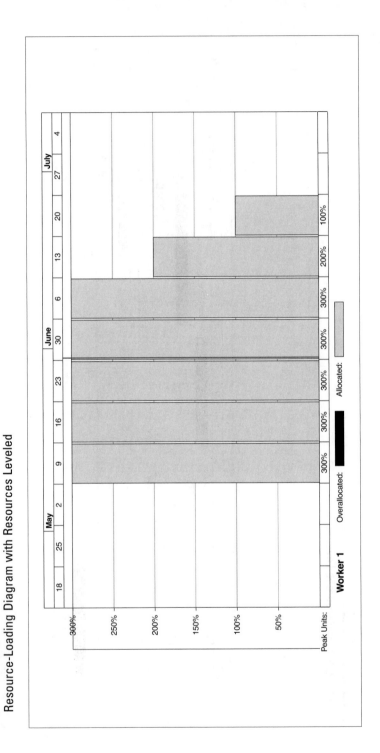

F I G U R E 9.6

Bar Chart with Specific Individuals Assigned to Tasks

F I G U R E 9.7

Schedule with Tom's Overload Resolved

ID	🛈	Task Name	Duration
1		Start	0 days
2		Task A	5 days
3		Task B	5 days
4		Task C	6 days
5		Task D	10 days
6		Task E	5 days
7		Task F	8 days
8		Finish	0 days

Critical Task

Task with Float

Schedule Leveled Under Resource-Critical Conditions

ID	⊡	Task Name	Duration
1		Start	0 days
2		Task A	5 days
3		Task B	5 days
4		Task C	6 days
5		Task D	10 days
6		Task E	5 days
7		Task F	8 days
8		Finish	0 days

Critical Task

Task with Float

As you can see, the end date has slipped. But what good is this schedule if you need to meet the earlier date?

Simple.

It gives you a bargaining chip. You can now show the project sponsor what is going to happen if trade-offs aren't made. You can reduce the scope of work, reduce quality, work people overtime, or slip the end date. Those are the choices. Of course, you may be told to work faster or use a more productive person, but if either solution were possible, you wouldn't be having a conversation with the sponsor in the first place. This approach gives you an analytical handle on the project. If you had no computer solution, but simply *felt* that you needed more help, you would have no credibility with the sponsor at all. Remember: You are always making trade-offs between the P, C, T, and S variables in every project, and values for all four cannot be dictated. Three can be assigned, but the fourth must be allowed to float.

The subject of resource allocation has only been touched on in this chapter. To give a full treatment of the topic requires an entire book. If you need help dealing with specific aspects of resource allocation, you must consult the software manual to find out how the software handles the particular problem.

For example, some programs allow activity splitting and some do not. With activity splitting, a person working on a 10-day task can work for 2 days, shift to something else, then come back and finish the original task. This way, a higher-priority task can be completed without being delayed. The only concern with activity splitting is that it is usually assumed that a split task will take the same time to complete as an unsplit one. That is almost never the case. Once you have been away from a task for a few days, you need to rethink where you were, and this setup time will add to the total time needed to do the job. If setup time is not taken into account, your project schedule may not be correct. Naturally, if setup time is trivial, then it can be ignored.

10
CHAPTER

Scheduling with PERT

PERT COMPARED WITH CPM

When most of the activities in a project are similar to other activities that have been performed a large number of times, CPM scheduling is generally used. With CPM, estimates of activity durations are based on historical data and are assumed to be the mean or average time that the activity has taken to perform in the past.

However, when a project contains a majority of activities for which no experience exists—that is, when no historical data is available—the estimating difficulty becomes significant. With no experience to serve as a guide, the only solution is to make the best possible guess, using *whatever* relevant experience available.

It seems clear, however, that the more unique an activity is, the less certain the estimate of its duration and, therefore, the more *risky* the project will be in terms of control. And since a lot of projects (such as research and development) fall into this category, the question naturally arises as to whether some method might be employed to reduce estimating risk.

It was in response to this problem that PERT was developed around 1957 as a joint effort between the U.S. Navy and the consulting firm of Booz, Allen, and Hamilton. The concept was originally applied to the Polaris submarine project.

Although estimates of activity durations for CPM projects are taken as averages based on history, once they are in place, they are often assumed to be more or less fixed or, to use the colloquial expression, they are "engraved in granite." The PERT system, however, is based on the recognition that estimates are uncertain, and therefore it makes sense to talk of *ranges* of durations and the *probability* that an activity duration will fall into that range, rather than assuming that an activity will be completed in a fixed amount of time.

EMPIRICAL FREQUENCY DISTRIBUTIONS

To understand the probability and statistics involved in PERT, consider an activity that has been performed in the past many times under essentially the same conditions. For the activity in question, duration times ranged from 7 to 17 days. Now suppose that you count the number of times the activity required 7 days to perform, 8 days to perform, etc., and you display the resulting information in the form of an empirical frequency distribution or histogram, as shown in Figure 10.1.

As we know from statistics, if an infinite number of observations were made, the width of the intervals in this figure would approach zero, and the distribution would merge into some smooth curve. This type of curve is the theoretical probability density of the random variable. The total area under such a curve is made to be exactly 1, so that the area under the curve between any two values of time t is directly the probability that the random variable r will fall in this interval. When this is done, the curve is called a *normal distribution curve*. It is also often called a bell-shaped curve. Readers who

Empirical Frequency Distribution

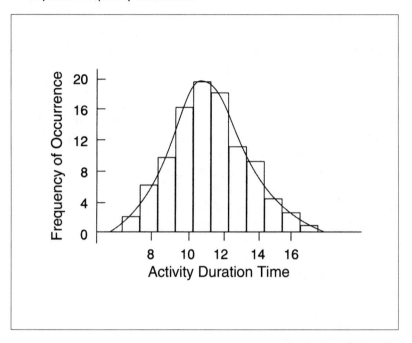

are well versed in statistics should note that normal distributions were not assumed in developing the PERT system, but it is much easier to understand the intent of the system if normal curves are used. For a rigorous treatment of the statistics, consult Moder, Phillips, and Davis (1983).

Once the normal distribution curve exists for an activity, it is then a simple matter to extract the average expected duration from the curve and to use that time as the estimate for how long the work will take. However, when no such distribution exists, we could still say that the problem is to arrive at our *best approximation of what the average expected duration would be* if we *could* perform the work over and over to develop the normal distribution curve. It is the answer to this question that forms the heart of the PERT system.

PERT SYSTEM OF THREE TIME ESTIMATES

Even though a project may consist of activities for which little or no experience exists, most planners will have some relevant experience, so in most cases it is possible to make an educated guess of the *most likely* time the work will take. In addition, estimates can be made of how long the work would take if things go better than expected and, conversely, if things go worse than expected. These are called the *optimistic* and *pessimistic* conditions, respectively. They are not defined as best- and worst-case conditions, however. See the definitions in Table 10.1 for their exact meanings.

The optimistic, pessimistic, and most likely time estimates can be thought of as representing aspects of the normal distribution curve that could be developed if the work were performed a sufficient number of times. Another way to think of them is to say they represent *information* or data about the work in question. Taken together, perhaps they allow a computation of the distribution *mean* to be made.

T A B L E 10.1

Terms Used in PERT Scheduling

Term	Definition
a	optimistic time: the time that would be improved only one time in 20, if the activity could be performed repeatedly under the same essential conditions.
m	most likely time: the modal value of the distribution, or value that is most likely to occur more often than any other value.
b	pessimistic time: the time that would be exceeded only one time in 20 if the activity could be performed repeatedly under the same essential conditions.

This is the essence of the PERT system, although what has been presented is an admittedly simplified presentation. As mentioned above, the interested reader should consult Moder, Phillips, and Davis (1983) for a more thorough treatment of the statistics involved. For our purposes, all that matters is the application of the method.

PERT COMPUTATIONS

In order to combine the three estimates to calculate the expected mean duration for the activity, the PERT developers derived a formula based on principles from statistics. The estimate of average expected time to perform an activity is given by the following expression:

$$t_e = \frac{a + 4m + b}{6}$$

where

t_e = expected time
a = optimistic time estimate
m = most likely time
b = pessimistic time

These values of t_e are used as the durations of activities in a PERT network. Given those estimated durations, the network calculations are identical to those for CPM. A forward pass computation yields earliest times for events and a backward pass provides latest times.

ESTIMATING PROBABILITY OF SCHEDULED COMPLETION

What is gained by PERT, compared with CPM, is the ability to now compute a *confidence interval* for each activity and for the critical path, once it has been located. To do this, the standard deviation of each activity distribution must be known. Such a computation is automatically made by PERT software. However, if CPM software is used to do scheduling, the calculations can be made externally, perhaps using a spread-sheet (which is very simple to construct, incidentally).

A suitable estimator of activity standard deviation is given by:

$$\hat{s} = \frac{b - a}{6}$$

where is the standard deviation of the expected time, te.

Once the critical path has been determined for the network, the standard deviation for the total critical path can be calculated by taking the square root of the sum of the variances of the activities on the critical path. Thus, the standard deviation is given by:

$$\hat{s}_{cp} = \sqrt{s_1^2 + s_2^2 + \ldots + s_n^2}$$

From statistics, we know that the probability of completing the project is 68 percent within plus-or-minus one standard deviation of the mean, 95 percent within two standard deviations, and 99.74 percent within three standard deviations. The normal curve is shown in Figure 10.2 for reference.

An Example

To illustrate how PERT works, we will consider a single activity, for which estimates are made by two different planners. The estimates given by each person are shown in Table 10.2, together with the calculated values for t_e and s.

Note that the standard deviation for the estimates made by planner 1 is only 0.5 day, meaning that the spread on the normal distribution curve is quite small. For planner 2, the standard deviation is 1.8 days. For convenience, we will call this 2.0 days even. The normal distribution curve, using these two different sets of numbers, is shown in Figure 10.3.

The impact on the activity estimate is that the *confidence interval* for planner 2 is four times wider than that for planner 1 for a *given probability* of completion of the task. To illustrate,

Normal Distribution Curve

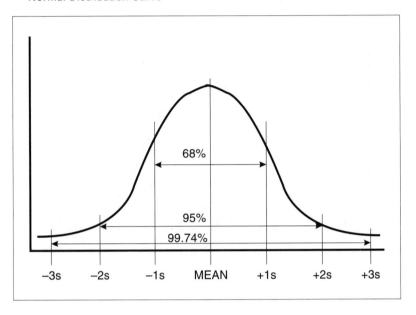

T A B L E 10.2

Estimates for an Activity Made by Two Planners

Description	Planner 1	Planner 2
m = most likely	10 days	10 days
a = optimistic	9 days	9 days
b = pessimistic	12 days	20 days
PERT time	10.166 days	11.5 days
Standard deviation	0.5 day	1.8 days

F I G U R E 10.3

Distribution with Confidence Intervals Shown

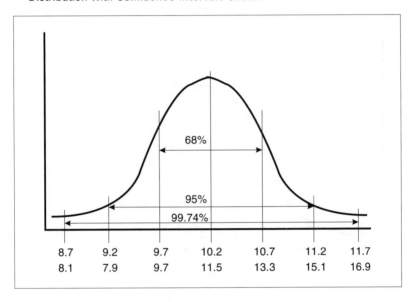

| 8.7 | 9.2 | 9.7 | 10.2 | 10.7 | 11.2 | 11.7 |
| 8.1 | 7.9 | 9.7 | 11.5 | 13.3 | 15.1 | 16.9 |

there is a 68 percent probability that the activity will be completed in the range of 9.7 to 11.7 days if the estimates made by planner 1 are used, whereas the 68 percent confidence interval is 9.5 to 13.5 days if the estimates made by planner 2 are used.

What these statistics mean is simply that planner 1 has greater confidence or less *uncertainty* about her estimates than planner 2. Does that mean planner 1 is more correct? No. It is simply a reflection of the different experiences of the two individuals.

Perhaps because planner 2 has had less experience with this particular activity than planner 1, he is not sure how long it will take. Therefore, the PERT system would tell him to use an activity duration of 11.5 days as his best estimate of mean duration, whereas planner 1 would use only 10.2 days. This can be thought of as automatically providing some "padding" for the person who has the least confidence in his estimates, although I am using the word "pad" here in a different sense than it is normally used.

USING PERT

As we have seen, PERT requires that three time estimates be made for each project activity and that these be plugged into formulas to calculate a time estimate and standard deviation. Because this means additional work compared with CPM, many planners consider PERT to be not worth the effort.

In fact, some people question the validity of the entire process. They argue that, if all three estimates are guesses, why should the weighted composite of three guesses be any better than just using the most likely estimate in the first place? Indeed, there is merit to this argument. As I see it, a principal advantage of PERT is that it makes everyone realize that durations used to specify the completion of work are not exact, but carry with them *probabilities*.

Should you choose to use PERT estimating with software that does not support it, you can download a spreadsheet from my Website that will do the computations for you. The address is www.lewisinstitute.com.

SECTION Four

PROJECT CONTROL
AND EVALUATION

CHAPTER

Principles of Project
Control and Evaluation

CONTROL AND EVALUATION PRINCIPLES

Proper project control and evaluation are necessary if project objectives are to be met. Therefore, the design of a project control system is very important, as is the practice of proper evaluation methods. Before such systems can be designed, it is essential to understand the basic concepts and principles of control and evaluation.

PROJECT REVIEWS

There are three kinds of project reviews that can be conducted: status, design, and process. Each has a different purpose. A status review concentrates on whether the P, C, T, and S targets are being met: Are we on schedule and on budget. Is the scope correct? Are performance requirements okay?

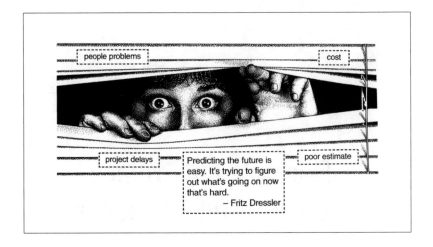

A design review applies only to those projects in which something is being designed, such as a product, service, or software. Some of the questions asked during such a review are: Does it meet specifications? Is it user-friendly? Can we manufacture it? Is the market still looking for what we are developing? Are return on investment (ROI) and other product justifications still in line?

A process review focuses on *how* we are doing our work. Two questions are asked: What are we doing well? What do we want to improve?

During status and design reviews, a project may also be evaluated. An evaluation is usually focused on software or hardware development projects and tries to determine if the required end result will be accomplished. Will the ROI target be met? Will the product be manufacturable? Can we sell it? The answers to these questions determine whether the project will be continued or canceled. Table 11.1 summarizes the three project reviews.

Following are some of the general reasons for conducting periodic project reviews:

- ◆ Improve project performance together with project management.

T A B L E 11.1

The Three Kinds of Project Reviews

Type of Review	Purpose
Status	Are P, C, T, and S okay?
Design	Does it work? Can we make it?
Process	What have we done well so far? What do we want to do better in the future?

- Ensure that quality of project work does not take a back seat to schedule and cost concerns.
- Reveal developing problems early, so that action can be taken to deal with them.
- Identify areas where other projects (current or future) should be managed differently.
- Keep client(s) informed of project status. This can also help ensure that the completed project will meet the needs of the client.
- Reaffirm the organization's commitment to the project for the benefit of project team members.

Process Reviews

The objective or purpose of a process review is to improve performance of the team. Note that in reviewing performance, we do not ask, "What have we done wrong?" Asking that question simply raises defenses in team members. People are going to try to hide anything they think is wrong, because they assume that they will be trashed for mistakes. The purpose of a process review is to learn from experience, so

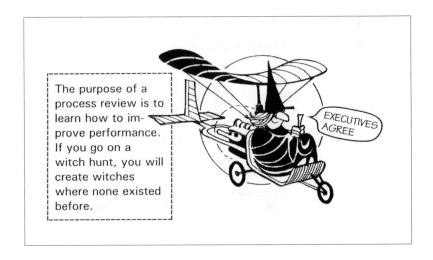

that we can avoid those things that were not done so well and continue doing those things that have been done well. It is not a witch-hunt. If you go about it in a "blame and punishment" way, people will hide their faults.

Another reason for not asking "What have we done wrong?" is that the answer may be "Nothing," and everyone may think that a review is unnecessary. This is not true. The best-performing team must always attempt to get even better, since competitors are not sitting idly by maintaining the status quo. They too are improving, and if you stand still for very long, they will pass you.

It is also a fact that the most dangerous place a team can be is successful. That may sound like faulty logic, and even may be a bit depressing, but it is true. A successful team can easily get complacent. Coaches of sports teams know this. When you have won every game of the season, your very next game is risky because you may get cocky and careless. For that reason, you can never be satisfied with the status quo.

It is very important to understand that process will always affect task outcomes! That is, the *way* you do something will always affect the results you get. As the saying goes, "If you always do what you've always done, you'll always get what you always got." And the corollary is, "Insanity is continuing to do what you've always done and hope for a different result." In terms of process, these statements mean, "If you aren't getting the results you want, change your process!"

> **Process will *always* affect task!**
> —Marvin Weisbord

In any project team, the processes we care about include those shown in the box. One of the most important of these is meetings. Projects cannot succeed without periodic meetings. However, as we all know, the large majority of meetings are badly run, leaving participants drained, frustrated, and wishing they never had to attend another one. In his video *Meetings, Bloody Meetings,* John Cleese makes a profound comment. He says, "The essence of management is in how we run meetings."

> **Team Processes**
> - Leadership
> - Decision making
> - Problem solving
> - Communications
> - Meetings
> - Planning
> - Giving feedback to team members
> - Conflict management

Now if that doesn't make you depressed, you haven't thought about the implications. Meetings typically lose focus, have no clear direction to begin with, last ad nauseum, and don't accomplish anything. If you can't manage a meeting, how can you manage an organization?

One of the best meeting-management models I have seen, developed at Xerox, is described by Tom Kaiser in his book *Mining Group Gold*. The process is also illustrated in a video by the same name, which is distributed by CRM Films (see the Resources). The essence of the model is that a premeeting agenda is published, with each agenda item time-limited. When the meeting starts, the agenda is reviewed to ensure that it is still valid. One member of the team serves the role of notekeeper (called the *scribe* by Kaiser). Notes are taken on flipchart pages so that members of the group can see them throughout the meeting. Taking notes on standard paper does not permit constant viewing.

Another member of the team serves as timekeeper, making sure the meeting stays on schedule. Finally, there is the facilitator, who has responsibility for controlling the meeting. All members are expected to be cofacilitators, however, so that if the meeting gets off track and the facilitator does not bring it back around, any member of the team can do so.

Another aspect of the model is that feelings must be processed before facts. If people get upset about something, they are asked to pause and reflect on why they are upset, then have an open discussion of their feelings. As Kaiser says, if you attempt to deal with facts while people are upset, you are just wasting your time.

This is a much more reasonable approach than telling people to keep feelings out of the meeting. Such a directive is totally unrealistic. People would not be people without feelings, so we must validate them and learn to deal effectively with them.

THE PROCESS REVIEW REPORT

When a project is reviewed, team members should share the lessons learned with other teams. By doing so, they can avoid past mistakes and take advantage of the things they are doing well. The lessons-learned report should contain as a minimum the following:

1. **Current project status.** Project status is best shown through earned-value analysis, as presented in Chapter 12. However, when earned value analysis is not used, status should still be reported with as great accuracy as possible.

2. **Future status.** The report should forecast what is expected to happen in the project. Are significant deviations expected in schedule, cost, performance, or scope? If so, the nature of such changes should be specified.

3. **Status of critical tasks.** The status of critical tasks, particularly those on the critical path, should be reported. Tasks that have high levels of technical risk should be given special attention, as should those being performed by outside vendors, subcontractors, or others over whom the project manager may have limited control.

4. **Risk assessment.** Have any risks been identified that highlight potential for monetary loss, project failure, or other liabilities?

5. **Information relevant to other projects.** What has been learned from this review that can or should be applied to other projects, whether presently in progress or about to start?

6. **Limitations of the review.** What factors might limit the validity of the review? Are any assumptions suspect? Is any data missing or suspect of contamination? Was anyone uncooperative in providing information for the review?

As a rule, the simpler and more straightforward a project review report, the better. The information should be organized so that planned versus actual results can be easily compared. Significant deviations should be highlighted and explained. The form in Figure 11.1 is designed for a milestone process review. For an end-of-project review, the form will be too small to capture all the data generated, so it should be

F I G U R E   11.1

Process Review Form

Project Process Review
Project:
Prepared by: Date:
For the period from   to:
Evaluate the following objectives: Performance was on target ❏, below target ❏, above target ❏ Budget was on target ❏, overspent ❏, underspent ❏ Schedule was on target ❏, behind ❏, ahead ❏
Overall, was the project a success? Yes ❏ No ❏
If not, what factors contributed to a negative evaluation?
What was done really well?
What could have been done better?
What recommendations would you make for future project application?
What would you do differently if you could do it over?
What have you learned that can be applied to future projects?

used as a guide for what questions to ask. See the project checklists in Chapter 30 for additional ideas.

PROJECT EVALUATION

As the dictionary definition suggests, to evaluate a project is to determine if the overall status of the work is acceptable, in terms of intended value to the client once the job is finished. Project evaluation appraises the progress and performance of a job compared with what was originally planned. That evaluation provides the basis for management decisions on how to proceed with the

> **e•val•u•ate:** To determine or judge the value or worth of.
> —*Random House Dictionary*

project. The evaluation must be credible in the eyes of everyone affected, or decisions based on that evaluation will not be considered valid. The primary tool for project evaluation is the *project evaluation or audit,* which is usually conducted at major milestones throughout the life of the project.

The audit is actually a special combination of the status and design reviews. As previously stated, it focuses on P, C, T, and S, and whether the outcome of the project will meet all objectives.

One concern that I have is with the word "audit." If you have ever been audited, you know that it was not a happy experience. People who audit you often seem to be out to get you. "Evaluation" is a kinder, gentler word, to use the popular phrase. We are not out to get the project manager when we evaluate a project, even though it is true that the outcome may be to cancel the project. On the other hand, no one likes to cancel projects because of the sunk costs involved, so most project evaluations are really aimed at validating the project rather than canceling it. I will use the term "evaluation," rather than "audit," throughout this chapter.

If an evaluation is to be effective, you must have an effective project control system, since no evaluation can be successful unless proper control methods are first employed. The requirements for such a control system are presented later in this chapter.

CANCELING PROJECTS

One of the most traumatic things you can do is cancel a project. Anyone who thinks it is a purely "business" decision has probably not been there. People get upset, especially members of the project team. "It's a good project," they protest. "How can you cancel it?"

Managers are in equal agony. "I hate to cancel it and lose all that money we've spent." But sunk costs are sunk and can't be recovered in many cases.

Marvin Patterson, former vice president of product development at Hewlett-Packard, wrote a book entitled *Accelerating Innovation* (1993), in which he discusses canceling product development projects. He says that, if you have never canceled a product development project, then you have undoubtedly brought to market some products that should never have seen the light of day, because no team is so good that it is 100 percent successful. On the other hand, if you cancel too many development projects, then there is something wrong with your project selection, product development, or project management processes. How many is too many? There is no way to give an exact answer, but in terms of normal distribution curves, you could expect that those out on the tail of the curve might fit. That might be a couple of percent.

Patterson offers a very simple way to address the issue of canceling projects, and I am unashamedly borrowing from him in the material that follows. There is no use reinventing a wheel when someone has produced a perfect one!

The analysis is based on cash flow in development projects, as shown in Figure 11.2. When cash flow is negative,

F I G U R E 11.2

Cash Flow in a Product Development Project

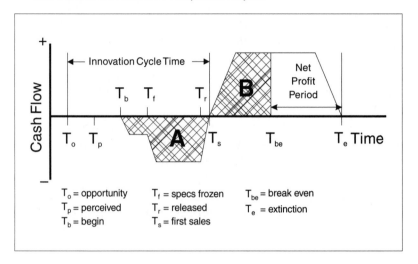

you are investing in development of the product (or software). When cash flow is positive, you are receiving money from sales. When money received (area B in the figure) equals total investment (area A), you have reached the breakeven point, and revenues to the right of area B represent profits.

Now notice the points on the horizontal time line. On the far left is a point labeled T_o, which represents the time when the *opportunity* for the product comes into being. Presumably, if we had the product at that time, customers would buy it, if they could afford it. The problem is, we don't know the opportunity exists. Our marketing people have responsibility for finding out about these things, but they never have perfect environmental "radar," so there is a delay between T_o and T_p, where the opportunity is finally *perceived*.

Now I'm sure you know that marketing people who find an opportunity to sell something will get very excited.

(This is appropriate: they should be excited about doing their job.) Furthermore, they will try to see if they can justify developing the product. To do so, they look at whether there will be an acceptable return on investment (total revenue generated by lifetime sales of the product, divided by area A). Interestingly, marketing people often make projections without talking to anyone else. They estimate both sales and development costs, and if the ROI is acceptable, they try to get the project approved.

It is, of course, curious how marketing departments estimate development costs without talking to the development group, but I have figured that one out. They use a mathematical function I call *Tater's Transform*, named after a fellow from South Carolina, Mark Tate, (Tater to his friends), who first made me realize how it works. Tater's Transform gives you an equation like this:

$$x \triangleright\triangleright y$$

The way you read this equation is "*x* becomes *y*." This means that whatever you put into the left-hand side becomes whatever you *want* it to be on the right-hand side. Furthermore, the equation is bilateral, so that you can also write:

$$y \triangleright\triangleright x$$

Now we have all known how to use Tater's Transform since infancy. I believe it is a genetic thing. It is wired in at birth. As proof, consider the fellow who wants to buy a $5000 hunting bow. His wife wants to know how he can justify spending so much money on a toy, and he assures her that the game and venison that he will bring home with his new bow will save them thousands in groceries over the years. He is using Tater's Transform.

So this is what the marketing folks do. But notice that even after they come in with their proposal, there is a delay before we begin working on the product. Why is that? If it is such a great idea, why don't we get on it immediately?

Generically, this delay can be called *organizational inertia*, and there are several possible sources of it. The first is the approval process itself. In some organizations, you need 27 signatures from people scattered all over the world before a project can get funding, and these 27 people all know intuitively that marketing people use Tater's Transform to justify their ideas. So it takes some time to convince everyone that the idea is valid. The second reason is budget. There is no money available to do the project, and if the marketing person happens to have the idea just after the close of next year's budget approval cycle, the job might have to wait a year for funding. By that time someone else has started working on the idea and beats you to market.

The third reason, pervasive in the United States today, is downsizing. There are no extra resources sitting around waiting for something to do, so even if it is a great idea and we could fund it, there is no one to work on it.

In any case, the project is finally approved and work is started. Now we are at T_b, the point at which work begins. At this point, cash flow goes negative, because the company is spending its own money—making an *investment* in the new product. Initially, the work done is an attempt to pin down the product specifications, so the point labeled T_f is the time at which the specs are frozen. This point, of course, is a myth. No product specifications are ever really frozen this early in the life cycle. The point at which they are really frozen is T_E, the time at which the product becomes *extinct* in the marketplace. By default, they are frozen then. So we should really consider T_f a tentative point.

Once the specs are tentatively frozen, development work begins in earnest, and the cycle proceeds to T_r, the point where the product is released to manufacturing. This point is quickly followed by T_s, which is supposedly the time at which first sales occur, but everyone knows that the sales department would never wait until now to sell a product. No. Sales sold it way back at T_p, took orders for it, and promised deliveries, all without consulting the product development group about whether the promised delivery date could be met. Sales also used Tater's Transform to arrive at the delivery date. So this point should really be called the point at which shipments occur.

Now cash flow turns positive, because the product is generating revenue, and continues to do so until T_E is reached. At this time, the product is extinct in the marketplace. Point T_{BE} is the time when revenue generated equals total investment, so the company is at the breakeven point, and all revenue to the right is net profit on the product. (This is *approximately* correct.)

This analysis would all be fairly straightforward if T_E were stable, but it is not. The extinction point can move around. A competitor introduces a new product that is better, faster, and cheaper, and your T_E moves to the left. A new market opportunity is found, and T_E is pushed out to the right. Or market saturation occurs—people have all the product they need. Or new regulations are passed and the product won't meet the requirements, so sales must be discontinued. Many such factors can cause the extinction point to move around. One of the best ways to push T_E to the right is to develop a world-class product in the first place.

Now consider a company that has just started working in earnest on developing a product. The marketing folks come in with gloom and doom written all over their faces. When asked what is wrong, they say, "We've just found out that a competitor is going to beat us to market, so that our product will be killed shortly after we release it." As Figure 11.3 shows, this means that the investment will never be recovered, so that if the program continues, the company will just throw away a lot of money. This is a no-brainer—cancel the project and start a new one. That may mean redefining the product and going from there, or trying to leapfrog the next generation. In any case, you simply can't continue with the product as presently defined, unless you like to waste money.

As logical as this sounds, it is a very traumatic situation, and there are organizations that refuse to do the "obvious."

F I G U R E   11.3

Extinction Time Moves Forward

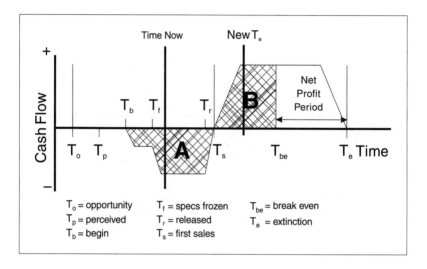

They can't bear to throw away all the money they have already spent (sunk costs). And engineers get very emotional and complain that their project is such a good one, it is a shame to cancel it. Both arguments are fallacious. Sunk costs are sunk costs, and you may as well admit that they can't be recovered, short of a miracle. Unfortunately, there aren't enough miracles in business worth banking on. It may be indeed a good product, but if it will never succeed in the marketplace, of what value is it, even to the engineer who is enamored with it? So the smart thing to do is kill the project and get on with something that promises a positive return on investment.

The question is, if you are vulnerable to this kind of market dynamics, what can you do to protect yourself? There are several things. First, you need to reduce the design cycle, as shown in Figure 11.4. There are two ways to reduce design time. One is by using state-of-the-art design practices, such as rapid prototyping. The second is by doing really good project

F I G U R E 11.4

Development Cycle Shortened

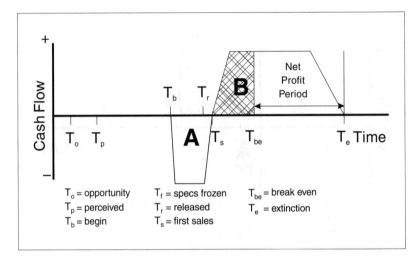

T_o = opportunity T_f = specs frozen T_{be} = break even
T_p = perceived T_r = released T_e = extinction
T_b = begin T_s = first sales

F I G U R E 11.5

Total Investment Reduced

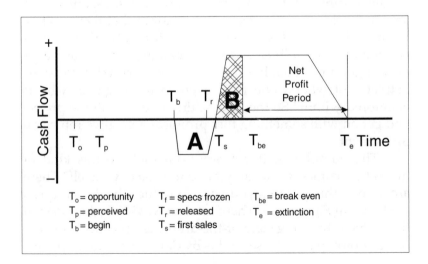

T_o = opportunity T_f = specs frozen T_{be} = break even
T_p = perceived T_r = released T_e = extinction
T_b = begin T_s = first sales

management. The ultimate objective is to shorten the design cycle and to simultaneously reduce the cost of the cycle. This is shown in Figure 11.5. If we can reduce total investment (area A), then we don't have to sell as much product to reach the breakeven point and become profitable. Good project management can help achieve this objective.

How? One way is by reducing rework through good planning. Estimates place rework at 30 percent of total product development costs. This means that one of every three engineers or programmers assigned to development is working full-time to redo what the other two did wrong in the first place. By eliminating the rework, you will improve your productivity by a corresponding amount.

This is, incidentally, a good way to show that you are improving your management of projects. When you are new to formal project management, it is usually difficult to show that you are getting better, because you don't have good history on previous projects. But if you start measuring rework in projects, you should see that measure improve, and this is evidence that project management is paying good dividends.

Another way to protect yourself from competitive forces is to move T_b leftward toward T_p. That is, reduce organizational inertia. Have some reserve capacity. Shorten the approval cycle. You also want to move T_p over toward T_o. You need the best market surveillance you can get. You do this by living with your customers, watching your competitors, and forecasting trends.

Finally, you place T_b to the left of T_o. This means that you develop the product before the opportunity comes into being. You are a market leader, rather than a follower. Examples include the automobile, telephone, Post-It™ note, Sony Walkman™, personal computer, and many other products. As Jack Trout has said, it is a well-known fact that you cannot do market research on something not in the market (Trout and Rivkin, 1999), so market leaders must proceed on faith that what they are developing will ultimately sell.

PROJECT CONTROL

The status review is used to help control a project. Control is on a day-to-day effort to keep project work on track. It consists of measuring the status of work performed, comparing that status with what was planned to be accomplished to date, then taking corrective action to get back on target if a deviation is discovered. The need for a good plan,

> **con•trol:** To compare progress against plan so that corrective action can be taken when a deviation occurs.

against which progress can be compared, was emphasized in Chapter 3. This chapter will focus on attempting to assess or measure actual progress, which is not always such an easy task, as we shall see.

One important distinction should be made here. The word "control" often refers to power, authority, command, or domination. Another meaning, however, is that of guiding a course of action to meet a predefined objective. This is the meaning of control that should be applied to project control systems. With these ideas in mind, let's look at some premises of management control systems.

- **Work is controlled—not workers.** The objective is to get the work done, not make workers "toe the line." Authoritarian management generally leads to an atmosphere that breeds resentment and stifles creativity—just the opposite of what is needed. Control should be viewed as a *tool* that the worker can use to perform more effectively and efficiently.

- **Control of complex work is based on motivation and self-control.** If control is not exercised by the person doing the work, it must be exercised by someone else. When this happens, a number of problems arise. Control is likely to degenerate into control of the worker,

rather than the work. Proper communication between the worker and controller may not take place. Finally, the controller probably does not know the work as well as the worker, and cannot establish reasonable checkpoints as required. The worker is in the best position to establish a course of action and monitor his or her own progress.

Self-control is part of the job of knowledge workers. This fact should be clearly spelled out to them. The best set of control procedures will not work unless the people involved are motivated to make it work.

- ◆ **Control is based on completed work.** Progress toward objectives is measured by examining the product. In the case of a complex task, the work is subdivided (to the work package level, for example) and the smaller units are monitored. Each task must have a well-defined output (or deliverable), and there must be standards for evaluating the completed work.

◆ **Methods of obtaining control data must be built into the work process.** That is, those doing the work must be able to tell where they are at any given time. When driving, we use road signs to tell us where we are, and we compare those against our map to see if we are on course. If a brick wall is being constructed, it is easy enough to count the bricks actually laid (or measure the height of the wall) so that the figure can be compared with the plan. As pointed out previously, however, knowledge work is harder to measure and usually will be an estimate of progress.

As a further consideration, only data that is actually required for control should be collected. The control process should not be a burden.

◆ **Control data must go to the person who does the work.** Consider a pilot. Do you give information about the plane's position to the pilot's boss? Of course not. In organizations, however, control data is often deflected, so that managers receive more information than they can possibly use.

◆ **A control system is designed for the routine.** A thermostat turns a furnace on or off to control temperature. It cannot compensate for an empty fuel tank. A control system is designed to cope with the routine: exceptions must be given special handling. It must, then, be decided what is routine and what is not.

◆ **Control of a complex process is achieved through levels of control.** That which is exceptional at one level may be routine at the next-higher level. Only the most pressing problems should find their way to the top level of control.

CHARACTERISTICS OF A PROJECT CONTROL SYSTEM

Activities

There are four basic activities that must be performed to have a satisfactory control system:

1. Planning performance
2. Observing actual performance
3. Comparing actual and planned performance
4. Adjusting as required

When work can be quantified, deviation from plan is called *variance*. When work cannot be quantified, comparing performance against plan becomes difficult. Each worker's performance must be judged subjectively. Usually such judgment is binary—that is, either the work is satisfactory or it is not.

Summary performance reports should be standardized for all projects. Data should also be presented in an effective way. There must be a balance between presenting too much and too little data.

Objectives

The control system must focus on objectives. The designer of the control system should answer these questions:

- What is important to the organization?
- What are we attempting to do?
- Which aspects of the work are most important to track and control?
- What are the critical points in the process at which controls should be placed?

The important should be controlled. However, what is controlled tends to become important. Thus, if budgets and schedules are emphasized to the exclusion of quality, only those will be controlled. The project may well come in on time and within budget at the expense of quality.

Response

A control system should focus on response: If control data does not result in action, then the system is ineffective. That is, a control system must use deviation data to *initiate corrective action*. Otherwise, it is not really a control system but simply a monitoring system.

Timeliness

The response to control data must be timely. If action occurs too late, it will be ineffective.

Human Factors

The system should be easy to use. In particular, the control system should be designed for the convenience of people, not machines.

Flexibility

One system is not likely to be correct for all projects. It may need to be scaled down for small projects and beefed up for large ones.

Simplicity

The smallest control effort that achieves the desired result should be used. Any control data that is not essential should be eliminated. However, one common mistake is to try to control complex projects with systems that are *too simple!*

COMPONENTS OF A PROJECT CONTROL SYSTEM

In its simplest form, a project control system can be represented by a first-order feedback system, as shown in Figure 11.6. The system has *inputs, outputs,* and a *process* for transforming those inputs to outputs, together with a *feedback loop* to ensure that the system continues processing inputs according to its design. The outputs are monitored and compared against some preset standard. If the outputs are off, that information is fed back as an input to the system to correct for the deviation.

The first-order feedback system is a very simple one. It is not very elegant, and it has some serious limitations as a model on how to achieve control in project management. For those readers unfamiliar with feedback systems, a good analogy for the first-order system is the thermostat in one's home. In the winter the system provides heat, and the desired room temperature is preset by adjusting the thermostat to the proper level.

It should be clear that every system is designed to work properly only under certain conditions. For example, the

F I G U R E 11.6

First-Order Feedback System

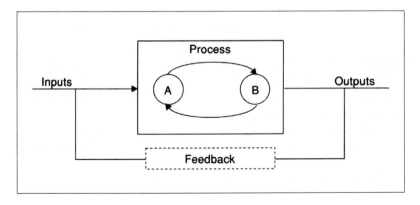

home heating system might be designed to maintain the
room at 70 degrees Fahrenheit so long as the outside temperature does not go below minus 30 degrees. When the outside
temperature drops below that level, the heater will run continuously, but the room temperature will begin to drop below the preset level of 70 degrees. To maintain the desired
room temperature, the system would have to increase its
heating capacity, but it cannot do this. Thus, it keeps running, without being able to adequately heat the house.

In a similar manner, a project may run into unexpected
obstacles that fall outside the boundaries for which the project control system was designed. People are following the
plan to the letter, but they are not getting the desired result.
What is needed is to change the approach. However, a
first-order control system does not have that capability.
Something more flexible is needed. The third-order system
shown in Figure 11.7 is the answer.

The system in Figure 11.7 has the same basic elements as
the first-order system of Figure 11.6. There are inputs, processes, outputs, and feedback. However, the third-order system feeds information about the system outputs to a
comparator, which weighs them against the original plan. If
there is a discrepancy, that information is passed to an *adjust*
element, which must decide if the discrepancy is caused by
something being wrong with the process, the inputs, or the
plan itself.

Once that determination is made, the adjust element
calls for a change in the plan, inputs, or process itself. Note
also that the adjust element has an arrow going back to the
monitor. If a deviation is detected, the monitoring rate is increased until the deviation is corrected; then monitoring is
decreased to its original level.

The real-world analogy is that if you are monitoring
progress on a project weekly and a problem occurs, you may
begin to monitor daily. If the problem becomes serious
enough, your monitoring rate may increase to several times

F I G U R E   11.7

Third-Order Feedback System

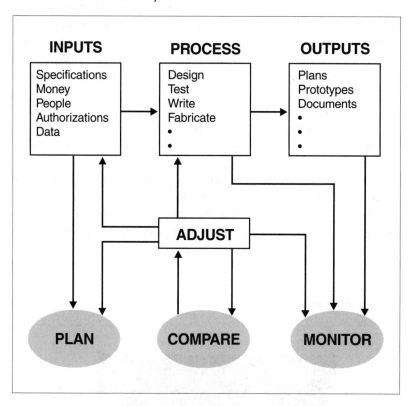

each day. Once the problem has been solved, you revert to your weekly monitoring.

Comparing performance against plan can be difficult when the work cannot be quantified. How do you know what percentage of a design is complete, for example? Or, if you are doing a mechanical drawing of a part, is the drawing 75 percent complete when 75 percent of the area of the paper is covered? Probably not. Measuring progress in *knowledge work*, to use Peter Drucker's term, is very difficult.

This often leads to strange results. Suppose a member of the project team has agreed to design a new golf club, and has promised to finish it in 10 weeks. At the end of week 1, she reports that the design work is 10 percent complete. At the end of week 2, the work is 25 percent complete. In week 3 the designer hits a small snag and gets a little behind, but by week 5 she has gotten ahead again. Figure 11.8 plots her progress.

Everything goes pretty well until week 8, when the designer hits another snag. At the end of that week, she has made almost no progress at all. The same is true the following week, and the following, and the following . . .

What happened? For one thing, the 80/20 rule got her. In the case of knowledge work, it says that 80 percent of the work will be consumed by 20 percent of the problems encountered, and they will always happen near the end of the

F I G U R E 11.8

Percent Complete Graph

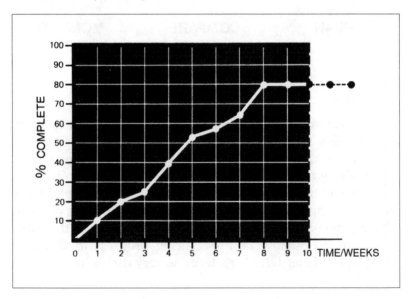

job. The real issue, though, is how she measured progress in the first place. Chances are, at the end of the first week, the designer reasoned somewhat like Cathy in the comics and said to herself, "I'm at the end of the first week on a 10-week job. I must be 10 percent complete." And she would be in good company, because

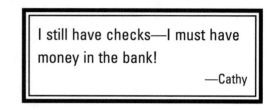

I still have checks—I must have money in the bank!

—Cathy

that is exactly what a lot of people do when *estimating* progress on knowledge work.

Note the word "estimate"! Assessing progress when work is not easily quantifiable is estimating, and subject to all the difficulties discussed in Chapter 6. This shows the limits of our ability to achieve control in management.

It is for this reason that two practices are advisable. First, work should be broken into small "chunks" that permit progress to be monitored fairly frequently, perhaps in intervals no greater than two weeks. Second, tangible deliverables should be used as signposts to show progress. In design, a drawing is tangible evidence of progress. In software development, printed code or written functional specs are evidence that work is complete. Having it "in one's head" is impossible to verify.

12

CHAPTER

Project Control Using Earned-Value Analysis

USING VARIANCE OR EARNED-VALUE ANALYSIS IN PROJECT CONTROL

Even though there are limits in assessing exactly how much work has been done on a project, there can be no control unless some assessment is done. The most robust method of measuring project progress is through *variance* or *earned-value* analysis. The method was originally developed to measure work accomplishment in manufacturing, and was later adopted as part of the cost/schedule control systems criteria (C/SCSC) for measuring progress in projects. If you have a knowledge of standard cost systems in manufacturing, you will be right at home with earned-value analysis.

For a fuller explanation of the C/SCSC system, see Chapter 13. What follows in this chapter is an abbreviated approach that should be appropriate for application to most projects, not just large government jobs. Readers who need a complete treatment of the C/SCSC system should consult Fleming (1988).

First, we define variance as any deviation from plan. Variance analysis allows the project manager to determine "trouble spots" in the project and to take corrective action. As was mentioned previously, there are four areas

> **var • i • ance:** Any deviation from plan.

of the project that the project manager is expected to control. These are the *performance, cost, time,* and *scope* objectives.

In this set of variables, cost refers to labor costs. Material and capital equipment costs will be tracked, but they are not part of this set, because they do not directly relate to scope, time, and performance. Also, whether you talk about labor costs in terms of money or simply head count, there is always a cost associated with the project. In some cases, when labor costs are not known, hours worked will be tracked. Cost is

Variance analysis allows the project manager to determine "trouble spots" in the project and to take corrective action.

General Approach to Progress Monitoring

When progress is monitored, three questions should always be asked:

1. What is the actual status of the project?
2. If a deviation exists, what caused it?
3. What should be done about it?

In answering the third question, there are three responses that can be made:

1. Ignore the deviation.
2. Take corrective action to get back on target.
3. Revise the plan.

If the deviation is not significant, it can be ignored, but note the word *significant.* As pointed out in a previous chapter, what is meant by significant should be determined in the planning stage of a project. In general, a deviation should exceed 5 percent to be considered significant, since most control systems cannot maintain a tighter tolerance.

---

the easiest of the four variables to measure. The others can become considerably more difficult.

Consider, for example, that you are building a brick wall. The plan calls for a vertical wall 10 feet high and 1 foot thick. You can inspect to see that the wall is vertical and that the mortar is clean—this is performance or quality of work done. You can also measure the height and thickness. If you find that the wall is only 8 feet high, you know that work on the wall is behind schedule. What is completed is only about 80 percent of what was planned. The measure isn't perfect, but it is much better than can be gained in knowledge work projects.

As an example, assume that a programmer is writing code. He estimates that he will have about 10,000 lines of code in the module, and he has written about 8000 lines. Is he 80 percent complete? Probably not. For one thing, you can't tell if unfinished code will work when it is finished, so you have no idea about quality. Also, you don't obtain a good measure of percent complete by taking a ratio of lines written to estimated lines required. So if you don't know scope or quality, you can't know anything about progress on schedule. The only measure that is accurate is cost. You know how many hours the programmer has worked on the code, but that is all.

This fact makes some people think that you shouldn't try to measure progress in programming, since it is so "iffy." One programmer I know claims that there is no value at all in unfinished code, so if you stopped work on it, there would be no salvage value, whereas the same is not true in making things. I don't agree. There is not much salvage value in an unfinished brick wall either. Yes, you could tear it down and reclaim the bricks, but progress is not measured to determine the salvage value of the bricks. It is measured solely to determine if the job is on schedule.

In general, engineering and programming work should be subdivided into one- to three-week increments, with markers that tell you if the increments have been completed. This means that at the end of the period being tracked, the worker gets credit for doing the work if it is complete, and no credit if it is not complete. We don't try to estimate percentages, since this causes the problems described in Chapter 11.

If we begin by measuring scope and performance, we can then determine if there are schedule and cost variances. These are defined as follows:

+ **Cost variance:** Compares deviations only from budget and provides no comparisons of work scheduled and work accomplished.

♦ **Schedule variance:** Compares planned versus actual work completed. This variance can be translated into the dollar value of the work, so that all variances can be specified in monetary terms.

In some organizations, project managers do not deal with costs, but rather with *labor-hours*. Once standard variance analysis has been presented in terms of cost, a method of dealing with working hours will be presented.

In order to assess cost and schedule variance, three measures are used. The definitions are provided below, together with examples of how the measures are calculated.

♦ **BCWS** (budgeted cost of work scheduled): The budgeted cost of work scheduled to be done in a given time period, or the level of effort budgeted to be performed in that period. This is the *target* toward which the project is headed. Another way to say it is that BCWS represents the *plan* that is to be followed. It is basically the product of labor-hours and the loaded labor rate that is paid during a given period of time, usually a day or week at a time. Loaded labor means that the direct pay has added to it the overhead rates that are used to cover heat, water, lights, rent, and so on. Loaded labor is the actual cost to do project work, and should be used to calculate project costs.

As an example, suppose that two people are to work on a project for one week (40 hours) at the loaded labor rate of $30 per hour each. In addition, a third person will work on the project for 30 hours during the same week, but at a loaded labor rate of $50 per hour. The budgeted cost of work scheduled for the week, then, is the sum of two products:

$$40 \text{ hours} \times \$30/\text{hour} \times 2 \qquad = \$2400$$
$$30 \text{ hours} \times \$50/\text{hour} \times 1 \qquad = \underline{\$1500}$$
$$\text{Total BCWS} = \$2400 + \$1500 \quad = \$3900$$

+ **BCWP** (budgeted cost of work performed): The budgeted cost of work actually performed in a given period. BCWP is also called **earned value.** It is a
  measure of how much work has been accomplished.

The BCWP figure is calculated as follows. For the example above, assume that the two employees who are assigned
to work for a full 40 hours each do indeed put in that amount
of effort. One worker actually gets her work complete, while
the other does not. He completes only about 80 percent of the
work supposed to be done. The worker assigned to put in
only 30 hours also completes his work as planned. We say
that the *earned value* of the work completed, then, is as follows:

40 hours x $30/hour	= $1200
0.8 x 40 hours x $30/hour	= $ 960
30 hours x $50/hour	= $1500
Total BCWP:	$3660

+ **ACWP** (actual cost of work performed): The amount
  of money actually spent in completing work in a
  given period. This is the amount of money paid to
  workers (wages only—no material costs are included
  in any of these figures) to do the work that was completed during the time period in question.

To continue with the above example, assume that the
work completed has actually cost the organization $3900. If
this figure were compared with BCWS, we might think the
project was in good shape. The scheduled work was supposed to cost $3900, and that is what has been paid in labor.
However, we also know that one person did not get through
with the work he was supposed to do. The value of his accomplishment is only $960, but was supposed to be $1200. In
order to see what this means for the project, the following
formulas are employed:

Cost Variance = BCWP – ACWP

Schedule Variance = BCWP - BCWS (dollar value)

Plugging numbers into these formulas, we have the following results:

Cost Variance = $3660 − $3900 = −$240

A negative cost variance means that the project is spending more than it should—thus, a negative variance is *unfavorable*.

Schedule Variance = $3660 − $3900 = −$240

Again, a negative schedule variance means that the project is behind schedule, and so is also *unfavorable*.

Looking at these two figures together tells us that the project has gotten behind schedule in the amount of $240 worth of work, and since the cost variance is identical to the schedule variance, we know that the cost variance is due *only* to the schedule variance. That is, the work being done is costing what it was estimated to cost. If labor rates had escalated, then the cost variance would be greater than the schedule variance.

Variance Analysis Using Spending Curves

Variances are often plotted using spending curves. Figure 12.1 is a BCWS curve for a project. It shows the *cumulative spending* planned for a project, and is sometimes called a *baseline plan.* Such curves can often be plotted automatically by transferring spending data from a scheduling program (which calculates labor expenses on a daily or weekly basis by multiplying labor rates times labor-hours expended) to a graphics program using a DIF file or some other file transfer format.

In the event that software is not available to provide the necessary data, Figure 12.2 shows how data for the curve is generated. Consider a simple bar chart schedule. Only three tasks are involved. Task 1 involves 40 labor-hours per week

F I G U R E 12.1

BCWS Curve

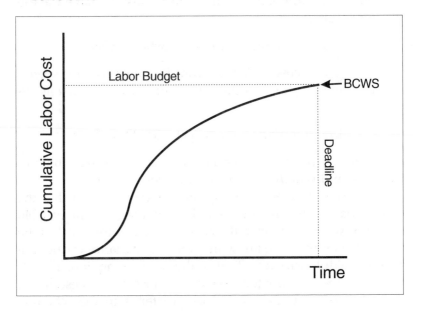

at an average loaded labor rate of $20 per hour, so that the task spends $800 per week. Task 2 involves 100 hours per week of labor at $30 per hour, or $3000 per week. Finally, task 3 spends $2400 per week, based on 60 hours of labor at $40 per hour.

At the bottom of the chart we see that during the first week $800 is spent for project labor; in the second week both tasks 1 and 2 are running, so the labor expenditure is $3800. In the third week, all three tasks are running, so labor expenditure is the sum of the three, or $6200. These are the *weekly* expenditures.

The *cumulative* expenditures are calculated by just adding the cost for each subsequent week to the previous cumulative total. At the end of week 1, $800 has been spent. At the end of week 2, the figure is $4600; at the end of week 3, it is $10,800; and so on.

Cumulative Spending for Schedule

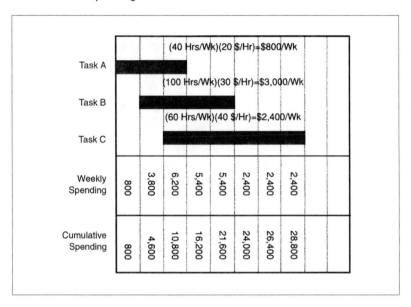

These cumulative amounts are plotted in Figure 12.3. This is the spending curve for the project, and is another BCWS curve. Since it is derived directly from the schedule, it represents *planned performance* and therefore is a baseline plan. Further, since control is exercised by comparing progress against plan, this curve can be used as the basis for such comparisons so that the project manager can tell the status of the program. Following are examples of how such assessments are made.

Progress Tracking Using Spending Curves

Consider the curves in Figure 12.4. On a given date, the project is supposed to have accomplished $50,000 in labor (BCWS). The people working on the project were supposed to do 1000 hours of work at a loaded labor rate of $50 per

Cumulative Spending Curve

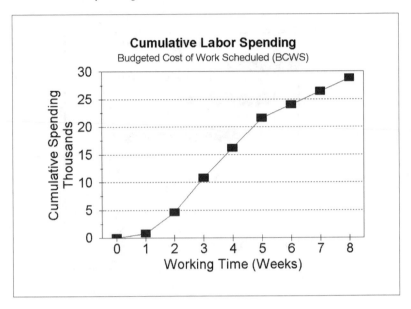

hour. When the project manager checks progress, he finds that the amount of work actually accomplished to date is 80 percent of what was supposed to be done. The value of this work to the organization is, then, 80 percent of the scheduled work (BCWS), or $40,000. This is shown in Figure 12.4.

The actual cost of the work performed (ACWP) is $60,000. This might be because the people doing work have put in 1200 hours at $50 per hour, or they put in 1000 hours of work but the labor rate escalated to $60 per hour. Actual cost variance, then, is a composite variance. Either way it occurs, it means that labor is costing more than was originally planned. These figures are usually obtained from accounting, and are derived from all the time cards that have reported labor applied to the project. Note that material or capital equipment costs are not included in these figures. They are kept in a separate account.

F I G U R E 12.4

Project Behind Schedule and Overspent

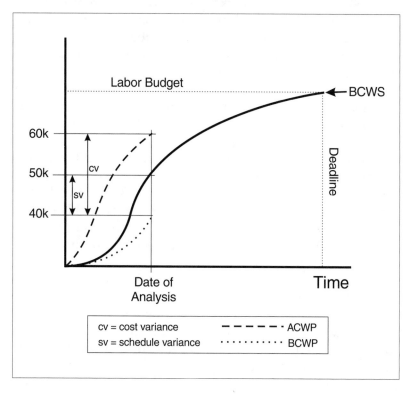

cv = cost variance .... ACWP
sv = schedule variance .... BCWP

The first question we ask is "What is the project status?" I always begin with schedule variance, which is BCWP – BCWS. In this case, $40,000 – $50,000, or –$10,000. That is, the project is $10,000 worth of work behind schedule. Note in Figure 12.4 that this variance can be obtained in dollars or time units. The project should have hit the $40,000 point earlier, so if you drop a perpendicular down to the time axis, you can see that the project is x units behind schedule.

The cost variance is BCWP – ACWP. Think always of BCWP as what you got for the effort expended. We are then taking the difference between what we got for our money

and what it cost us. In this case, we have $40,000 – $60,000, or
–$20,000. If we say it in words—"We spent $60,000 to accomplish $40,000 worth of work—we see that we are not getting
enough for our expense. Note that the $20,000 variance is the
sum of two variances. We are $10,000 above budget (BCWS)
and $10,000 behind schedule, so the total cost or spending
variance is the sum of the two.

Thus, we are behind schedule and overspent. This is the
worst situation a project can be in. It is bad enough to be behind schedule *or* overspent, but to be both at the same time is
really a problem and, unfortunately, it happens.

The second question we must answer is, "What caused
the deviation?" We generally don't know for certain. The estimates could be wrong. The work turned out to be harder
than we expected, or there were unforeseen problems that
caused the work to take longer and cost more than originally
estimated. Or the people may have been unproductive. We
don't know in many cases.

The third question that must be answered is, "What
should be done about the variance?" There are a number of
possibilities. Figure 12.5 plots trends for the BCWP and
ACWP curves. If nothing changes, this appears to be where
they are headed. Note that the BCWP curve must eventually
hit the total labor figure of x, and if it continues as shown, the
project will be late by x.

The ACWP curve must intersect the finish date, so at its
present rate it will go up to approximately x dollars, which
means that the project will end up late and overspent by x
dollars. But what if it is unacceptable to slip the end date?
Can it still be met?

There are two possibilities. Note in Figure 12.5 that if the
scope were reduced to x dollars, the project could be finished
on time, even though it would be overspent by x dollars. If
such a solution is acceptable to all stakeholders, then we could
continue the project so that it would finish in this manner.

However, if it is not acceptable to be late *or* to reduce
scope, then we are going to have to accelerate the work, mak-

F I G U R E 12.5

Trends for the Project If Nothing Changes

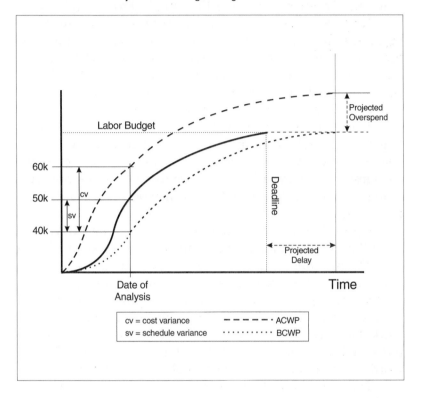

ing the BCWP curve turn upward, so that it will intersect the finish point on the required date. As shown, it is likely to cost us more money to do this, so the project will wind up spending x dollars.

Now you may ask if it isn't somehow possible to finish on time without taking such a big hit on spending. The answer is, it is highly unlikely. It has been found that if a project is in trouble only 15 percent of the way along the horizontal timeline, it is going to stay in trouble. A study of more than 800 defense contract projects that were behind schedule or overspent at the 15 percent mark showed that not one ever recovered. The reason? Think about where the BCWS curve came from. It is based on all our estimates of how long work will take. Another word for estimating is *forecasting*.

Now, with all due respect to weather forecasters, we know that if they can't tell us what will happen tomorrow, there is not much reason to believe that their long-term forecasts will be accurate. The same is true for projects. If you can't forecast the near-term work accurately, why should you believe your end-of-project estimate will be right?

This is a good news, bad news story. The good news is that you can tell early in a project that it is likely to be a "bad" project, and you can take steps to cancel or make changes to the plan early. The bad news is that, if a project is doing well at the 15 percent mark, it won't necessarily continue to do so.

Figure 12.6 illustrates another scenario. The BCWP and ACWP curves both fall at the same point, $60,000. Beginning with the first question, "What is the project status?" we see that the project is ahead of schedule, but spending correctly for the amount of work done. When we say it in words, we have spent $60,000 and have accomplished $60,000 worth of work. However, the plan called for $50,000 worth of work, so the schedule variance (BCWP – BCWS) is positive $10,000 worth of work, meaning the job is ahead of schedule.

The second question we ask is, "What caused the deviation?" The most common cause is that extra resources were applied, but at the planned labor rate (since there is no spending variance). Then the question is where the project manager came up with the extra people. In a shared-resource environment there are two possibilities: Either someone else had problems, couldn't use certain resources, and gave them to the project manager or the manager diverted them to the project at someone else's expense. In construction projects this situation often occurs because weather delay days are built into the schedule, and the weather remains good, so people are able to do work they didn't think they would be able to do, but it is costing the correct amount.

Project Ahead of Schedule, But Spending Okay

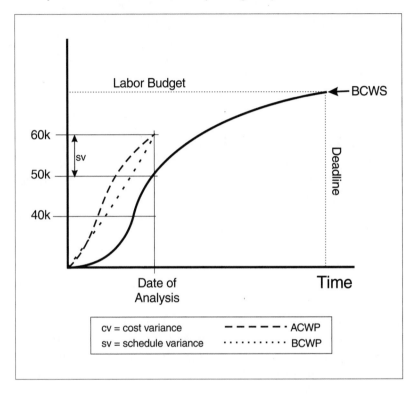

The next question we ask is, "What should be done about the variance?" If you are like most people, your first thought is, "What does he mean, what should be done about it? I'm ahead of schedule and spending correctly, so I'm not going to do anything about it." I know, it sounds crazy to think you might need to slow down, but you might.

The reason? Ask yourself if being ahead of schedule could cause problems in the project, and you will see that it is possible. If you are producing something, your customer might not be able to use it if you finish early, and you have to pay to store it. Or you may reach a point in the project at which the people now have nothing to do, and you have simply delayed the inevitable.

Another consideration is cash flow. Even though the project is ahead of schedule, can it be funded at the rate being spent? If not, then the work would have to be decelerated. This might be true in construction projects, where contractors want progress payments for the work they have done, and your controller can't pay the bills because money isn't coming in at the same rate as it is going out.

I know the scenario is a little depressing. Just when you thought you were doing a good job—you got ahead for the first time in your life—people start telling you to slow down. Naturally, it is a matter of degree. If you are a tiny bit ahead, no one is going to get excited. However, the variances I have shown in the figures are fairly large percentage deviations, and you may need to slow down in that case.

The next set of curves illustrates another situation. In Figure 12.7 the BCWP and ACWP curves are both at $40,000. This means the project is behind schedule and underspent. The most likely cause? This project is starved for resources (perhaps the victim of another project manager being ahead). Labor is costing what it is supposed to cost, but not enough work is being done to stay on schedule. In asking what you want to do, most of the time you want to get back on schedule. The problem here is that the project manager will probably go over budget in trying to catch up, since premium labor will most likely be required.

Finally, Figure 12.8 looks like Figure 12.4, except that the ACWP and BCWP curves have been reversed. Now the project is ahead of schedule and underspent. The accomplished work has an earned value of $60,000, but the actual cost of that labor has been only $40,000. At first glance, this looks wonderful. But ask yourself how the variance happened.

There are three possible explanations for how this project manager achieved the result shown:

Project Behind Schedule, But Spending Okay

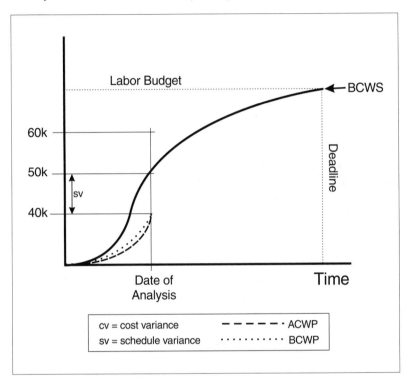

1. Actual labor rates were considerably lower than expected and/or the people were more efficient than anticipated.
2. The project team had a "lucky break." The team had expected to have to work really hard to solve a problem, but it turned out to be very easy.
3. The project manager "sandbagged" his estimates. He padded everything, playing it safe.

If you believe situation 1, you will believe anything. It is very unlikely that both variances would happen at the same

F I G U R E 12.8

Project Ahead of Schedule and Underspent

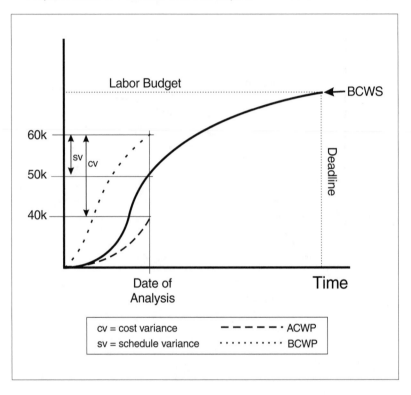

time. Situation 2 happens occasionally. When all the planets are aligned—about once in a zillion years, you say. You bet!

Situation 3 is the most likely explanation. The project manager was playing it safe. And he would tell you that there is no problem. After all, if he continues along this course, the project will come in ahead of schedule and underspent, which means the manager will give money back to the company. No problem.

But is that true? First of all, I can almost guarantee that the project manager won't give any money back. He will find a way to spend it—by adding bells and whistles to the project, by buying unplanned equipment or supplies, or by throwing one huge party! No sane project manager wants to give the money back, because he knows that his next project budget will be cut.

However, suppose the manager did give back the money. Would that be okay? No. The reason is that the organization would have lost the opportunity to use that money to fund some other project. In fact, the first scenario we looked at was for a project that was behind schedule and overspent. The forecast showed that the project was going to be very late and over budget. It may well be that the project will be canceled, since it may no longer meet acceptable ROI ratios, or we simply say we can't fund it because no money is available.

But the money is available. It is tied up in the underbudget project. If that project were rescheduled and rebudgeted, the money would be available to keep the other project going, assuming that the ROI is still justified.

The question is, naturally, "What is reasonable?" We certainly cannot expect to have zero variances in a project. And this is true. It all depends on the nature of our business. Well-defined construction projects can be held to very small tolerances—as small as plus-or-minus 3 to 5 percent. Research and development projects are likely to run higher tolerances, perhaps in the range of 15 to 25 percent. Each organization has to develop acceptable tolerances from experience.

Cross-Charging

There is another way to deal with the projects that are above and below on spending. You tell people working on the overspent project, "Don't charge any more time to this one. Charge your time to the underspent project." That way, both projects will come out right on target, and everyone will think you are doing a super job of managing.

This is called cross-charging. If you are doing defense contracting, you will be put in jail if you are caught. Why? Because you are lying about what you have actually done. Progress payments (see Chapter 13) are based on the BCWP that you report. If you cross-charge, you are reporting more work being accomplished on one job than you actually did, and less on the other.

But whether or not you are doing defense contracting, you are contaminating both project databases, and at the end of the job you won't know what either one really cost you. Does it matter? Of course. If it is new-product development you are doing, part of the pricing formula is the cost to develop the product. One product is going to appear lower than it is and the other will appear higher. The pricing of both will be wrong. Further, if a competitor enters the market, the salespeople don't know for sure if they can lower the selling price and still make a profit. They also don't know when the breakeven point is reached.

Worse yet, the status information on the project is used to decide whether to cancel the job if it is in trouble, and if you start charging time to other projects, you make it impossible for that decision to be made. The proper way to deal with this situation is to do aboveboard transfers of money. You reduce the budget for the project that is doing well, and increase the budget for the other. That way, the databases are not contaminated.

The fear that project managers have is that once they give money back, they can't recover it should an unforeseen problem occur. Then they will come in over budget, which would not have happened if they had held on to the money.

It is a dilemma, and there is no easy answer. The question always is whether you expect to continue as you have already performed. If so, then give some of the money back. If not, then keep it. However, the best predictor of future performance is past performance, and I would generally not expect a successful ongoing project to suddenly start getting in trouble, unless I knew that there were potential risks ahead.

Note that I said give *part* of it back. It is proper risk management practice to have a small contingency in a project to cover normal variances. All targets are estimates, and you can be sure that the variances won't be zero. As I pointed out previously, if you can hold tolerances of 5 percent, keep that much in reserve. If your tolerances are larger, keep a larger reserve account. No matter how you do it, this account should be aboveboard. It should be agreed to by everyone involved.

REFINING THE ANALYSIS

The only problem with the analysis presented here is that it is an *aggregate* figure, and does not permit determination of what area of the project a problem exists in. It may even hide a problem completely. For that reason, the variance analysis needs to be conducted on a task-by-task basis. This is usually done at whatever level in the work breakdown structure you have scheduled the work.

The importance of this was brought home to me by a client who had been using aggregate analysis to gauge project status for some time. The client discovered that a $100,000 overspend in one area of a project was being counterbalanced by a $100,000 underspend in another area. Such a project looks like it is in good shape, but the huge variances indicate a lack of control, and should be addressed.

Figure 12.9 shows how individual tasks are tracked. The form has been filled in with some data to illustrate the various combinations of numbers and their meanings.

The project status report[1] shows the levels of project costs and work completed to date for each work package (or whatever level you wish to use to report progress). The report is configured as a QuattroPro® spreadsheet. The columns contain the following information:

---

[1] This report can be downloaded free from my website: www.lewisinstitute.com.

F I G U R E 12.9

Earned-Value Tracking Report Form

Earned Value Report

Project No.:
Description:
Prepared by:

Date: 06-Jun-99
Page _____ of _____
Signed:

FILE: PROJRPT2

WBS # or Name	Cumulative-to-date			Variance		At Completion			Critical Ratio	Action Required
	BCWS	BCWP	ACWP	Sched.	Cost	Budgeted (BAC)	Latest Est. (EAC)	Variance		
				0	0			0	NA	NA
				0	0			0	NA	NA
				0	0			0	NA	NA
				0	0			0	NA	NA
				0	0			0	NA	NA
				0	0			0	NA	NA
				0	0			0	NA	NA
				0	0			0	NA	NA
				0	0			0	NA	NA
				0	0			0	NA	NA
				0	0			0	NA	NA
				0	0			0	NA	NA
				0	0			0	NA	NA
TOTALS:	0	0	0	0	0	0	0	0	NA	NA

NOTE: Negative variance is unfavorable !! If Critical Ratio < 0.6, INFORM MANAGEMENT!   ( ) = NEGATIVE VALUES

- Column 1: Work package number.

- Column 2: BCWS (budgeted cost of work scheduled to date). Look again at Figure 12.2. For task 1, at the end of the first week, the BCWS figure is $800. At the end of the second week, it is $1600. Note that for task 2, nothing will be entered into this cell until week 2.

- Column 3: BCWP (budgeted cost of work performed to date). This is the *earned-value* figure defined previously.

- Column 4: ACWP (actual cost of work performed to date). This is the actual cost of labor to date, as previously defined.

- Column 5: Schedule variance. This is the difference between BCWS and BCWP, calculated by the spreadsheet.

- Column 6: Budget Variance. This is the difference between ACWP and BCWP, calculated by the spreadsheet.

- Column 7: At-completion target cost for the work. For task 1, the at-completion cost for labor will be $2400 (three weeks at $800 per week). For task 3, the at-completion cost will be $14,400 (six weeks at $2400 per week). Naturally, labor spending will not always be uniform. This example uses uniform spending for simplicity.

- Column 8: The latest estimate of what the work will cost when complete. If we find on task 1 that we are actually having to spend $22 per hour for labor rather than the $20 that was originally budgeted, but we expect the work to be completed in the same number of working hours as originally estimated, then the budgeted-at-completion (BAC) figure will be 22 x 40 x 3, or $2640, rather than the originally budgeted $2400. The result is an overspend of $240.

It is also possible for the BAC to differ from the original estimate because more or fewer labor hours will
be needed, but labor costs will be what were originally planned. The BAC figure is extremely important when decisions are being made as to whether to
continue or terminate a project.

- Column 9: At-completion budget variance expected.
  This is the difference between columns 7 and 8, calculated by the spreadsheet.

- Column 10: Critical ratio—calculated as described
  below.

- Column 11: Action required. This is determined by
  the spreadsheet using an "IF formula." The rules are
  explained below.

The Critical Ratio

Part of the C/SCSC system involves calculation of two ratios
that indicate how well the project is doing. One of these is
called a *cost performance index* (CPI) and the other is called a
schedule performance index (SPI). The CPI is the ratio of BCWP
and ACWP (BCWP/ACWP). The SPI is the ratio of BCWP
and BCWS (BCWP/BCWS). Meredith & Mantel (1985) describe a control-charting method that can be used to analyze
progress in projects. They calculate the *critical ratio* as a product, using the following formula:

$$Critical\ Ratio = SPI \bullet CPI$$

or

$$Critical\ Ratio = \frac{BCWP}{BCWS} \bullet \frac{BCWP}{ACWP}$$

As is true for control charts used to monitor manufacturing processes, rules can be devised for responding to the
critical ratio. Meredith and Mantel (1985) suggest limits and
actions as shown in Figure 12.10. These limits are only sug-

F I G U R E 12.10

Control Chart for Tracking the Critical Ratio

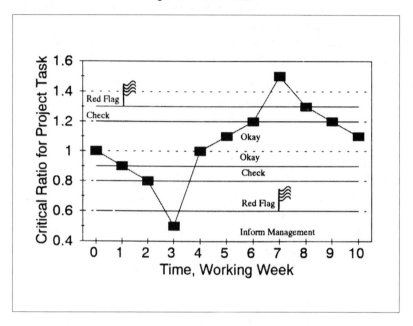

gestions, and project managers will have to devise limits that are appropriate for their own programs.

Using a spreadsheet allows the process of interpretation to be automated. The progress report in Figure 12.9 is set up with an IF formula in the final column. This formula looks at the critical ratio calculated in the previous column and subjects it to tests. On the basis of those tests, the formula returns the words "OK," "CHECK," "RED FLAG," or "NA," meaning no critical ratio has yet been calculated in the cell being tested. The tests are simple. In words:

Print "OK" if the critical ratio (CR) is between the values 0.9 and 1.2.

Print "CHECK" if the CR is between 0.8 to 0.9 or 1.2 to 1.3.

Print "RED FLAG" if the CR is above 1.3 or below 0.8.

In addition, if the ratio falls below 0.6, company management should be informed, since progress is so much better than expected that some changes probably should be made to the project plan.

Following is the IF formula for a spreadsheet with the critical ratio in cell K10 and the IF formula in cell L10:

@IF(K10>1.3#OR#K10<0.8,"RED FLAG",
@IF(K10>1.2#AND#K10<1.3#OR#K10>0.8#AND#K10<0.9,
"CHECK","O.K."))

Note that the example is set up so that the bottom-line summary for the project looks very good. The critical ratio for the overall project is 0.96, indicating that everything is fine. However, there are three work packages with RED FLAGS and two with CHECKS indicated, which means that some parts of the project are in trouble. If this were my project, I would be concerned.

However, a complete assessment of the project cannot be done using just this report. We also need to know exactly where in the project these work packages fall. Are any of the ones with problems on the critical path? If so, we know we have a more serious problem than indicated by the summary analysis. Even if none are critical, are any of them behind far enough to be running out of float? If so, then they will soon be critical. (See, for example, work packages 504 and 510. These are far enough behind that they could be in real trouble.)

THE NEED FOR ALL THREE MEASURES

Occasionally project managers fall into the trap of trying to track their projects using only BCWS and ACWP. As long as they see no difference between what they had planned to spend and what has actually been spent, they think the project is running smoothly. However, we saw from the above examples that this may not be true, and the manager may not spot a problem until it has been serious.

In fact, a controller from one organization told me that he constantly sees this happen in his company. For a long time the project goes along being underspent or right on target. Then the project manager realizes that the work is not getting done as required, and a big effort is applied to catch up. The usual result is that spending overshoots the planned target. This is illustrated by the curves in Figure 12.11.

F I G U R E 12.11

Overshoot Curve

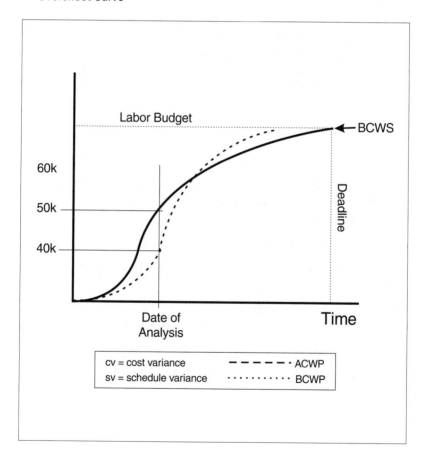

VARIANCE ANALYSIS USING HOURS ONLY

In some organizations, project managers are held accountable not for costs, but only for the hours actually worked on the project and for the work actually accomplished. The argument used to justify this way of working is that project managers usually have no control over labor rates. This is because an individual may be assigned to the project by a functional manager simply because she is the only person available who can do the job, but her rate is 25 percent higher than what the project manager expected to pay when the original estimating was done.

The other cause of problems is that the accounting department may change burden allocation (overhead) rates (for valid reasons), which causes total labor costs to go above original estimates. This naturally creates a cost variance in the project, but one over which the project manager had no control, so the argument is that the manager should not be held accountable.

In this case, the same analysis can be conducted by stripping the dollars off the figures. This results in the following:

BCWS becomes total planned (or scheduled) hours.

BCWP becomes earned hours (scheduled hours × percent of work accomplished).

ACWP becomes actual hours worked.

With the new numbers, it is possible to compute the following variances:

$$\text{Schedule Variance} = \text{BCWP} - \text{BCWS} =$$
$$\text{Earned Hours} - \text{Planned Hours}$$

$$\text{Labor Variance} = \text{BCWP} - \text{ACWP} =$$
$$\text{Earned Hours} - \text{Actual Hours Worked}$$

13
CHAPTER

Progress Payments and Earned-Value Analysis[1]

SOME BACKGROUND ON PROGRESS PAYMENTS

One of the major challenges facing all prime contractors is managing the risks of contract performance: the cost, schedule, and technical risks. With the progressively larger share of contract dollars now going outside of prime contractors down to their subcontracting base, many prime contractors are looking outward at their suppliers to share some of the "glory" of the risks of contract performance.

There are a multitude of ways to minimize the risks associated with prime contractor performance. One of the more obvious is by preparing high-quality specifications for a program—system, performance, process, development, and procurement, to mention just a few. Another key factor in risk management is the ability to define an airtight statement of work, both for internal budget performance and most particularly for subcontracted (external) supplier performance.

However, many times it is not possible to precisely define either a tight specification or even an adequate statement of work. In these cases the prime contractor may attempt to transfer some of its own risks to subcontractors by selecting an appropriate contract type for the occasion—choosing from the two broad families of contract types, either a fixed-price or a cost-reimbursable contract.

The importance of selecting the appropriate type of contractual arrangement for a given subcontract is a critical one for all procurements. The type of contract selected depends on many factors. Perhaps none is more important to both parties than the amount of "cost risk" that the buyer (the prime contractor) wishes to transfer to the seller (the subcontractor) and, conversely, how much of the cost risk the seller is willing to assume.

If the prime contractor is willing to retain the risks of cost growth, for whatever reason, then it will likely choose a cost-reimbursable contract. If, however, it is the buyer's intent to transfer the maximum potential cost risk to the subcontractor, then some type of fixed-price contract would be used, likely a firm fixed-price (FFP) subcontract.

Under an FFP subcontract, a supplier is obligated to assume the complete risk of any resulting cost growth and losses. This is the normal arrangement, but there is one very important condition, almost an exception, that should be understood. When the subcontract includes a "progress payment" clause, there is some likelihood that the cost risk factor *may* have remained with the prime contractor and did not transfer to the supplier. And, although not a widely publicized fact, there is a history of—shall we say—"unfortunate cost experiences" (called losses) in the industry as a direct result of the poor management of progress payments. For example, one of the more obvious ways for a prime contractor to lose money is to make progress payments in advance of the supplier's physical performance, and then have the supplier close its doors.

Proper management of progress payments begins before the subcontract is awarded, and must continue throughout the life of the subcontract. A prime contractor that uses progress payments is particularly vulnerable if its buyers fail to understand the importance of doing the right things both prior to and after the subcontract is awarded.

Today progress payments are commonplace in the government contracting business, and prime contractors are "encouraged" by the government to flow these financial arrangements downward to all their subcontracting team members. Thus, the subject of progress payments and the associated risks must be clearly understood in order to best protect the interests of prime contractors and, of course, the U.S. government.

JUST WHAT ARE PROGRESS PAYMENTS?

In their simplest form, progress payments may be viewed as a temporary interest-free loan from a buyer (the prime contractor) to a seller (the subcontractor). They are based on costs incurred by the supplier in the performance of a specific order and are paid directly to the supplier as a stipulated and agreed-to percentage of the total costs incurred, as defined in the federal acquisition regulation (FAR). The supplier promises to "pay back" the temporary progress payment loan by (1) making contractual deliveries or completing contractual line items, and (2) allocating some portion of the proceeds of the delivered unit price or completed line-item values to liquidate the loan, based on the established subcontract unit price of the articles or services delivered.

Note that there is an important distinction to be made between the "loan" value (the progress payment rate) and the repayment of the loan (the "liquidation" rate for the progress payments). Progress payments are paid as a percentage of *costs* incurred by a supplier—for example, 80 percent of the costs incurred. By contrast, the liquidation of the loan is based on a percentage of the unit *price* of article or service deliveries, which includes the supplier's fee. As such, the loan liquidations will include both the supplier's costs as well

In their simplest form, progress payments may be viewed as a loan from the buyer to the seller.

as the supplier's profit (i.e., the full subcontract unit values of the delivered articles).

Thus, the delivery of contract units and the completion of line items once started will result in a dramatic reduction of the outstanding progress payment loan. However, contract deliveries must first happen, and subcontractors must make physical progress in order to liquidate or repay the loan. This sometimes is the very heart of progress payment difficulties.

Progress payments are a form of contract financing to be used on *fixed-price* contracts. The payments cover the period from when a supplier begins to incur costs against an authorized order to when the supplier is making unit deliveries or completing contractual tasks. This results in a supplier getting paid on the basis of established unit or line-item task prices. The intent of progress payments is to prevent an "impairment" of the working capital of industrial suppliers doing business under U.S. government contracts.

With this introduction in mind, we now turn to how the earned-value approach is used to control progress payments. For a complete treatment of progress payments, the interested reader is referred to the book by Fleming and Fleming, from which the material for this chapter was taken. (See the end-of-chapter notes for a complete citation.)

PROGRESS PAYMENTS AND THE
EARNED-VALUE (C/SCSC) CONCEPT[2]

On January 7, 1991, Secretary of Defense Richard B. Cheney canceled the A-12 Avenger program. Because of this single action—reportedly the largest contract ever terminated by the Department of Defense (DOD)—upward of 9000 employees immediately lost their jobs.

Without debating the rightness or wrongness of the Cheney decision, we may consider its value in understanding the link between progress payments and the earned-value concept. To those of us who are interested in management control systems for government programs, particularly major programs, the A-12 Avenger cancellation provides a case study that will likely be discussed for years. To those of us who are specifically interested in the subset elements of "progress payments" and "earned value" performance management, the A-12 incident provides a lessons-learned opportunity of major importance.

The exact circumstances surrounding the A-12 cancellation will not be available to the general public for several years. It was what is called a secret SAR (special access required) program, which kept it out of the main monitoring processes of the DOD and certainly the general public. Nevertheless, enough public information has surfaced for us to draw certain conclusions.

The prime contracts were awarded on January 13, 1988, under a fixed-price incentive contractual arrangement that contained a target price of $4.379 billion, a target cost of $3.981 billion, and a ceiling price of $4.777 billion.[3] Full compliance with the cost/schedule control systems criteria (C/SCSC) and periodic cost performance reports (CPRs) were required from the two prime contractors: McDonnell Douglas, St. Louis, and General Dynamics, Fort Worth.[4] Progress payments were included in the fixed-price contractual arrangement.

Reliable DOD sources have acknowledged that the C/SCSC management control systems were implemented properly, and were functioning well at both the principal contractors.[5] But as early as April 10, 1991 (some 90 days after cancellation), it was reported that the government was demanding a return of $1.35 billion in "overpayments" made to the prime contractors.[6] And by June 8, 1991 (five months after cancellation), the two contractors had filed a 78-page lawsuit against the government, arguing that they were entitled to keep the questioned overpayment of funds.[7] Stay tuned—this saga will be continued.

Final settlement of this "major difference of opinion" between the U.S. government and two of its largest contractors will likely take years in the courts. However, if it is generally acknowledged that (1) the C/SCSC management control systems were working well with both of the prime contractors and (2) there was an overpayment of one-third of the total program's target costs only part way through the contractual period, then one can only conclude that the C/SCSC administrators appear not to have been communicating well with the progress payment administrators! Thus, contractor progress payments would appear not to have been linked with earned-value (C/SCSC) performance measurement. Time will tell.

This chapter will not focus on the A-12 program cancellation. The A-12 merely provides us with a case study, a role model, of what can go wrong, and perhaps some examples of future practices we will want to do differently ourselves, if at all possible.

Rather, in this chapter we will address four basic subjects in a generic sense, attempting to "link" the activities of progress payments with the earned-value performance measurement concept:

1. A brief overview of the earned-value (C/SCSC) performance measurement concept.
2. Relating progress payment data to earned-value performance measurement data when full C/SCSC *is* formally imposed on the subcontractor.
3. Relating progress payment data to performance on firm fixed-price (FFP) subcontracts when *no* formal C/SCSC is imposed on the supplier.
4. Methods (the formula) used by earned-value (C/SCSC) practitioners to forecast an independent estimate of costs at completion (EAC), based on the actual cost and schedule performance of the subcontractor.

The Earned-Value (C/SCSC) Concept in a Nutshell

In spite of the heading, the earned-value performance measurement concept is a complex subject that is difficult to present in a "nutshell." One of the best introductions to the theory of the earned-value concept comes from one of its founders, in an article he wrote after retirement from the government:

> Since 1967, the DOD has employed the cost/schedule control systems criteria (C/SCSC) as a means to ensure that major contractors' internal management systems are sound and can provide government program managers with reliable, objective cost performance information for use in management

decision making. The "criteria approach" allows contractors to adopt the systems and controls of their own choosing, provided those systems can satisfy the criteria. Compliance is determined by government teams which review the systems in operation after contract award.

The C/SCSC require that a contractor establish an integrated cost and schedule baseline plan against which actual performance on the contract can be compared. Performance must be measured as objectively as possible based on positive indicators of physical accomplishment rather than on subjective estimates or amounts of money spent. Budget values are assigned to scheduled increments of work to form the performance measurement baseline (PMB).

In order to measure contract performance, budgets for all work on the contract must sum to the contract target cost (CTC) so that each increment of work is assigned a value (budget) that is relational to the contract value. When an increment of work is done, its value is earned; hence the term earned value. By maintaining the budgetary relationship to contract target cost, variances from the budget baseline reflect ongoing contract cost performance.[8]

To properly put the earned-value performance measurement concept into historical perspective, we must go back in time some three decades and trace the evolution of cost/schedule control systems criteria (C/SCSC) from its two ancestors: PERT/time and PERT/cost.

The program evaluation and review technique (PERT) was introduced by the U.S. Navy in 1957 to support the development of its Polaris missile program. PERT attempted to simulate the necessary work to develop the Polaris missile by creating a logic network of dependent sequential events. Its purpose was threefold: to plan the required effort, to schedule the work, and to predict the likelihood of accomplishing the objectives of the program within a given time frame. The initial focus of PERT was on the management of time and predicting the probability of program success.

There was great excitement surrounding the new PERT program management concept. Unfortunately, the technique's successes fell far short of its proponents' expectations. Part (perhaps most) of the difficulty with PERT was not with the concept itself, but rather with the computers at the time. Both computer hardware and software were not up to the required challenges in the late 1950s. Computers were scarce, and PERT network processing had to compete with the processing of the company's payroll; somehow the company payroll always won. Also, the software programs, evolving initially out of simple linear network concepts, just could not provide the needed flexibility to support the program management requirements at the time.

Although the PERT planning, scheduling, and probability forecasting concepts have survived to this day, PERT's intended use as a program management tool initially "suffocated" a few short years after its introduction. The technique was too rigid for practical applications with the computer hardware and software available at the time. There was also the problem of the overzealous government mandate to use PERT. Industry management rightfully resented being told what tools to use in the management of their contracts.

Then, before PERT was accepted by program management in industry, the U.S. Air Force came up with an extension of PERT by adding resource estimates to the logic networks. PERT/cost was thus born in 1962, and just plain PERT was thereafter known as PERT/time. Needless to say that if PERT/time as a management technique was too rigid for practical applications at the time, PERT/cost with the added dimension of resources only exacerbated the problem. PERT/cost as a management control tool had a lifetime of perhaps two years.

What was significant about PERT/cost, however, was not the technique itself, but rather what evolved from it. The earned-value measurement concept was introduced to industry in March 1963 when the government issued its *Supplement No. 1 to DOD and NASA Guide, PERT/Cost Output Reports*, which provided industry with a simple definition of the earned-value concept:

VALUE (work performed to date): The total planned cost for work completed within the summary item.[9]

Thus, instead of relating cost plans to cost actuals, which historically had been the custom, PERT/cost related the *value* of work performed against the cost actuals, to determine the utility/benefits from the funds spent. What was **physically accomplished** for what was **actually spent** was a simple but fundamentally important new concept in program management. Hence, the earned-value concept was introduced in 1963, but had to wait until the issuance of the formal C/SCSC to have its full and lasting impact on American industry.

For various reasons the U.S. Air Force gave up on the PERT/cost technique in the mid-1960s, but correctly held on to the earned-value concept. When the Department of Defense formally issued its C/SCSC in 1967, the earned-value concept was solidly contained therein. With the subsequent adoption of these same criteria by the Department of Energy in 1975, and the reaffirmation of the criteria by the Department of Defense in its major 1991 defense acquisition policy statement, the earned-value concept of cost and schedule management was firmly established in the U.S. government acquisition process.[10]

A detailed discussion of the 35 specific criteria contained in the C/SCSC is beyond the limited scope of this book. There are full textbooks, week-long seminars, and practitioners/consultants available to cover these matters. Here we will merely attempt to summarize some of the more significant features in order to relate the earned-value concept to our primary subject: progress payments to fixed-price subcontractors.[11]

The C/SCSC are divided into five logical groupings, which contain the 35 criteria:

1. **Organization** *(5 criteria)*: To define the required contractual effort with use of a work breakdown structure (WBS), to assign the responsibilities for performance of the work to specific organizational components (i.e., the organizational breakdown

structure (OBS)), and to manage the work with use of a single "integrated" contractor management control system.

2. **Planning and Budgeting** *(11 criteria)*: To establish and maintain a performance measurement baseline (PMB) for the planning and control of the authorized contractual work.

3. **Accounting** *(7 criteria)*: To accumulate the actual costs of work performed (ACWP) and materials consumed in a manner that allows for comparison with the actual performance measurement (BCWP).

4. **Analysis** *(6 criteria)*: To determine the earned value, to analyze both cost variances (CV) and schedule variances (SV), and to develop reliable estimates of the total costs at completion (EAC).

5. **Revisions and Access to Data** *(6 criteria)*: To incorporate changes to the controlled performance measurement baseline (PMB) as required, and to allow appropriate government representatives to have access to contract data for determining C/SCSC compliance.

We will briefly discuss some of the critical elements of these five criteria groupings to provide a quick overview of the earned-value concept. Each of the acronyms used above will be defined in the discussion that follows.

Criteria Group 1

The five criteria required by the **organization** section can best be illustrated by a review of the diagram in Figure 13.1. The first criterion (1a) requires the use of a work breakdown structure (WBS) to define the required effort, whether it be a contract, a subcontract, a company funded internal project, or other undertaking. The WBS approach allows program management to comprehensively define and then perform a given contract within the maze of a company's functional organization. The use of a WBS to define the program is illustrated in Figure 13.1, at the extreme left side.

F I G U R E   13.1

Work Breakdown and Organizational Breakdown Structures

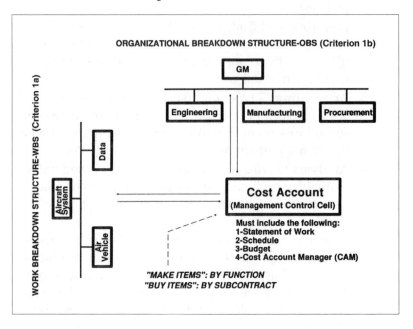

The second criterion in group 1 (1b) requires assignment of the defined WBS work tasks to the organizational breakdown structure (OBS) for performance. This concept is illustrated in the upper portion of Figure 13.1. Internal functional organizations (OBS) will perform the contract tasks as defined by the WBS.

The third criterion (1c) requires integration among the contractor's management control functions as well as their integration with the defined WBS and OBS elements. This requirement is achieved by the creation of "management control cells," which are referred to in the C/SCSC as cost accounts, and are displayed in Figure 13.1. Tasks that are "make items" (work to be performed internally by the contractor) must be identifiable to both the WBS and the OBS. Likewise, "subcontracts" must be identifiable to both. Thus the hundreds (or more) of these self-contained management control cells (cost accounts) in the C/SCSC must all be relatable either by the WBS to comply with the precise language of the prime contract's statement of work or by the OBS to satisfy the requirements of internal functional management within a given company.

Each management control cell (cost account) must have four elements to maintain the integrity of the management control unit and to carry out the performance measurement of data contained therein: (1) a statement of work for the cell, (2) a time frame or schedule for the cell, (3) a budget of financial resources, and (4) a responsible manager, typically referred to as the cost account manager (CAM). The cost account concept or management control cell is fundamental to the C/SCSC and is displayed in the lower-right corner of Figure 13.1.

Criteria Group 2

The 11 criteria contained in the **planning and budgeting** section require the formation of a baseline against which the supplier's performance may be measured. This requirement can be illustrated by a review of Figure 13.2. There are 12 specific components of what is called the C/SCSC performance measurement baseline (PMB). To follow the discussion, we need some understanding of what is meant by each of the elements contained in the baseline. Therefore, these 12 PMB elements are defined below, relatable by number to the elements displayed in Figure 13.2.

1. **Contract (or subcontract) target price (CTP)**: The negotiated estimated cost plus profit or fee for the contract or subcontract.
2. **Fee/margin/profit**: The excess in the amount realized from the sale of goods, minus the cost of goods.
3. **Contract (or subcontract) budget base (CBB)**: The negotiated contract cost plus the contractor's (or subcontractor's) estimated cost of authorized but unpriced work.

F I G U R E 13.2

The Performance Measurement Baseline

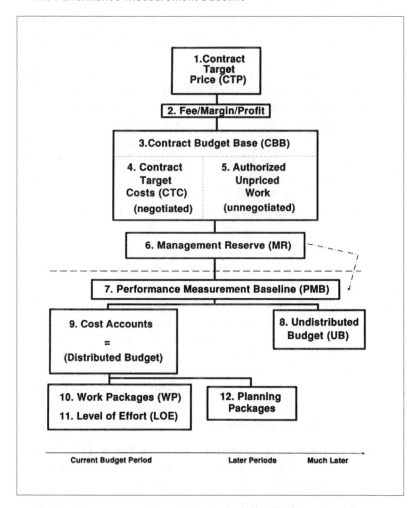

4. **Contract (or subcontract) target cost (CTC):** The negotiated cost for the original definitized contract and
   all contractual changes that have been definitized,
   but excluding the estimated cost of any authorized,
   unpriced changes.

5. **Authorized unpriced work**: The effort for which definitized contract costs have not been agreed to, but for which written authorization has been received by the contractor or subcontractor.

6. **Management reserve (MR)**: A portion of the contract budget base (CBB) that is held for management control purposes by a contractor to cover the expense of "unanticipated" program requirements. MR is not initially a part of the performance measurement baseline (PMB), but is expected to be consumed as PMB prior to completing a contract. Any MR not consumed at program completion becomes pure profit (item 2 above) and some portion may be returned to the buying customer under an incentive-type arrangement.

7. **Performance measurement baseline (PMB)**: The time-phased budget plan against which project performance is measured. It is formed by the summation of budgets assigned to scheduled cost accounts and their applicable indirect budgets. For future effort that is not currently planned to the cost account level, the performance measurement baseline also includes those budgets assigned to higher-level WBS elements. The PMB normally equals the contract budget base less management reserve.

8. **Undistributed budget (UB)**: The budget applicable to contract effort that has not yet been identified to WBS elements at or below the lowest level of reporting to the government or prime contractor.

9. **Cost account (CA)**: A natural intersection point between the work breakdown structure (WBS) and the organizational breakdown structure (OBS), at which functional management responsibility for the work is assigned, and actual direct labor, material, and other direct costs are compared with earned value for management control purposes. Cost accounts are the focal point of cost/schedule control.

10. **Work package (WP)**: A detailed short-span job or material item, identified by the contractor for accomplishing work required to complete a contract. Work packages are discrete tasks that have specific end products or end results.

11. **Level of effort (LOE)**: Work that does not result in a final product (e.g., liaison, coordination, follow-up, and other support activities) and that cannot be effectively associated with a definable end product process result. It is measured only in terms of resources actually consumed within a given time period.

12. **Planning package**: A logical aggregation of far-term work within a cost account that can be identified and budgeted but that is not yet defined into work packages. Planning packages are identified during the initial baseline planning to establish the time phasing of the major activities within a cost account and the quantity of the resources required for their performance. Planning packages are placed into work packages consistent with the "rolling wave" scheduling concept prior to the performance of the work.

It may come as a surprise to some that the C/SCSC performance measurement baseline (PMB) represents a value less than the total contract or subcontract amount. However, this fact is true only for the initial PMB. Profit or fee is not intended to be used in the performance of the contract, or else the result will be zero profit to the contractor or subcontractor. By contrast, management reserve (MR) is expected to be consumed during contractual performance, and when it is needed, MR is shifted into the PMB. Any management reserve remaining at the end of the contract is used to offset unfavorable variances, or may represent contract underrun and/or profit.

Criteria Group 3

The 7 criteria in the **accounting** group require that both cost actuals and schedule performance be relatable in the same time period with the earned-value achievement, or what PERT/cost called simply "value." Important point: By definition in the C/SCSC, a cost variance (CV) is the difference between the earned value achieved and the cost actuals for the same period. A schedule variance (SV) is the difference between the value of the scheduled work for the period and the earned value achieved in the same period. Let us discuss this simple but fundamental concept with a review of the data displayed in Figures 13.3 and 13.4.

F I G U R E 13.3

Conventional Cost Control

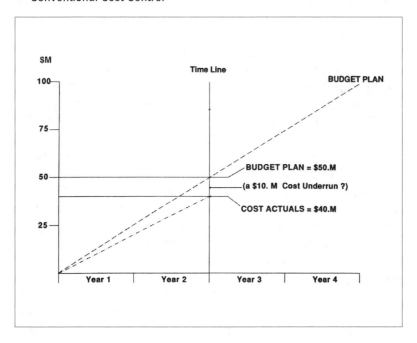

Figure 13.3 presents an imaginary four-year, $100 million contract, using the "conventional" cost control method. The plan calls for the expenditure of exactly $25 million each year for the four years. At the end of exactly two years of performance we find we have spent $40 million, compared with our plan, which called for the expenditure of $50 million. How are we doing? Truthful answer: We really do not know, using the "conventional" planned costs versus actual costs method.

An optimist might look at the data in Figure 13.3 and say we have accomplished $50 million dollars of work with only $40 million in actual costs; therefore, we have underrun our costs to date by some $10 million. And remember, most program managers and senior executives and CEOs are optimists by their very nature!

A pessimist might look at this same chart and conclude that we have completed $40 million of our planned work and have exactly $40 million in actual costs; therefore, we are the equivalent of $10 million of work behind our schedule. On the other hand, our cost performance is just fine!

In reality, we cannot tell how well or poorly we are doing by simply using the "conventional" cost control method of comparing planned cost expenditures with actual cost expenditures. Our conclusions can, and will likely, be most deceiving. Under the traditional methods of cost management, we cannot tell if we have overrun or underrun our costs, or are ahead of or behind our schedule. And being optimists, pessimists, or realists will not improve the process. We need to know what physical work we have accomplished against our physical work plan, for the actual dollars we have spent in a given time frame. We need earned-value performance measurement to be able to make an objective assessment of our program accomplishments.

Figure 13.4 has added the critical third dimension of earned-value performance measurement. The results are shocking. We have accomplished only $25 million in physical work. Therefore, since we have spent $40 million, we are in

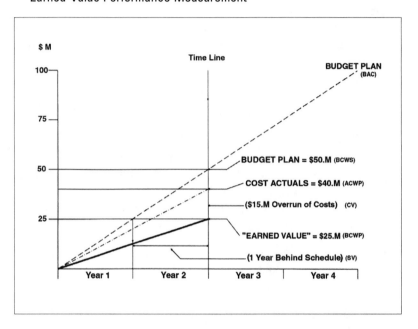

F I G U R E 13.4

Earned-Value Performance Measurement

fact $15 million overrun in costs. To add to our distress, of the $50 million in work we had planned to accomplish in the initial two years, only $25 million has been accomplished. We are thus $25 million in equivalent work behind schedule; stated another way, we are one year behind schedule!

By equating our cost dollars spent to our earned value, we know (sometimes painfully) exactly how well or poorly we are doing in our cost performance. By equating the planned schedule with earned value, we know (sometimes painfully) how much of the authorized contract work we have accomplished against our own schedule. Earned-value performance measurement is "objective" measurement. It takes the guesswork out of the cost and schedule management of contracts or subcontracts. Perhaps of greatest importance, the supplier's actual cost and schedule performance can be used to intelligently forecast (1) the final estimate of costs to complete the effort and (2) the necessary time to complete the effort.

To follow the discussion covered in the final section of this chapter—on using C/SCSC performance data to predict the final outcome—we will need to master some of the C/SCSC jargon. However, if we look at these very specific terms here and immediately relate them to the data in Figure 13.4, perhaps we can minimize the pain. Nine definitions of specific C/SCSC terms are needed:

- ◆ **Budgeted cost for work scheduled (BCWS)**: The sum of the budgets for all work packages scheduled to be accomplished (including in-process work packages) plus the amount of level of effort scheduled to be accomplished within a given time period.

The BCWS is nothing more than the "plan," against which contractor performance will be measured. In Figure 13.4 the plan or BCWS through year 2 was $50 million.

- ◆ **Budgeted cost for work performed (BCWP)**: The sum of the budgets for completed work packages and completed portions of open work packages, plus the appropriate portion of the budgets for level of effort. Also known as "earned value."

The BCWP is the "earned value," the physical value of the work done at a given point in time. In Figure 13.4 the BCWP or earned value at year 2 was $25 million.

- ◆ **Actual cost of work performed (ACWP)**: The costs actually incurred and recorded in accomplishing the work performed within a given time period.

The ACWP is the "actual cost" for a given period. The ACWP through year 2 was $40 million.

- ◆ **Cost variance (CV)**: The numerical difference between earned value (BCWP) and actual cost (ACWP).

The CV is the earned value () less the actual cost (ACWP). In Figure 13.4 the BCWP is $25 million, less the ACWP of $40 million, for a CV of –$15 million. Note the important difference in C/SCSC performance measurement: There is no comparison of the plan (BCWS) with the actual cost (ACWP), as there is with the "conventional cost" method.

♦ **Schedule variance (SV)**: The numerical difference between the earned value (BCWP) and the budget plan (BCWS).

The SV is the difference between what was scheduled to be done (BCWS) and what was accomplished, or the earned value (BCWP). In Figure 13.4 the BCWP is $25 million, less the BCWS of $50 million, for an SV of –$25 million.

♦ **Budget at completion (BAC)**: The sum of all budgets (BCWS) allocated to the contract. It is synonymous with the performance measurement baseline (PMB).

The BAC is important as a comparison with the estimate at completion, which will take place during the period of performance. In Figure 13.4 the BAC is $100 million at the end of four years, synonymous with the BCWS in this case.

♦ **Estimate at completion (EAC)**: A value periodically developed to represent a realistic appraisal of the final cost to complete an effort. It is the sum of direct and indirect costs to date, plus the estimate of costs for all authorized work remaining.

EAC = ACWP + Estimate to Complete

Thus, whenever we apply sound business practices to ourselves, or with progress payment administration, or with C/SCSC performance measurement, periodically we will want to make an estimate of what it will take to complete a given job. In Figure 13.4 no EAC is forecasted by the supplier. However, with a CV of –$15 million and an SV of –$25 million only halfway through the contract period, a realistic EAC is definitely in order.

- ◆ **Cost performance index (CPI)**: The cost efficiency factor achieved by relating earned value (BCWP) performance to the actual dollars spent (ACWP).

The CPI is the critical indicator of program performance under the earned-value technique. The CPI is derived by dividing the earned value (BCWP = $25M) performance by the dollars actually spent (ACWP = $40M), which provides the cost efficiency factor for work accomplished after two years. The result of $25 million divided by $40 million provides an efficiency factor of .625%. Stated another way, for every dollar spent to date, this program achieved a benefit of only .625 cents on the dollar!

- ◆ **Schedule performance index (SPI)**: The schedule efficiency factor achieved by relating earned value (BCWP) against scheduled work (BCWS).

The SPI is a critical corollary index to the CPI, and is often used in conjunction with the CPI to forecast the final outcome. The SPI is derived by dividing the earned value (BCWP-$25M) performance by the scheduled work (BCWS-$50M), which provides the schedule efficiency factor for work after two years. The result of $25 million divided by $50 million equates to a factor of only 50%. Stated another way, for every dollar of equivalent work planned, this contract accomplished only one-half of it.

Thus, we must conclude that the work initially scheduled to be done in years 1 and 2 will now be performed in an extended contract period into years 5 or even 6. And we all know the simple truth that work done in later periods likely will cost more to accomplish, thanks to inflation.

With these nine definitions, related back to the data contained in Figure 13.4, we will be in a position to better understand the forecasting techniques in the final EAC section below.

Criteria Group 4

The **analysis** section contains six criteria that require the contractor or subcontractor to make an assessment of what has occurred with its cost and schedule performance to date. Most important, however, this criteria group requires the supplier to analyze the cost and schedule performance to date, and then to estimate the cost and schedule requirements necessary to complete the effort, to forecast the EAC. Estimates at completion will be covered thoroughly later in this chapter.

Criteria Group 5

The **revisions and access to data** section contains six criteria that require the supplier to maintain the performance measurement baseline (PMB) throughout the life of the contract by incorporating all new work into the PMB in a timely manner. Obviously, the maintenance of the baseline is vital to the integrity of any performance measurement system. Also, this group requires the contractor to give the customer's representatives access to performance data so they can verify strict compliance with the criteria.

Since the Defense Department issued the C/SCSC in 1967, the application of the concept has been intentionally limited to those contracts in which the customer (the buyer) has retained the risks of cost growth (i.e., on cost or incentive-type contracts and subcontracts). The dollar thresholds for formal C/SCSC implementation vary from period to period and are set by the buying customer. Currently they are generally imposed at $50 million on prime contracts ($25 million for subcontracts) for developmental work, and $160 million ($60 million for subcontracts) for production efforts. Any full application of C/SCSC calls for a periodic report (typically monthly) called the "cost performance report" (CPR).

For smaller contracts, the lesser cost/schedule status report (C/SSR) or cost performance report no criteria (CPR/NC) is now generally set at $5 million in contract value and a minimum of 12 months in program duration. However, program and subcontract management should weigh the risk factors involved in a given effort and decide the earned-value applications on a case-by-case basis.

This overview was out of necessity a very limited discussion of a very large subject. One last question needs to be addressed: Does the earned-value (C/SCSC) performance measurement concept really work, or is it just another government requirement? To best answer this question, we should review the results of an impressive Department of Defense study.

Covering the period 1977–1990, more than 400 DOD contracts in which formal C/SCSC was implemented were studied. The results of the analysis are most impressive, and without exception the findings are consistent for all 400-plus contracts monitored.

Once the C/SCSC performance measurement baseline (PMB) is in place and at least 15 percent of the planned work has been performed, the following conclusions can be drawn on the future performance of a given program:

- The overrun at completion will not be less than the overrun to date.
- The percent overrun at completion will be greater than the percent overrun to date.
- The conclusion: You can't recover.
- Who says: More than 400 major DOD contracts since 1977.
- Why: If you underestimated the near term, there is no hope that you will do better on planning in the far term.[12]

Before closing this section on the basics of the earned-value concept, we should consider the objectives sought to be gained through the performance measurement concept to monitor and manage contractors and subcontractors. Once again, let us call upon one of the originators of the concept who did so much to implement the technique during his tenure with the DOD and later with the DOE. Robert Kemps summarizes the four objectives we can obtain from employing the earned-value (C/SCSC) performance measurement concept on our programs:

+ Sound contractor systems
+ Reliable, auditable data
+ Objective performance measurement
+ No surprises[13]

Four simple programmatic objectives, not always easy to obtain.

Comparing Progress Payment Data with C/SCSC Cost Performance Report (CPR) Data

The reporting of differences from a contractor or subcontractor will likely be the norm, not the exception, when we compare the cost data contained on progress payment invoices with the cost data contained in the formal C/SCSC cost performance report (CPR) or the lesser C/SSR or CPR/NC. Two issues require a reconciliation when differences exist:

1. Comparison of the *cost actuals* (ACWP) reported to date—between those contained in the progress payment invoice and the cost actuals reflected on the CPR.
2. Comparison of the *estimates to complete* (EAC) the effort—between those forecasted on the progress payment invoice and those forecasted on the CPR.

For purposes of this discussion we will consider the three distinct C/SCSC cost and schedule performance reports (CPR, C/SSR, and CPR/NC) as being identical for the purpose of reviewing the data contained therein. Any generic differences in these three reports deal with other matters, not the actual cost (ACWP) or the estimate at completion (EAC) contained in the report.

We would expect that some direct relationship exists, or should exist, between what a contractor or subcontractor reports as its cost actuals position on a progress payment invoice and what it reports reflect on other cost summaries (e.g., a CPR). After all, the cost data do come from the same supplier, reporting its cost status from a single accounting system.

However, in practice, it is not unusual to receive multiple cost reports from a supplier reflecting different financial actuals for the same reporting period. Any time this happens, it is incumbent on the buyer to request a reconciliation from the subcontractor, requiring an explanation of any differences in the cost reports.

Such discrepancies can be attributed to several factors that make the data contained in any of these cost reports unique. These factors are:

1. Different cutoff dates for the reports, or the data contained or reported therein. In some cases the date on the report reflects a specific accounting closure date, but at other times it reflects the date of report submittal. Not infrequently, the progress payment closure date will have a different cutoff from the general ledger closure date.

2. Cost data only (which exclude fee or profit) versus "price" data, which include some estimate of earned fee or profit on lower-tier subcontracts. Often there are distinct professional differences of opinion between a buyer and seller as to how much profit or fee a given supplier will likely have earned on the effort at a given point in time.

3. Progress payments to lower-tier suppliers. These may be included or excluded in the cost actuals being reported.

4. Negotiated statement of work versus unnegotiated statement of work—that is, changes. Unnegotiated work will often be placed into several categories,

such as (1) authorized, priced, and proposed; (2) authorized, unpriced, and unproposed; and (3) unauthorized and still under discussion. Not infrequently, there are legitimate differences of opinion between buyer and seller as to the correct value of the "yet to be negotiated" work.

5. The projected estimated supplier costs at completion, in absolute overrun or underrun terms, with the cost-sharing impact on a supplier's earned profits under an incentive-type contractual arrangement.

6. Termination liability projections at any given point in time, which will include either a supplier's open commitments or its expenditures only. Remember, small businesses may include accounting accruals as cost actuals for purposes of requesting progress payments. Large businesses must actually pay the bills in order for the payments to qualify as actual expenditures.

7. Materials purchased (e.g., raw stock, nuts, bolts, chemicals), received, and placed directly into inventory, but not yet charged to work in process. The costs of these materials may or may not be incorporated into the cost actuals reported.

There are doubtless additional factors, all legitimate reasons, which may cause differences in the reported data between the progress payment request (SF1443) and the C/SCSC cost performance report (CPR). These seven items are not intended to be all-inclusive.

What all this means to the buyer and the seller is that they should insist that those who prepare such cost reports invest them with a few choice narrative words that clarify any assumptions they may have made when the data were submitted. This is particularly true when multiple cost reports rely on similar financial terms that can have different meanings to the practitioners. However, any time different values are reported, the buyer has a programmatic responsibility to understand the reasons for these discrepancies prior to authorizing funds for the progress payment invoice.

Comparing Progress Payment Data without the Formal C/SCSC on Firm Fixed-Price (FFP) Subcontracts

How do you get earned-value performance measurement on subcontracts that do not have formal C/SCSC requirements imposed? One approach is to impose full C/SCSC requirements on all contracts and subcontracts that are funded by the U.S. government. One government official, William Hill, has suggested exactly that in his timely article on managing contractor progress payments. Note that in the following excerpt, "flexible" refers to cost or incentive-type contracts and "inflexible" refers to firm fixed-price (FFP) contracts:

> The DOD would be well advised to insist validated cost/schedule procedures be implemented on all large dollar contracts—flexible and inflexible, prime and subcontracts—that require payments reviews by the government. Validated cost/schedule reporting will ensure proper program controls and provide the government with a more effective and efficient method of conducting government payment reviews.[14]

Hill makes the point that since hundreds of contractors have fully validated C/SCSC systems, and since it is important to connect the approval of progress payments with the physical performance of a contractor, why not extend C/SCSC to all programs that are funded by the government? This is certainly a valid point, but it is not recommended for a number of reasons.

In the first place, although there are currently more than 200 actively validated C/SCSC management control systems in the United States, that number represents only a small fraction of all the contracts and subcontracts covered by government progress payments. Most of the firm fixed-price (FFP) contracts and subcontracts would not be affected by such an edict, because most suppliers do *not* possess a validated

C/SCSC management control system. Two hundred approved management systems out of several thousand suppliers is but a small percentage of the total.

Of greater significance, extending full C/SCSC to all programs that have progress payments would simply increase the costs of the government's procurement of major systems. The formal C/SCSC, with their 35 specific criteria, have too much "nonvalue-added" requirements to be universally and indiscriminately applied to all programs that have progress payments. Full C/SCSC applications should be limited to cost or incentive-type contracts, with their inherent cost risks, which can benefit from having an early-warning monitoring system.

In 1967, when C/SCSC was introduced, there was some confusion as to the types of contracts or subcontracts that should be governed by the criteria. It was decided at that time to limit the formal application of C/SCSC to those efforts in which the risk of cost growth was on the buyer (i.e., to cost or incentive type contracts). That principle is still valid today. There are better, less costly ways to achieve the same goal of linking progress payment approvals to the physical performance of the supplier requesting payment.

When a supplier requests progress payments and the buyer is prudent enough to require the creation and monthly submittal of a Gantt chart, the prime contractor (buyer) has all that is needed to employ at least a modified version of the earned-value concept. Even a modified earned-value approach can be significant for monitoring fixed-price suppliers, who traditionally have refused to allow any performance monitoring by prime contractors.

It is important to have the subcontractor prepare a Gantt chart for a project. The subcontractor should list all the planned tasks necessary to perform the purchase order. Each of the listed tasks must receive a weighted value, the sum of which must be 100 percent of the purchase order price. The Gantt chart with weighted values provides, in effect, a simple form of an earned-value plan, which in the C/SCSC vernacular is the budgeted costs for work scheduled (BCWS). With the supplier's own plan, we can quantify each task with its value into a time frame to form a cumulative percentage curve. Figure 13.5 illustrates the approach with data that would be supplied by a subcontractor to quantify its own performance plan and its own BCWS, monthly and cumulative.

Each month, as the supplier reports actual performance against Gantt schedule, it must report a percentage completion against the plan. Suppose that previously the supplier had reported 28 percent complete as of October 1991, and then 34 percent as of January 1992. This analysis compares unfavorably with our assessment of the data in Figure 13.5. To best illustrate what this supplier is reporting to us in its schedule performance, we should lay out the data as in Table 13.1.

Figure 13.5 shows what the subcontractor originally planned to do. We can immediately see that with the passage of time, this supplier is getting progressively behind in accomplishing the work set out in the original plan. And by measuring the schedule position with earned-value performance indices, we can quantify precisely how well or poorly the supplier is doing. Its schedule performance index (SPI)

T A B L E 13.1

Layout of Supplier's Performance Plan

	October 1991	January 1992
BCWS plan (from Figure 13.5)	37%	46%
BCWP performance (from previous reports)	28%	34%
Schedule variance position	−9%	−12%
SPI (BCWP divided by BCWS)	76%	74%

Establishing the BCWS

Hypothetical Engines, Inc.

Item#	Task	%	J	F	M	A	M	J	J	A	S	O	N	D	J	F	M	A	M	J	J	A	S	O	N	D	J	F	M	A	M	J
1	Des.Mod.	5	1	2	2																											
3	Qual.Test	5				5																										
5	Pur.Mat.	20				4	4	4	4	4																						
7	Fab.Parts	10								2	2	2	2	2																		
9	Comm.Assy	12										1	2	1	2	1	2	1	2													
11	#1	4																		2	2											
12	#2	4																			2	2										
13	#3	4																				2	2									
14	#4	4																					2	2								
15	#5	4																						2	2							
16	#6	4																							2	2						
17	#7	4																								2	2					
18	#8	4																									2	2				
19	#9	4																										2	2			
20	#10	4																											2	2		
21	#11	4																												2	2	
22	#12	4																													2	2
BCWS	Month%	100	1	2	2	9	4	4	4	6	2	3	4	3	2	1	2	1	2	2	4	4	4	4	4	4	4	4	4	4	4	2
BCWS	Cum.%		1	3	5	14	18	22	26	32	34	37	41	44	46	47	49	50	52	54	58	62	66	70	74	78	82	86	90	94	98	100

went down from 76 percent of accomplishing planned work in October 1991 to 74 percent 90 days later.

What this percent-complete estimate provides is a sort of modified earned value, or BCWP (budgeted costs for work performed) in the C/SCSC terminology. The difference between the planned BCWS versus what was accomplished in the BCWP provides the schedule performance (SV) position for a subcontractor. It tells the prime contractor whether the supplier is accomplishing the work it had set out to do, and in a timely fashion. The performance of Hypothetical Engines is not going well, 12 months into a 30-month effort.

Now let us relate the earned value (percent complete) to the costs this supplier is experiencing. Each month as the supplier submits a request for progress payments, it must complete an SF1443 invoice form. Line 12a of the SF1443 contains the supplier's total actual costs incurred, cumulative to date. The amount listed on line 12a is equivalent to the actual cost values in C/SCSC, or what is called the ACWP (actual costs for work performed). When we relate the ACWP to the earned value (BCWP), we have the cost variance (CV) for performance by a supplier. With this information we can deduce the cost performance efficiency factor for the supplier (BCWP divided by ACWP) to determine how much a supplier has earned for every dollar it has spent. If the supplier spends $1.00 but accomplishes only $.85 in earned value, the subcontractor should be watched closely. It could be heading for a loss, which will require the application of the loss ratio to all progress payments made once the total "projected" cost penetrates the subcontract price value.

Thus, by requiring that a subcontractor put in place a few elementary cost and schedule plans prior to a subcontract award, a buyer can employ a simple but effective earned-value performance measurement concept. With this, the performance of even firm fixed-price suppliers may be monitored during the life of their subcontracts to provide a linkage between progress payment approvals and earned-value measurement.

Using C/SCSC Performance Indices to Predict the EAC

The best estimate at completion (EAC) forecast for a given program is typically referred to as a "bottoms-up" or "grassroots" EAC. Here, each of the remaining tasks to be worked is examined by the very functions that will perform the tasks, and a detailed estimate to complete all the work is prepared. However, to accomplish a legitimate bottoms-up EAC takes a lot of program resources—the very same resources that are trying to complete the job in a timely manner. Therefore, grassroots EACs can be accommodated only once or twice each year per program in order for such exercises not to interfere with the primary mission of completing the contractual effort. At the upper extreme, a grassroots EAC may be done quarterly, but that frequency may well overtax the limited resources of any program and have an adverse impact on successful contractual performance.

However, and this is the good news, the cost and schedule performance data generated by the earned-value C/SCSC activities provide an effective way of complimenting the periodic (annual, semi-annual, or quarterly) grassroots EACs done by the functional organizations. Without disrupting personnel in the performing organizations, and with the help of computer software programs in place today, a monthly (or even weekly) full range of EAC forecasts may be efficiently provided, based upon the actual C/SCSC performance data.

In addition, work being performed by all subcontractors should be submitted to monthly EAC analysis, independent of what the supplier may be "officially" forecasting. Periodic subcontractor EACs should be verified independently by the responsible cost account manager (CAM). One of the best ways to accomplish this is by examination of the supplier's earned-value performance. Another benefit of the analysis—should the CAM be the same individual who approves all progress payment invoices—is to establish a critical linkage between the two management processes. Finally, the preparation of an independent EAC forecast for subcontractors provides better assurance to the government that a "loss ratio adjustment" will be invoked at the appropriate time to preclude any overpayment of government funds.

In 1991, when the Department of Defense made its long-awaited changes to the C/SCSC requirements documentation and incorporated them directly into a new acquisition policy statement in DODD 5000.1 and DODI 5000.2, there were no changes to the C/SCSC. There were, however, two important changes in the analysis of the C/SCSC data, particularly as related to providing the estimates of costs at completion (EAC) on a given program.

The first change requires a "range of EAC estimates" to be provided by the military service program manager who is responsible for the management of a given acquisition system. The service program manager must, from the cost/schedule performance data:

(1) Enter the range of estimates at completion, reflecting best and worst cases.[15]

The second DOD change to the C/SCSC requires a justification, again from the military service program manager, whenever an estimate of costs at completion forecasts a final value that is *less* than an amount forecast by the cumulative cost performance index (CPI):

(2) Provide the estimate at completion reflecting the best professional judgement of the servicing cost analysis organization. If the contract is at least 15 percent complete and the estimate is lower than that calculated using the cumulative cost performance index, provide an explanation.[16]

The "15 percent" thresholds relate to the DOD empirical study, covered earlier, of more than 400 contractors that performed under the C/SCSC.[17] What a contractor has achieved after performing 15 percent of a contract is likely to be the *lower-end* value of what it will do by the end of the contract.

With the added emphasis on using earned-value performance data to forecast the final cost/schedule outcomes of contracts, we would be wise to make sure that we fully understand some of the formulas available to forecast a "range of estimates." Although C/SCSC practitioners utilize a multitude of EAC formulas, we will address only the basic three, since these constitute the more accepted methods in use:

1. The *low-end* estimate at completion (mathematical EAC).
2. (a) The *middle-range* estimate at completion (CPI EAC).
   (b) What CPI performance factor it will take "to complete" an effort, called the to-complete performance index (TCPI), in order to achieve the CPI EAC forecast.
3. The *high-range* estimate at completion (CPI × SPI EAC).

We will examine each of these mathematical forecasting methods individually, building on the definitions of C/SCSC terms covered earlier in this chapter. To follow this discussion, we need to return to the C/SCSC jargon covering the display of data in Figure 13.4—particularly, the cost performance index (CPI) and the schedule performance index (SPI). A perfect CPI is 1.0, which means that for each dollar actually spent, one dollar of physical work was performed. A perfect SPI is also 1.0, which means that for each dollar of work planned to be accomplished, one dollar of physical work was accomplished.

If a contractor achieves what it sets out to achieve in its cost and schedule baseline plans (PMB), that is considered acceptable or even "perfect" efficiency in a performance measurement environment. This concept is illustrated in Figure 13.6.

If after establishing the performance measurement baseline (PMB) the contractor achieves a cost performance factor of 1.0, this is considered excellent results. For every dollar spent, the contractor has one dollar in physical earned-value accomplishments. Anything less than 1.0 is considered negative performance. Anything greater than 1.0 is considered positive or even exceptional efficiency.

F I G U R E 13.6

Gantt Chart to Support Progress Payment Evaluations

How might a contractor actually achieve a greater than 1.0 performance? On occasion, a contractor may perform slightly under 1.0 in the first part of a contractual period, then exceed 1.0 in the final stage. This may be the result of conservative planning of the performance baseline, where the final 100% achievement of various tasks is restrained in order to stimulate exemplary performance by program personnel.

However, if a contractor claims achievement "significantly" greater than 1.0, perhaps 1.5, then someone might want to pay the supplier a visit and find out how such "miracles" have occurred. Often, but not always, a performance attainment much greater than 1.0 is the result of an improper original performance measurement plan. And sometimes, exceptional performance is just plain "gamesmanship" by those who are preparing and/or approving the cost/schedule reports.

Likewise, schedule performance of 1.0 is considered as good as it can get, under normal circumstances. For every one dollar of work planned to be accomplished, one dollar of performance was achieved.

Now let's look at the range of EAC possibilities. The low-end EAC forecast is called the mathematical EAC, as displayed in Figure 13.7. Some people refer to the mathematical EAC formula as being useless, or unrealistic, or even optimistic. Yet many firms in the industry have been using this EAC method since the C/SCSC were issued in 1967. The formula for the mathematical EAC is budget at completion (BAC), less the cumulative earned value (BCWP), plus the cumulative actual costs to date (ACWP). What this EAC does in effect is to "buy out" any poor performance to date, but assumes that starting tomorrow, all remaining work will be performed at perfect or 1.0 efficiency (on the average).

Although the mathematical EAC is not an accurate device for forecasting what a program will likely cost at the end, it does provide a "floor" EAC, that value which represents the absolute minimum cost for the program. Such revelations

F I G U R E 13.7

Monitoring Earned-Value Performance

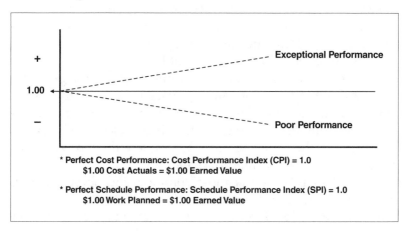

F I G U R E 13.8

"Mathematical" Estimate at Completion (EAC)

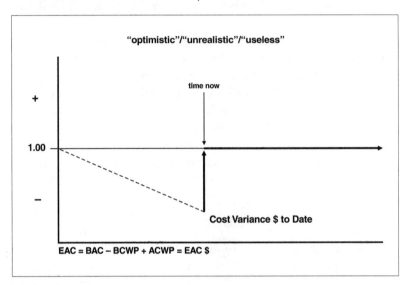

sometimes come as a shock to management, and do provide the lower-end range of EAC possibilities.

The middle-range EAC forecast is called the cumulative CPI EAC, as displayed in Figure 13.8. The formula is the budget at completion (BAC) divided by the cumulative cost performance index (CPI). There are a number of variations for this midrange EAC, but none offers value to us in this limited discussion of the subject. Some people use only the last 3 or 6 months of the CPI, to reflect a recent trend or change in the direction of the CPI. For our purposes we need only understand that the total budget available is divided by the cumulative performance efficiency factor. If that efficiency factor is less that 1.0, then the estimate to complete the job will grow from the original allocated budget.

The CPI EAC is the most common and accepted EAC method. Some people consider this method to reflect the "most likely" EAC forecast, while other, more conservative individuals feel it reflects only the "minimum" EAC. What-ever. In the recent acquisition policy statement DODD 5000.2-M, as quoted earlier, the military service program manager must now "provide an explanation" for any EAC forecasts that predict a final performance value that is less than that using the cumulative CPI EAC method.

One of the most important tools in C/SCSC forecasting does not deal with how much it will cost, or how long it will take to complete the job. Rather, the to-complete performance index (TCPI) has its utility in determining what performance efficiency factor it will take to do what you say you will do. Simply put, if you complete half a job with a CPI of .95 per-cent, then in order to complete the job within the approved budget for the remaining work, you must achieve a CPI of 1.05 percent for the balance of the effort. This concept is illus-trated in Figure 13.9, along with the formula to calculate the TCPI.

F I G U R E 13.9

"Cumulative CPI" Estimate at Completion

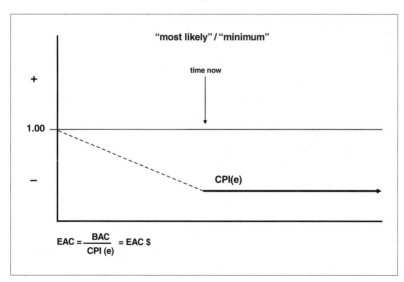

The value of the TCPI formula is that it can be used to answer a number of questions, all related to achieving some future objective. For example, what efficiency factor will it take (1) to stay within the budget at completion (BAC), (2) to stay within the latest estimate at completion (EAC), (3) to stay within the latest over-the-target budget (OTB), or (4) to stay within the fixed-price incentive (FPI) ceiling? The TCPI is used to "puncture" blind optimism, which sometimes inflicts company management, particularly more senior management.

The high-end EAC forecast is called the CPI x SPI EAC forecast. It adds the dimension of scheduled but unfinished work—work that was in the original plan, but has not been completed. This concept is illustrated in Figure 13.10. The formula is the work remaining to be performed (BAC less BCWP), divided by the product of the cost performance index (CPI) times the schedule performance index (SPI), plus the ACWP. Obviously, if you performed under 1.0 in both the CPI and SPI, the resulting estimate at completion will be substantial.

This EAC method can get to be quite emotional to those involved in managing programs. Some consider this technique to represent the "most likely" EAC, while others call it the "worst case" scenario. Some program managers, attempting to keep their costs under control, refer to this technique irreverently as a "self-fulfilling prophecy." Whatever.

This method is generally considered to be the high-end EAC method, and was used by the DOD cost analysts on the A-12 program to forecast its total estimate at completion. It is a most valuable high-end EAC forecasting technique.

Now, what do all these EAC methods do for us when we attempt to forecast the final costs of a given program? If we take each of the formulas as displayed in Figures 13.7 to 13.10 and relate them to the data provided from the performance in Figure 13.4, perhaps we can discern the value in employing these EAC techniques.

Starting from the low-end EAC method, we can line up a range of EAC forecasts:

Performance Index TCPI

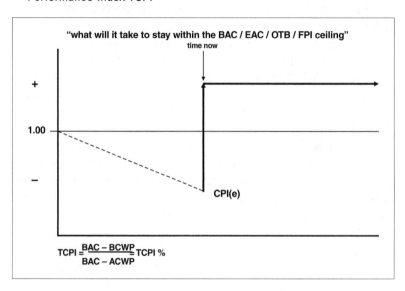

The Mathematical EAC

$$BAC - BCWP + ACWP = EAC\$$$
$$\$100M - \$25M + \$40M = EAC\ \mathbf{\$115M}$$

The CPI EAC

$$BAC\ /\ CPI = EAC\$$$
$$\$100M\ /.625\% = EAC\ \mathbf{\$160M}$$

The TCPI

$$(BAC - BCWP)\ /\ (BAC - ACWP) = TCPI\%$$
$$(\$100M - \$25M)\ /\ (\$100M - \$40M) = \$75M\ /\ \$60M = TCPI\ \mathbf{1.25\%}$$

The CPI × SPI EAC

$$(BAC - BCWP)\ /\ (CPI \times SPI) + ACWP = EAC\$$$
$$(\$100M - \$25M)\ /\ (.625\% \times .500\%) + \$40M = EAC\ \mathbf{\$280M}$$

The low-end EAC method (mathematical EAC) tells us we will spend $115 million, the minimum floor. The midrange EAC (CPI EAC) forecasts a total cost requirement of $160 million, and if anyone predicts a lesser amount, a military program manager will have to justify the lesser amount in order to comply with the new DODD5000.2-M. The high-end EAC (CPI x SPI EAC) tells us we will need $280 million to complete the job, quite an increase over our budget of $100 million! With these formulas we can provide a full range of EAC estimates.

What is also significant is the fact that in order to stay within the original approved budget of $100 million, we must achieve a CPI performance efficiency factor of 1.25 percent for all our remaining effort. A very ambitious goal for any mortal person or group to achieve.

The various EAC forecasting tools available to us when earned-value methods are employed can be most beneficial in the management of our contracts or subcontracts, and provide a complimentary adjunct in the effective administration of contractor progress payments.

IN SUMMARY

There is no universal acceptance of the concept that a linkage should or must exist between the progress payments being made to suppliers and the physical performance they are achieving on such work. Nonetheless, the A-12 program experience will likely require such relationships in the future. This important linkage will likely improve both management processes: progress payments and cost/schedule performance measurement.

By linking physical performance measurement to the approval of progress payments, the prime contractor should avoid the potential cost risks of making overpayments to the supplier. Also, the federal acquisition regulations covering progress payments specifically require that there be some monitoring of the supplier's performance in order to know when it might be necessary to adjust the repayment rate, or to suspend further progress payments, or to invoke the loss ratio, among other things.

By linking progress payments with C/SCSC performance measurement, the buyer will have a better understanding of what the suppliers are actually achieving in satisfying their statement of work. To exclude progress payment data from the actuals being reported in the cost performance report (CPR) does nothing but distort the desired earned-value measurements. And with the subcontracted portions (the buy content) becoming such a major part of most prime contractor dollars (upward of 80 percent in some cases), the exclusion of progress payment data in performance measurement can reflect major distortions in the data being reported. A better approach, it is felt, is to measure the physical performance of all suppliers involved in progress payments, including firm fixed-price suppliers, and to incorporate these actual dollars into all CPRs.

We touched on a couple of issues rather hurriedly in the discussion above, and it might be beneficial here to reemphasize these points. It is important that the buyer—the individual who has delegated procurement authority to issue the subcontract—be given the responsibility for the review and approval of each and every progress payment invoice before any such payments are made. This is a fundamental issue. Also important, it is believed, is the concept that this same buyer be held responsible for the total management of his or her subcontract, including that of functioning in the role of cost account manager for the performance measurement of the supplier.

If a prime contractor thus places the responsibility for (1) the full administration of progress payments, including the approval or disapproval of all payment invoices, and (2) the management of a subcontract earned-value cost account in a single individual, then the prime contractor will have achieved a "linkage" of both activities. This critical coupling should prevent any future overpayment of suppliers, in advance of their actual physical work accomplishments, and improve the over-all subcontract management processes.

We hope we have made the case for employing this approach.

N O T E S

1. This chapter is a composite of Chapters 1 and 5 of *Subcontract Project Management and Control: Progress Payments,* by Quentin W. Fleming and Quentin J. Fleming (Chicago: Probus, 1992). Used by permission of the authors.

2. The material that follows is taken from Chapter 5 of *Subcontract Project Management and Control: Progress Payments,* by Quentin W. Fleming and Quentin J. Fleming (Chicago: Probus, 1991).

3. Chester Paul Beach, Jr., Inquiry Officer, in a memorandum for the Secretary of the Navy, "A-12 Administrative Inquiry," November, 28, 1990, p. 2.

4. Ibid. pp. 3 and 4.

5. Wayne Abba, Office of Acquisition Policy and Program Integration, Office of the Secretary of Defense, in public remarks made on the A-12 program to the management systems subcommittee of the National Security Industrial Association, Costa Mesa, CA, January 16, 1991.

6. Eleanor Spector, Director of Defense Procurement, Office of the Secretary of Defense, in Congressional testimony, April 9, 1991.

7. *Los Angeles Times,* from Reuters, June 8, 1991.

8. Robert R. Kemps, Humphreys & Associates, Inc., formerly with the Department of Defense and later the Department of Energy, in "Solving the Baseline Dilemma," an article he wrote for the Performance Management Association's newsletter, Autumn 1990.

9. Russell D. Archibald and Richard L. Villoria, *Network-Based Management Systems (PERT/CPM)* (New York: John Wiley & Sons, 1967), p. 475.

10. Department of Defense Directive 5000.1, dated February 23, 1991, "Defense Acquisition"; Department of Defense Instruc-

tion 5000.2, same date, "Defense Acquisition Management Policies and Procedures."

11. See Fleming, *The C/SCSC System.*

12. Gary E. Christle, Deputy Director for Cost Management, Office of the Undersecretary of Defense for Acquisitions, in a paper entitled "Contractor Performance Measurement-Projecting Estimates at Completion," Atlanta, GA, October 26, 1987. Data updated from 200 to 400 contracts from the Beach report, November 28, 1990, p. 6.

13. Robert R. Kemps, Director of the Office of Project and Facilities Management for the Department of Energy (DOE), in "Cost/Schedule Control Systems Criteria (C/SCSC) for Contract Performance Measurement," a paper delivered at the Performance Management Association Conference in San Diego, CA, April 1989.

14. William J. Hill, "Toward More Effective Management and Control of Contractor Payments," in Defense Systems Management College's *Program Manager* magazine, January–February 1991, p. 21.

15. DOD 5000.2-M, p. 16-H-6.

16. DOD 5000.2-M, p. 16-H-6.

17. See note 12.

14

CHAPTER

Project Change Control

THE NEED FOR CHANGE CONTROL

One of the fallacies of project management is that, once a project plan has been assembled, the world will stand still while the plan is executed. This was probably not true in the past, and it certainly is not true today. Any project that lasts longer than a few months is almost certain to be affected by some change in the environment, and the project manager must respond to

> One of the fallacies of project management is that once a project plan has been assembled, the world will stand still while the plan is executed.

that effect. The objective is to deal with the change in such a way that all stakeholders know what is going on and approve of the response.

As an example, consider the situation in which someone is having a house built. Midway through the construction project, the customer says to the builder, "I've been thinking that it would be nice to pave the driveway to the house, rather than just putting in a gravel drive like we originally intended."

"No problem," says the builder. "I can do that for you."

"Can you still be finished on time?" asks the customer. "I have a lease on my apartment and don't want to have to renew it, so it's important that we be able to move into the house as originally scheduled."

"No problem," says the builder.

"Okay," the customer continues, "that sounds fine. But how about construction quality? That won't be affected will it?"

"Oh, no," the builder says with confidence. "No problem with quality."

"Well, then, I just have one more question," the customer replies. "How much will it cost?"

"Oh, it won't be much," the builder says casually.

You know, of course, that if the customer leaves it at that, there is bound to be a problem later on. The builder knows that, as driveways go, this is not an expensive driveway. It will be around $10,000. The customer, who knows nothing about the cost of driveways, is thinking about $2500. When he sees a bill for $10,000, he is bound to explode.

Here, the builder has an obligation to let the customer know how this change in scope will affect the project. That way, the customer can make an informed decision about what to do. He may say, "That's more than I want to pay, so just forget it," or he may say, "Well, it's a lot more than I expected, but go ahead." Either way, there are no surprises at the end of the job.

Note also that in alerting the customer the builder is protecting herself from possible repercussions if the customer is hit with an unexpected high driveway cost at the end of the job. You might say that the project manager (the builder in this case) has an obligation both to the customer and to herself, to protect both.

Now, does this mean that every time someone asks for a small change to a project, the manager should say, "It will cost you!"? I don't think so. Behaving that way will get you a reputation for being a nitpicker. It is best to absorb a few changes.

However, small changes add up to a big impact, and at some point you may have to say, "I've absorbed all the changes I can, so I'll have to charge you now." This is, of course, the way that *scope creep* works—small changes are made repeatedly, until the final project is much larger than it started out to be.

THE CHANGE CONTROL PROCESS

Every organization should have a formal project change control process or procedure. I believe very strongly in the KISS principle ("Keep it simple, stupid"), so the procedure should be no more burdensome on the organization than is necessary to protect against even worse long-term effects of changes. Here are some factors that should be considered when a change is requested:

- ◆ Will the change affect scope, cost, performance, or schedule?
- ◆ Will tooling or capital equipment be affected?
- ◆ How about inventory levels of parts or finished goods?
- ◆ In product development projects, will the change affect form, fit, or function of the product?
- ◆ Will the change make the product more or less desirable in the marketplace?
- ◆ Will the change affect return on investment or net present value? If so, can the project still be justified at this level of ROI or NPV?

- How is the change justified? Needed for competitive advantage? Mandated by some regulation? What is the business need?
- Is the change required to get the project back on track? Or is the project so far off its original target that the change is simply documenting where we are now and will serve as a baseline against which to track future progress?

Now let's look at some guidelines for change control are:

- Changes should be made only when required by stakeholder input or by significant deviations from the original plan. Note that the level representing *significant* should be defined at the beginning of the project. For example, if you can maintain only a plus-or-minus 10% tolerance around your schedule or budget, and you are off 20 percent and see no way of recovering, then the plan should be changed. The 10% boundary should have been established at the beginning.
- Causes of all changes should be documented in a factual way for the future. The objective is not to place blame or administer punishment, but to learn from history so that improved performance can be achieved in future projects.

Who should approve the change? One guideline that I find very practical is that only those stakeholders affected by the change need to approve it. By following this guide, you avoid slowing down the approval process by having too many signatures. The change approval form shown in Figure 14.1 allows flexibility, by having a check placed by the individuals who must sign the form. In this way, if a given individual is not affected by this specific change, then he or she does not have to sign it.

F I G U R E 14.1

Project Change Approval Form

Project Change Approval		
Project Name:	Project Number:	Date: May 19, 1999
Project Manager: Requested by:	Department:	Change in: ☐ Scope ☐ Schedule ☐ Budget ☐ Performance

Deviation Information

Description of change being requested:

Reason for change:

Effect on schedule:

Effect on cost (budget):

Effect on performance (quality):

Effect on scope:

Justification:

Class	Distribution of Estimated Cost Deviation	The Requested Change is:	
Capital		☐ Absolutely necessary to achieve desired results	☐ Scope reduction that will not impact original targets
Non-capital		☐ Discretionary - provides benefits beyond the original target	☐ Scope reduction that will impact original targets

Required Approvals ☐

☐ Project Leader/Manager (type name)	Sign:	Date:
☐ General Manager (type name)	Sign:	Date:
☐ Concerned Dept. Manager (type name)	Sign:	Date:
☐ Controller (type name)	Sign:	Date:
☐ Concerned Vice President (type name)	Sign:	Date:
☐ President (type name)	Sign:	Date:
☐ Other (type name)	Sign:	Date:

CAUSES OF PROJECT SUCCESS AND FAILURE

15 CHAPTER

Defining Project Success and Failure

Under ordinary circumstances, I'm sure that no one sets out to fail in managing a project. We all want our projects to be successful. However, it is not at all clear what is meant by success or failure. What is needed is an operational definition of these terms. An operational definition is based on criteria that all parties involved can agree to use to define the outcome.

The most frequently used definition is that a project is a failure when it does not meet its performance, cost, time, or scope (P, C, T, or S) targets. However, there are a couple of things wrong with this definition. First, where did the targets come from? When they are just "pulled out of the air" and are therefore unrealistic, should failing to meet those

> When you don't meet a target that was just pulled out of the air, should that be called a failure?

targets be considered a failure? Second, even if all of these targets are met, does the project solve the problem it was intended to solve? Does the customer use it? If not, was it really a success? As you can see, these are nontrivial questions.

Schultz, Sleven, and Pinto (1987) have identified four errors that can be made in solving problems. Since project management is problem solving on a large scale, their concept applies equally well in this area. These are:

1. **Type I error:** Not taking an action when one should be taken.
2. **Type II error:** Taking an action when none should be taken.
3. **Type III error:** Taking the wrong action (solving the wrong problem).
4. **Type IV error:** Addressing the right problem, but not implementing the solution.

Using their definitions, we can say that a project that meets its P, C, T, and S targets but is not used is either a Type III or a Type IV error. In some cases, it is the fact that a Type III error has been made that ultimately causes the project to be a Type IV error. That is, we have solved the wrong problem, so no one uses the project. This happens on internal software projects when we talk to department managers about their requirements and implement the system they recommend, but their people won't use the system because it does not really meet their needs.

OTHER PERSPECTIVES

In their book *Learning from Failure: The Systems Approach*, Fortune and Peters (1995) say, "A simple definition of failure is something that has gone wrong, or not lived up to expectations. Moving a little way beyond this simple statement, various types or categories of failure can be identified."

They go on to establish four types of failures, much like Schultz et al., as shown in Table 15.1. Type 1 failures are those

A simple definition of failure is that something has gone wrong or has not lived up to expectations.

T A B L E 15.1

Types of Failures

	Failures
Type 1	Objectives not met
Type 2	Undesirable side effects
Type 3	Designed failures
Type 4	Inappropriate objectives

that we encounter every day. Examples are software that never worked properly and new products that won't sell.

For Type 2 failures, the original objectives are met, but there are undesirable consequences or side effects. In step 4 of the Lewis Method of project management outlined in Chapter 2, the candidate strategy is subjected to a number of tests, one of which is "Are the consequences acceptable?" This question is designed to help project managers avoid Type 2 errors.

Most of today's environmental problems are the consequences of solutions to problems we had yesterday. Fortune and Peters cite the drug thalidomide as an example. Here was a product that seemed beneficial but caused numerous birth defects. The unanticipated side effects of breast implants provide a more recent example; the outcome has nearly destroyed Dow-Corning. So we are surrounded by many Type 2 errors.

The next category of failure is one that is intentional, and therefore is not considered bad. A fuse is designed to blow (fail) when a certain current level is exceeded. Sprinkler systems fail to hold water in pipes when a fire breaks out. These are Type 3 failures.

Type 4 failures are similar to Schultz et al. Type III errors: They involve solving the wrong problem. Included here are products that work well but don't meet the needs of the market. For example, a conveyor installed to reduce breakage of manufactured goods does not solve the breakage problem, but moves goods around the factory just fine. Similarly, the Apple III computer, which was probably technically superior to the IBM PC at the time, was not accepted in the marketplace because of IBM's superior name and also because no software was available to run business applications. We might say the same about Beta format in video players. The format was technically superior to VHS, but because Sony tried to keep it proprietary, most manufacturers adopted VWH—and Beta eventually died in the home entertainment market. (Most studio-quality recorders still use Beta format.)

As Fortune and Peters go on to say, almost all judgments about failure are subjective; they are colored by personal perception, circumstances, and expectations. Thus, the actual person a project team works with in a customer organization may regard the work as successful, while that person's boss will call it a failure. No doubt this is often true when multiple stakeholders are involved, and it illustrates how important it is to develop mutually agreed-upon criteria as definitions of success before such projects are started.

> ☞ It is extremely important that criteria be developed that are mutually agreed upon as definitions of success by major stakeholders before projects are started.

DELIVERABLES, RESULTS, AND EXPECTATIONS

There are three outcomes of a project that we need to consider as influencing the judgment of success or failure. These are project *deliverables,* the *results* achieved, and whether *expectations* of stakeholders were met. Consider the combinations shown in Figure 15.1.

We can say that outcome 1 is a totally successful project. Deliverables and results are as promised, and stakeholder expectations have been met. Outcome 2, however, suffers from political fallout. Deliverables and results are as promised, but stakeholder expectations have not been met. This might happen if the stakeholder pool changes midway through a project and the newcomers have different expectations from the original stakeholders. The outcome highlights the need for project managers to monitor changing expectations, rather than considering them to be engraved in granite from the beginning.

All Combinations of Deliverables, Results, and Expectations

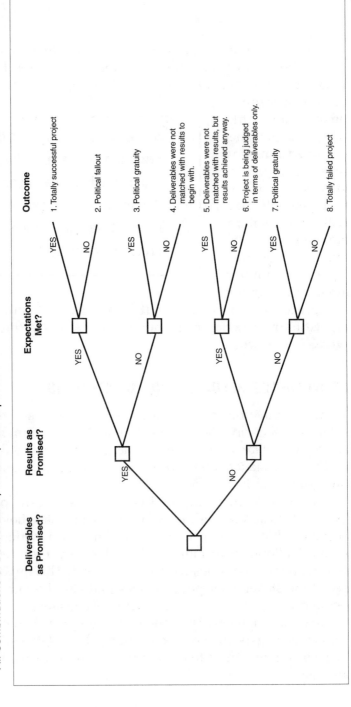

As an example of changing expectations, consider computer technology. In the days of the first personal computers, most users were in awe of how fast a spreadsheet recalculated rows and columns. A few years later, users complained about how slow many computers were. The reason? Expectations for performance actually grew. At one time we were satisfied with a postal system that took a month to deliver a letter across the country. Then along came Federal Express, and next-day delivery was born. Now we have fax machines and e-mail, both of which speed the process so that it is almost instantaneous. What a great time for those of us who like to procrastinate! We can now wait until a few milliseconds before the deadline and send our message electronically!

Outcome 3 is interesting. Deliverables were as promised but did not get results, yet expectations were met. First, we need to consider that deliverables were not matched with results. That is, we thought that what we delivered would get results, but we were wrong. If expectations were met, it either means that the stakeholder was very forgiving or that everyone decided ahead of time that results would not be forthcoming.

Outcome 4 is similar to 3, except that the stakeholder was not forgiving.

Outcome 5 is strange. Deliverables were not as promised, yet results were achieved and expectations met. This could mean that people realized partway through the project that original deliverables should be changed if results were to be achieved.

For outcome 6, deliverables were not correct, yet results were okay, but expectations were not met. Here the stakeholder appeared to hold the project manager to original promises for deliverables, ignoring the fact that desired results were achieved in spite of the disconnect.

In outcome 7, we have a truly forgiving stakeholder. Neither deliverables nor results were as promised, yet expectations were met. This is probably a project run by one of the stakeholder's relatives.

Finally, in outcome 8, we have a totally failed project, and it should well be considered as such.

RESEARCH FINDINGS

Murphy, Baker, and Fisher (1974) reported the results of a study of more than 650 projects to determine the factors that affect project success. The study is also summarized in the *Project Management Handbook* (Cleland and King, 1988). The researchers asked two key questions: "Why are some projects perceived as failures when they met the P, C, T, and S targets?" And "Why are others considered successes even when they are late and over budget?" From the results of their study, they decided that success must be defined as follows:

> If the project meets the technical performance specifications and/or mission to be performed, and if there is a high level of satisfaction concerning the project outcome among key people in the parent organization, key people in the client organization, key people on the project team, and key users or clientele of the project effort, the project is considered an overall success. (Baker et al., 1988.)

It is a matter of "perception." If the right people perceive the project to be a success, then it is, for all practical purposes. Note that the definition does not include schedule and cost performance as criteria for success. According to Baker et al., one reason is that the research was conducted on completed projects.

> If the right people consider a project a success, it is, for all practical purposes.

When a job is in progress, cost and schedule targets are an ongoing source of pressure. However, once the job is complete, if it satisfies the needs of a lot of key people, the missed cost and schedule targets become less important.

The study identifies a number of variables that are important for perceived project success and a number that contribute to perceived project failure. An important finding is that for a project to be perceived as successful, many, if not most, of the variables associated with success must be present. Similarly, most, if not all, of the variables associated with failure must be absent.

The study also confirms something that contradicts what many managers seem to believe about project management: It is not just scheduling! PERT/CPM do contribute to project success, but the importance of scheduling is far outweighed by other factors, including use of tools known as system management concepts. Among these tools are work breakdown structures, life-cycle planning, systems engineering, configuration management, and status reports. In fact, the overuse of PERT-CPM was found to hamper success! The reason is that the project manager spends so much time updating the schedule that day-to-day managing suffers.

Factors Contributing to Perceived Project Success

A regression analysis of the data suggests that seven broad factors contribute to project success. Taken together, these seven factors explain 91 percent of the variance in perceived project success—a finding that is strongly compelling. Table 15.2 shows the standardized regression coefficient, together

T A B L E 15.2

Regression Analysis

Determining Factor	Regression Coefficient	Cumulative R^2
Coordination and relations	+.347	.773
Adequacy of project structure and control	+.187	.830
Project uniqueness, importance, public exposure	+.145	.877
Success criteria salience and consensus	+.254	.886
Competitive and budgetary pressure	−.153	.897
Initial overoptimism, conceptual difficulty	−.215	.905
Internal capabilities buildup	+.084	.911

with the cumulative R^2 for each variable. All seven factors are statistically significant to a probability of less than 0.001.

Note that a negative regression coefficient means that the direction of the effect is reversed. In other words, whereas increased coordination causes an increase in project success, an increase in competitive pressure will cause a *decrease* in project success.

Because coordination and relations alone account for 77 percent of the variance in perceived project success, it is instructive to take a closer look at just what this means. Below is a summary of the factors that make up the overall coordination and relations variable.

Coordination & Relations Factor

- Unity between project manager and functional managers
- Project team spirit, sense of mission, goal commitment, and capability
- Unity between project manager and public officials, client contact, and manager's superior
- Project manager's human and administrative skills
- Realistic progress reports
- Supportive informal relations of team members
- Authority of project manager
- Adequacy of change procedures
- Job security of project team
- Project team participation in decision making and major problem solving
- Parent company enthusiasm
- Availability of backup strategies

Factors Contributing to Perceived Project Failure

There are a number of factors that cause people to perceive a project as a failure. Again, you must *perform* those things that cause perceived project success and *avoid* those things that cause perceived project failure. The following factors affect perceived failure:

Characteristics That Affect Perceived Project Failure

- Insufficient use of progress or status reports
- Use of superficial status reports
- Inadequate project manager administrative, human, and technical skills
- Insufficient project manager influence and authority
- Poor coordination with client
- Lack of rapport with client and parent organization
- Client disinterest in budget criteria
- Lack of project team participation in decision making and problem solving
- Excessive structuring within the project team
- Job insecurity within the project team
- Lack of team spirit and sense of mission within the project team
- Parent organization stable, nondynamic, lacking strategic change
- Poor coordination with parent organization
- New "type" of project
- Project more complex than parent has handled previously
- Initial underfunding
- Inability to freeze design early
- Inability to close out the effort
- Unrealistic project schedules
- Inadequate change procedures

One final note about the study. Project managers are
inclined to believe that the "adverse nature" of a situation
will prevent them
from succeeding.
Baker et al. report
that project man-
agers actually can
achieve high levels
of perceived pro-
ject success, even
under adverse cir-

> Project managers can achieve
> high levels of perceived success,
> even under adverse
> circumstances.

cumstances, if they properly attend to the factors listed
above.

TARGETS AND VARIATION

I mentioned at the beginning of this chapter that failure is often defined as not meeting the P, C, T, or S targets. However, I
question whether not meeting targets that have been based on
wishful thinking truly is failure. Unless targets are realistic to
begin with, everyone associated with a project is getting set
up. If I, as a project manager, agree to meet targets that I am
pretty sure are unrealistic, because my manager puts pressure
on me to do so, then we are both being set up. Eventually,
when I can't meet the unrealistic target, my manager is going
to be in trouble as well. So I have an obligation to insist on
committing only to targets that are believed to be realistic.

How do we know if a target is realistic? We know only
if the target is based on some history. Until we make estimates at a level in a work breakdown structure where tasks
are somewhat repeatable, and we have some history on similar tasks, we are guessing. Even then, there are tolerances on
all estimates. We should understand that working times for
all activities are probabilistic, not deterministic. Yet we assign
durations to activities on the basis of best guesses, then link
them together, and do deterministic calculations to find critical paths, float, and so on.

If we think about it, there is reason to wonder how any project is successful, as defined by coming in on schedule. I believe the only way we are ever successful is by varying the effort applied to meet the times. However, if we were to track both schedule performance and actual hours worked against original estimated hours, I think we would find that the price paid is in large variances of actual compared with estimated working hours. Consider the many causes of variation shown in Table 15.3.

Here, too, there are unrealistic expectations about what magnitude of variance is likely in project work. Many managers who have experience with departmental budgeting think that project budgets should be held to the same tight tolerances that are possible with departments. But projects aren't budgeted the same way that departments are. In a department, you budget for next year by looking at forecasted headcount. You tally up the salary increases you plan to give, add in the cost of rubber bands, paper clips, computers, and

T A B L E 15.3

Sources of Variation in Project Work

Source	Example
Estimate of task duration is based on a small sample (it has been done only a few times before).	People are pulled off the project to put out fires on other projects.
The person for whom the original estimate was made is not available to do the work when the time comes.	Long stretches of overtime cause fatigue, which causes errors, which leads to more overtime, which leads to . . .
Sharing resources on multiple projects causes increased setup time, with a corresponding decrease in work efficiency.	Work has to be done over because mistakes are made as a result of poor planning, communication errors, and so on.
Unexpected technical problems cause tasks to take longer than expected.	Illness, serious personal problems, child care, and jury duty lead to delays.

other supplies, and away you go. A department budget can often be held to a few percentage points.

A project, on the other hand, is based on how much work has to be done, and that exact quantity is not well known at the outset, so labor costs cannot be accurately determined. Figure 15.2 illustrates the well-known saying: The ultimate certainty of project cost increases the closer you get to the end.

The one thing that we must all do is accept variability. It is a part of any process. We can reduce it over time, but we can never eliminate it. There is an injunction that is sometimes heard in organizations: You cannot go over budget—but neither can you come in under budget. Such an injunction is asking that people violate a law of nature. If they do it—that is, come in right on target—it is always through fancy footwork or pure accident. It is not because they were able to actually control work to achieve the result.

F I G U R E 15.2

Ultimate Certainty of Project Cost

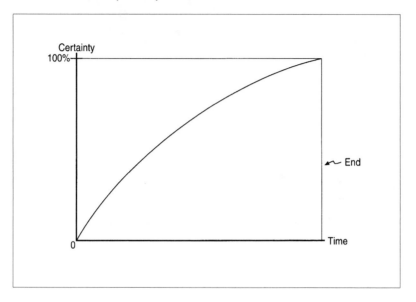

16

CHAPTER

Causes of Project Failure

THE HIGH COST OF PROJECT FAILURE

It has been estimated that nearly half the work done in some organizations is of a project nature. That means, clearly, that if many projects are failures, the organization as a whole is on its way to disaster.

And fail they do.

According to the Standish Group, which surveys information systems projects yearly, only 17 percent of projects meet their original targets, 50 percent have to have their targets changed, and the remaining 33 percent are canceled. The cost to U.S. companies is around 80 billion dollars a year.

Why so many failures?

There are 13 fairly common causes. If these are understood, then presumably some steps can be taken to avoid them. At least that is the intention of this chapter: to alert the project manager to the typical causes of failure with prevention as the objective.

CAUSES AND RECOMMENDATIONS FOR SOLUTION

1. The problem is not properly defined. The importance of problem definition was noted in Chapter 1. As J.M. Juran says, a project is a problem scheduled for solution. If the problem is not well understood, then we may make the classic error of developing the right solution to the wrong problem. This can be avoided by attempting to understand the *real* reason for doing the job, then writing a problem statement to reflect that objective.

For example, a group is given the assignment of relocating an office to another part of the building. The group may see its job as just moving furniture and partitions. But what is the real intention of moving the office? Perhaps it is to achieve better coordination between the people being moved and those nearby the new location. Is there an optimum layout that will make the move more effective? Only by understanding the real purpose of the move can the team answer or address this question.

2. Planning is based on insufficient data. For example, a planned engineering project will involve significant use of a test facility. What the team doesn't know is that the test facility is to be relocated at exactly the time when the testing is scheduled to start.

Or, as often occurs with system development projects, the client has an "itch" that needs scratching. Unfortunately, the client knows very little about the capability of software, and the programmers know very little about the user's operation. As they get into the project, they both begin learning, and the scope of the job begins to grow.

3. Planning is performed by a planning group. Although this is necessary in some environments, it can lead to disaster. Recall the plight of the project manager who forgot the site preparation work on a construction job. The result was a $600,000 overspend on a job originally estimated at $2 million. The cause? The project manager planned the job by himself, thus violating the rule that *the people who must do a job should participate in planning it.*

4. No one is in charge. Sometimes the project manager's role is not well defined or is not accepted by everyone in the organization. This can mean that no one person is really responsible for the project, so that things "fall through the cracks." When the project manager's role is weak, the manager may be given no approval authority over expenditures; the result is a "blank check" for people in the organization. Managing a project by committee can also be a problem, especially if people have no skills in reaching consensus, making decisions, and so forth.

5. Project estimates are best guesses, made without consulting historical data. Sometimes there simply *is no historical data!* In many companies, good records of past projects do not exist, so no one can refer to them for planning the next project. Or the reporting of labor hours becomes contaminated because salaried people do not report overtime (since they are not paid for it), and the current project was planned using the labor figures on the books.

6. Resource planning is inadequate. For example, no one bothers to check whether a person with certain specialized skills will be available when needed in the project. Or a functional group is expected to do work for several projects, but no one notices that the composite workload will require 300 percent more labor-hours than are actually available in the department. Poor resource planning may very well be the most frequent cause of project failures.

7. People don't see themselves as working on one team. When a project is divided up into different functional areas, participants sometimes lose sight of the fact that the ultimate result requires the combining of all the parts. They build walls around themselves, don't communicate, and fail to coordinate their efforts with members of other subgroups. The result is chaos. A project manager faced with this problem has to work on team building.

8. People are constantly pulled off the project or reassigned with no regard for impact. Functional managers are "rewarded" for making their departments run smoothly, not for achieving project objectives. Again, this is because people in organizations do not see the importance of project work or the project manager. Rewards must be consistent with what the organization wants to happen, since it is a psychological given that *what is rewarded gets done.*

9. The project plan lacks detail. When a project is planned with too little detail, it is difficult to anticipate what kinds of problems may develop. Further, it is hard to manage resources, make proper estimates of time or costs, and develop workable schedules. Invariably this "broad brush" approach to planning results in numerous conflicts and changes, and creates interference with other projects being executed at the time. One caution, however: The opposite approach is equally undesirable. A basic rule is that no project should be planned in more detail than can be managed. Clearly, a balance is required.

10. The project is not tracked against the plan. This seems inconceivable, but it happens. There are two general reasons. First, the plan may be so broad and undefined that it is not worth following—in which case the team winds up having no control, since control can be exercised only by following a plan. Second, even if a detailed plan is developed, people may go into a panic mode and forget the plan as soon as a problem arises. Again, they lose control. Planning should not be done just to satisfy some requirement that it exist. A plan that is not followed is useless.

All too often, people adopt the attitude that since the plan keeps changing, they may as well abandon it. This is like saying that, since we have encountered several detours on our drive across the United States, we may as well throw out the map and just "wing it." Such thinking is clearly nonsense, unless we don't care where we are at any given time.

11. People lose sight of the original goal. Product development engineers sometimes become so enamored of the technology that they forget they are supposed to be developing a product. Or they become perfectionists and waste time trying to make the product better than the specification calls for. Project managers must continuously monitor project activities and, if necessary, remind contributors of the purpose of their work.

12. Senior managers refuse to accept reality. Sometimes senior managers base their requirements for a job on knowledge of a previous job or some other factor. When a project manager turns in an estimate that is out of line with what the senior manager thinks it should be (with the estimate being higher, of course), the manager insists that it be reduced. If the project manager is coerced into agreeing to targets in this manner, the project is likely to fail.

In line with this approach is the tendency to dictate performance, cost, schedule, and scope targets simultaneously, thus violating the rule that only three of the four can be pinned down—the remaining factor must be allowed to float, since the four targets are interdependent.

13. Ballpark estimates become official targets. Sometimes a project manager is asked for a *ballpark* estimate,

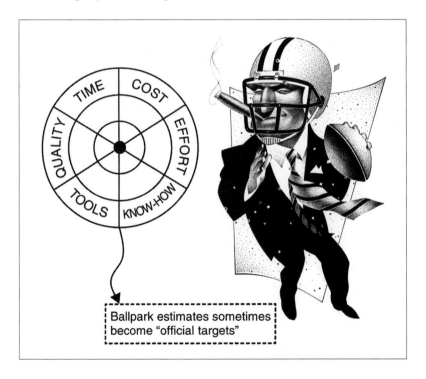

Ballpark estimates sometimes become "official targets"

which is to be used for a go/no-go decision. Since people are only at the thinking stage, details are sketchy. The estimate is based on that sketchy information. A decision is then made to do the job, but now more detail is available, and it turns out that the ballpark figure was way too low. At this point, however, the manager cannot go back to higher-ups and report that the job will cost more, since they were originally told a lower figure and have come to think of that figure as *the* correct figure. So the ballpark becomes the target. To avoid this problem, always document all assumptions. Make it known *in writing* that the estimate is a ballpark figure, with tolerances of plus or minus X percent, so it is clear from the beginning that the figures are subject to revision. (Of course, the ballpark estimate may still become the target, but at least you have documented your original position.)

17

Managing Project Risks

Perhaps the most famous "law" of all is Murphy's Law, which is usually stated as "Whatever can go wrong *will!*" Given that this statement reflects the experience of most peo-

PROJECT SUCCESS

It's a piece of cake!

Principle: We are all inclined to overestimate our ability and underestimate difficulties. As someone has said, "Even Murphy was an optimist!"

ple, it seems reasonable to ask how we should deal with Murphy's Law.

It seems clear that, when something goes wrong, we have *the possibility of suffering harm or loss*, which is defined as *risk.* I therefore de-fine risk as any-thing that can go wrong in a project that will affect pro-ject targets. Since the impact on tar-gets is of concern, we now need to ask how we can *manage* risks in projects.

> **risk:** Anything that can go wrong in a project that will affect project targets.

In my experience, this is a neglected area in managing projects. It is sometimes caused by an overzealous "can do" approach to managing. A lot of managers subscribe to this at-titude. Those who voice concerns about being able to meet targets are immediately la-beled whiners or worse. They are told that if they can't get the job done, management will find someone who can. This is the macho attitude cap-tured by the quote "Damn the torpedoes! Full speed ahead!"

> It is an unhappy fact of life that there are usually more things that can go wrong with a project than can unexpectedly go right.
> —John R. Schuyler (1995)

There are certainly times when the can-do approach is justified, but there are many more when it is not. There is a difference between being foolhardy and taking a reasoned approach to real risks. I am certainly not advocating that people adopt an "Ain't it awful" attitude toward projects, in which identified risks lead to paralysis. I am advocating that identified risks be *managed*. I would also say that adopting a can-do approach that ignores risks is project mismanagement.

One reason for managing risk is that, when things go wrong unexpectedly, they throw you off balance and cause major crises for your projects. Trying to deal with a problem that has hit you without warning is always more difficult than laying out contingencies before the problem has occurred.

As an example, I have seen design engineers put all their effort into a design that they couldn't make work. They never even *considered* the possibility of failure! It may be that merely to reflect on being unable to make the design work would be to admit their fallibility, and that might be too much for some perfectionist types to bear. Whatever the reason, those engineers who encounter design problems are often thrown into the panic mode and may have to start over, since they have put "all their eggs into one basket." Naturally, such a setback can have a serious impact on the project.

Another example was related to me by a participant in one of my seminars. The woman's husband was managing a project to install a new manufacturing line in a plant. The equipment was being made in Italy. A few days before the ship date, Air Italia (the scheduled carrier) went on strike, and all its cargo had to be shifted to other carriers. The mean had a terrible time getting his shipment across. Whether he could have anticipated this risk is doubtful, but suppose he had. What might he have done? Arranged for an alternative carrier? Advanced the ship date so the machine could be sent over by marine transport rather than by air? Both are possibilities.

If you refer to my project management model in Chapter 2 (Figure 2.1), you will see that there are two places in which risk needs to be managed. The first is in planning project strategy. The second is in implementation planning.

In planning strategy, you are trying to develop an approach for managing the project that may involve the choice of technology as well as an execution method. I have called these *project strategy* and *technical strategy* in Chapter 5. Both strategies have risks in most cases. When proven technology is being employed, the risks of failure are usually low. However, if cutting-edge technology is being applied, the risks are much higher. Further, some project strategies have higher risks than others. For example, a farm-out project strategy may be more risky that one in which all work is done internally.

Either way, the first step in analyzing risk is to identify what might go wrong. (This is true at both steps 4 and 6 of Figure 2.1.) When I work with a team, I have people brainstorm a list of risks and record them on a flipchart with no discussion or evaluation. To help the group identify risks, I simply ask, "What could go wrong that could impact time, cost, performance, or scope in the project?"

THREATS VERSUS RISKS

You will notice that in step 4 of the project management model you are supposed to test a strategy against risks and SWOT analysis. SWOT stands for **S**trengths, **W**eaknesses, **O**pportunities, and **T**hreats. Unless you can manage risks, offset weaknesses, and contend with threats, your project strategy is likely to fail. The question is: What is the difference between threats and risks?

If you adopt a purist definition, risks are things that can happen without any deliberate intention to cause harm behind them. Examples of risks are accidents; earthquakes, fires, floods, and other acts of nature; losing key members of the team; escalating labor rates or inflation; exchange rate fluctuations for international projects; and political instability. A threat is a step taken by a competitor or adversary to offset whatever you have done. For example, when an airline tries to capture a route by offering a very low fare, it is usually unsuccessful because the competition simply matches the lower fare and nobody gains any more market share. Although threats and risks are technically different, for the purposes of managing projects, they can be lumped together in the same analysis.

It seems reasonable to say that it is always better to avoid risk than it is to manage it (Levine, 1995). This should be done through better planning, not by avoiding a good opportunity. As I said above, you begin by identifying what can go wrong that might affect time, cost, performance, or scope in your project. Then you ask what might be done to avoid these effects. If it is not possible to avoid an effect, can you reduce its impact?

As an example, weather can hold up projects, and cannot be avoided. The solution is to examine the weather history for the area and time of year and to build into the schedule a reasonable amount of delay. If the weather is better than usual, you will get ahead of schedule, and conversely.

On the other hand, I would rather avoid the risk of putting an inexperienced project manager on a highly important project than try to manage the risk once I have done so. Prevention is always less expensive than failure.

QUANTIFYING RISKS AND THREATS

It is helpful to have some measure of the impact that a risk or threat might have on a project. Naturally most risks and threats cannot be quantified in any objective way, but we can use a subjective method that seems to work fairly well. The approach was first devised by engineers to identify where product designs might fail, and is therefore called failure mode effects analysis (FMEA). For any of you who are math-challenged, this terms sounds foreboding, but don't be intimidated by it. The approach is really very simple and requires nothing more difficult than multiplication.

I am going to call the approach *project risk analysis and management*, because I want to emphasize that it is not enough simply to identify risks—you have to manage them as well. Furthermore, I am lumping risks and threats together, so I don't have to keep saying "risks and threats" every time. From now on, you will understand that *risks* refers to both.

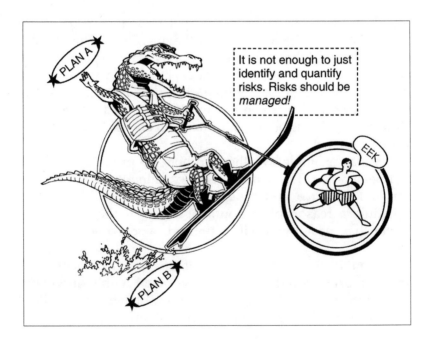

T A B L E 17.1

Probability of Occurrence

Probability of Occurrence	Possible Occurrence Rate	Rank
Very high: occurrence is almost	≥ 1 in 2	10
certain	1 in 3	9
High: repeated occurrences possible	1 in 8	8
	1 in 20	7
Moderate: occasional occurrences	1 in 80	6
	1 in 400	5
	1 in 2,000	4
Low: relatively few occurrences	1 in 15,000	3
	1 in 150,000	2
Remote: occurrence is unlikely	≤ 1 in 1,500,000	1

Assessing Probability

Once we have brainstormed a list of risks, we have to estimate the probability that they will occur. To do so, we use Table 17.1. In the FMEA terminology, something that goes wrong is a failure. I have changed that word to "occurrence," since the word "failure" does not always apply. For example, political unrest in a country that might affect an international project is not a failure but an occurrence or event. You will note that the probability scale is logarithmic, whereas the remaining scales are linear.

Estimating Severity

The next thing that we need to consider is how severely the event or occurrence will affect the project. An event that has a high probability of happening but a low impact on the project is of little concern, whereas an event that is low probability but severe impact is of great concern. In Table 17.2, you

T A B L E 17.2

Severity of the Effect

Effect	Criteria: Severity of Effect	Rank
Hazardous— without warning	Project severely impacted, possible cancellation, with no warning.	10
Hazardous— with warning	Project severely impacted, possible cancellation, with warning.	9
Very high	Major impact on project schedule, budget, or performance; may cause severe delays, overruns, or degradation of performance.	8
High	Project schedule, budget, or performance impacted significantly; job can be completed, but customer will be very dissatisfied.	7
Moderate	Project schedule, budget, or performance impacted some; customer will be dissatisfied.	6
Low	Project schedule, budget, or performance impacted slightly; customer will be mildly dissatisfied.	5
Very low	Some impact to project; customer will be aware of impact.	4
Minor	Small impact to project; average customer will be aware of impact.	3
Very minor	Impact so small that it would be noticed only by a very discriminating customer.	2
None	No effect.	1

will note the word "customer" being used several times. For this analysis, "customer" can mean an actual customer for the project or your company management, whichever is appropriate.

Can It Be Detected?

In conventional FMEA analysis, detection capability has to do with whether a fault can be detected before a design is completed or a product is shipped. Using that meaning in assessing project risks leads to a 1 for the detection value most of the time, making this component useless. This is because you almost always know after the fact that a problem has occurred. However, if you change the meaning of detection to mean that a problem can be detected *before* it occurs, then you have a more useful definition.

As an example, if the oil runs out of your car while you are driving it, the effect will be severe. If you have an oil gauge or indicator light that comes on at some threshold level, you should be able to see that the oil pressure is getting low and take action before the situation becomes serious. If you have a broken oil gauge or indicator light, it is not as easy to detect the problem beforehand.

In projects, things like bad weather can be predicted with some accuracy, so that steps can be taken to compensate. Accidents, however, tend to happen without warning, so they are harder to deal with. Table 17.3 is used to measure

T A B L E 17.3

Detection Capability

Detection	Rank
Absolute uncertainty	10
Very remote	9
Remote	8
Very low	7
Low	6
Moderate	5
Moderately high	4
High	3
Very high	2
Almost certain	1

the detection capability of a risk in a project. Note that this scale is reversed. That is, the more certain it is that you can detect a hazard, the lower the number.

THE RISK PROBABILITY NUMBER

For each risk that you have identified, you now have three measures—a probability level (P), severity measure (S), and detection capability index (D). These three numbers are multiplied to obtain a risk probability number (RPN). The higher that number, the more serious the risk. To show how this works, consider the three risks shown in Figure 17.1.

The general approach to dealing with high RPNs is to ask whether any of the three individual components can be reduced. That is, can risk or severity be lowered and/or can detection be increased (which will lower its number)? As an example, we can reduce the probability of weather delays by doing a project during a calendar period that historically has good weather. We can reduce the severity of weather delays by padding the schedule, and we can increase our ability to detect forthcoming bad weather by paying close attention to weather forecasts.

F I G U R E   17.1

Risk Analysis for a Project

Identified Risk	P	S	D	RPN
Bad weather	3	2	4	24
Loss of key team member	2	8	8	128
Technology won't work	6	10	8	480

For the examples listed, the RPN for bad weather is so small that it can be ignored. However, the other two risks have significant RPNs, and we should consider what to do. First, let's examine loss of a key team member. Although it has a probability of only 2, it has a high severity and high detection. As a rule, whenever severity is high, regardless of the RPN, special attention should be given to this particular risk.

This principle was illustrated tragically by the *Challenger* space shuttle disaster. Some members of the project team believed that the probability of O-ring failure at the low launch temperature was quite low. However, the severity of failure was a 10, because the astronauts on board would be killed. Because of this fact alone, greater caution should have been exercised. It has been my experience that when people think the probability of something is low, they throw caution to the wind. Thus, people who think the probability of having an automobile accident is very low may take chances with their driving—and get killed or seriously injured.

The severity of losing a key team member can be reduced if we have someone available as a backup. This is what live theatrical productions do. They have an understudy who can play the part of a regular performer in the event of illness or accident. We might not be able to reduce detection in this case, but reducing severity alone might be enough.

The third risk in Figure 17.1 is that technology won't work. There are a couple of possibilities in this case. First, the probability of failure is shown as 6 points, which is moderate. This might not give us too much cause for concern. However, if the probability of technology failure were higher—say, around 8 or 9 points—I would suggest that a feasibility study be conducted before any kind of application of that technology be attempted. A basic premise is that discovery and development should be separated, if you are to have control over project schedules.

Even if the probability of failure is low, the severity of a technology failure can be very high. One way to deal with this is to be ready with an alternate. In some very high-risk projects, where it was not possible to do feasibility studies, companies have launched parallel development paths. The first technology that could be made to work was the one the company continued with. The approach obviously costs a lot of money, and would be done only in those situations where time is more important than costs.

Finally, can we detect failure of technology with any ease? Perhaps not. However, it might be prudent to establish some decision criteria about how many failures will be tolerated before an approach is abandoned in favor of one that is more certain. Setting limits on failure can be a blow to the ego of a professional, but in business we must do what is prudent, rather than what is necessarily self-serving. A possible exception is an attempt to develop a vaccine for a disease such as AIDS. However, even here, we must ask if repeated failures at a particular approach might not dictate adopting an alternative strategy.

DEVELOPING CONTINGENCY PLANS

As I stated earlier, it is not enough to identify and quantify risks. The idea is to manage them. This might be done in three ways:

1. Risk avoidance
2. Mitigation (reduction, such as using air bags)
3. Risk transfer (such as loss prevention through insurance)

Risk Avoidance

With risk aversion or avoidance, we want to avoid the risk altogether. In the case of the *Challenger,* a decision to delay the launch until the temperature warmed up would have been of risk avoidance.

Japanese manufacturing has for many years employed "foolproofing" as a risk avoidance strategy. The idea is to

set up the assembly process so that it cannot be done incorrectly. For example, a manufacturer occasionally would
start to install a gas tank in a car, only to find that one of the
four mounting brackets had not been welded onto the tank.
The solution was to set up a fixture to hold the tank while
the brackets were being welded onto it. Feelers were at-
tached to detect the presence of the brackets. If all four
brackets were not in place, the welding machine would not
weld any of them.

In construction projects, we pad the schedule with rain
delay days, guided by weather history for the area and time
of year. This way, we avoid the risk that we will be delayed
by bad weather. In engineering projects, as noted, parallel design strategies are launched to avoid missing a deadline because one strategy proves difficult to implement. In any
project, risk aversion or avoidance may be the most preferable strategy to follow.

Mitigation or Risk Reduction

If we can think of contingencies in the event that a risk takes
place, we can mitigate the effect. Placing air bags in cars is an
attempt to reduce the severity of an accident, should one occur. Stafford Beer (1981) has argued that seat belts and air
bags in cars actually give drivers a false sense of security. We
have defined the problem as protecting the driver from being
harmed in case of an accident. Beer argues that it may be
better to redefine the problem as keeping a driver from having an accident in the first place (risk avoidance). He suggests
that if we line the dashboard of the car with spikes, making it
very clear that an accident has serious consequences, drivers
may have an incentive to be more careful. His suggestion is
not without merit.

In projects that involve procurement, using a sole source
is a risk to consider. The alternative is to second-source all
procured parts or equipment. That way, if a supplier can't
deliver on time or at the specified price, the second supplier

may be able to. The approach can be thought of as either risk avoidance or mitigation.

Temporary workers are used as backups for critical personnel who become ill or are injured. Overtime is used as a contingency when tasks take longer than estimated. This is one reason why overtime should not be planned into a project to meet original targets. Rather, it should be kept in reserve as a contingency. Another form of mitigation is to reduce scope to permit the team to meet the original target date, then come back later and incorporate deferred work to finish the job.

Risk Transfer or Insurance

Insurance is one way of protecting against loss in the event that a risk materializes. Having alternative sites available into which a group can move in the event of a disaster is a loss prevention strategy. Having a fire evacuation plan in a building can also be thought of as a loss prevention plan. Backup personnel provide a form of insurance against loss. If someone else can do the work, then when a key person is ill, there will be no loss to the project. Of course, it is difficult to find adequate replacements with highly skilled personnel.

Another form of insurance is setting up a cost contingency management reserve account. Too often, management reserve is considered protection against poor performance. This is incorrect. Management reserve is a fund that is part of a project budget. All projects should have a work budget, to cover the cost of identified work, and a management reserve—to cover work not yet identified. In addition, on projects that are paid for by a customer, there will be a component of the total job cost called *margin*. This is the intended profit for the job. Poor performance eats into margin, not management reserve.

The management reserve account is not touched unless new, unscheduled work is identified. This is a change in scope, of course. At that point, money is transferred from the management reserve account into the work budget, and performance is subsequently tracked against the revised budget.

A log should be maintained of all scope changes and their effect on the work budget, management reserve, and margin (if the change has such an effect). In customer-funded projects, the customer may be required to pay for scope changes, so that there is no impact to the management reserve account.

Schuyler (1995) has developed a list of possible ways to mitigate or avoid risks, as presented in Table 17.4.

T A B L E 17.4

Schuyler's Ways of Mitigating or Avoiding Risks

Portfolio Risks

Share risks by having partners

Spread risks over time

Participate in many ventures

Group complementary risks into portfolios

Seek lower-risk ventures

Specialize and concentrate in a single, well-known area

Increase the company's capitalization

Commodity Prices

Hedge or fix in the futures markets

Use long- or short-term sales (price and volume) contracts

Tailor contracts for risk sharing

Interest Rate and Exchange Rate

Use swaps, floors, ceilings, collars, and other hedging instruments

Restructure the balance sheet

Denominate or index certain transactions in a foreign currency

Environmental Hazards

Buy insurance

Increase safety margins

Develop and test an incident response program

Operational Risks

Hire contractors under turnkey contracts

Tailor risk-sharing contract clauses

Use safety margins; overbuild and overspecify designs

Have backup and redundant equipment

Increase training

Operate with redirect and bailout options

Conduct tests, pilot programs, and trials

Analysis Risks (Reducing Evaluation Error)

Use better techniques (i.e., decision analysis)

Seek additional information

Monitor key and indicator variables

Validate models

Include evaluation practices along with project postreviews

Develop redundant models with alternative approaches and people

Involve multiple disciplines and communicate across disciplines

Provide better training and tools

THE PROJECT MANAGEMENT APPROACH
AS A FUNCTION OF RISK

As Jean Couillard (1995) has written, much of the literature on managing projects proposes a uniform set of tools and methods to manage all kinds of projects. A study by Couillard confirms a suggestion by McFarlan (1983) that the nature of the project should dictate the proper tools and methods. Risk, in particular, is a characteristic that should determine the best management approach.

Couillard found that, if project risk is not considered, standard PERT/CPM techniques, project monitoring, and control do not have a significant influence on project success. However, in high-risk projects, using PERT/CPM to increase the frequency of project monitoring and control does improve the likelihood of project success. Couillard concluded that

> **When technical risk is high, matrix is better than pure-project organization.**

high-risk projects should be more closely planned, monitored, and controlled than low-risk projects.

The study also showed that when technical risk is high, pure-project organization structure (see Chapter 18) has a significant *negative influence* on project success. It turns out that matrix structure is better for such projects, presumably because technical expertise can be more easily drawn from a matrix structure than from pure-project structure.

To measure success, Couillard employed the factors shown in Table 17.5. Following the findings of Baker et al. (1974), he used measures appropriate to judging the *perceived* success of a project, since the quantitative measures alone (performance, cost, time, scope) do not always correlate with whether a project is deemed successful. As you can see, Couillard is explicit in calling the measures *subjective*.

Altogether, Couillard used 17 factors to indicate aspects of project management. These are shown in Table 17.6.

T A B L E 17.5

Project Success Measures

Measure	Description
Tech1	The subjective measure of technical success relative to the initial requirement
Tech2	The subjective measure of technical success compared with other projects
Cost	The subjective measure of budget overrun or underrun
Time	The subjective measure of schedule overrun or underrun
Overall	The subjective measure of overall project success

Source: Adapted from Couillard (1995). Used with permission.

T A B L E 17.6

Management Factors

Project Manager Experience	Project Management Method	Project Management Tools and Techniques
Number of projects managed	Understanding of project goals	WBS utilization
Responsibility index	Level of project manager authority and responsibility	PERT/CPM utilization
	Level of project director authority and responsibility	C/SCSC utilization
	Organizational structure	Periodic technical reports
	Senior management involvement	Periodic cost reports
	Communication patterns	Periodic schedule reports
	Problem handling	Frequency of project monitoring
	Project team support	

Source: Adapted from Couillard (1995). Used with permission.

Using regression analysis, Couillard concluded that communication patterns and understanding of project goals significantly influence all six measures of project success. This finding supports the frequent suggestion in the literature that you must have a clear, shared understanding of the project mission in order to be successful. Good communication within the team is also essential.

The authority given to the project manager to make decisions at the project level is also a factor, as are support received from the project team and problem handling by the team. This offers some support to the complaint by project managers that they have a lot of responsibility and no authority. On the basis of this finding, senior managers should be sure to give the project manager the needed authority to deal with project issues directly.

Project managers in the study were also asked to assess project risk with regard to three objectives: technical performance, cost, and schedule. Couillard used a three-point scale in which risk was rated as low, medium, and high. It was found that more experienced project managers are generally assigned to the high-risk projects. Also, PERT/CPM, C/SCSC, and periodic technical reports are more frequently used in high-risk projects.

Technical Risk

When technical risk is high, project success is influenced by project manager authority, communication, team support, and problem handling. As previously mentioned, pure-project structure is also negatively correlated with success when technical risk is high.

Cost Risk

When cost risk is high, project success is influenced by team understanding of project goals, project manager authority, team support, and communication.

Schedule Risk

If schedule risk is high, two factors are important: the project manager's experience and the frequency of monitoring progress.

CONCLUSION

Many success factors in projects center around human relationships. Thus, project managers must master these skills no matter what the project risk. High-risk projects need more careful planning, monitoring, and controlling than do low-risk projects. In general, if you have any one or a combination of technical, cost, or schedule risks, it seems prudent to follow these guidelines:

1. Emphasize team support.
2. Give the project manager appropriate authority.
3. Improve problem handling and communication.
4. Avoid the pure-project structure.
5. Increase the frequency of project monitoring.
6. Use the WBS, PERT/CPM, and C/SCSC.
7. Establish clear project goals for the team.
8. Select an experienced project manager.

SECTION

OTHER ISSUES IN
PROJECT MANAGEMENT

18

CHAPTER

Sociotechnical Systems and Project Organization[1]

TRADITIONAL PROJECT ORGANIZATION

Over the years a number of structures have been tried for organizing projects. Some of these are illustrated in Figure 18.1. At present, only two of the structures are widely used: pure hierarchy (sometimes called pure-project form) and matrix. In fact, a number of writers appear to consider matrix to be synonymous with project organization, though in practice this is by no means true. Many projects are still organized in hierarchical form when speed is of the essence in product development. Some of these efforts are called *skunkworks* projects.

The strengths and weaknesses of both forms of organization are described in Chapter 9, so they will not be repeated here. Rather, this chapter examines project organization in the light of sociotechnical systems design principles, and offers

---

[1] I wish to acknowledge the contribution of Michael C. Thomas, Ph.D., to my thinking in writing this chapter.

F I G U R E 18.1

Project Organization Structures

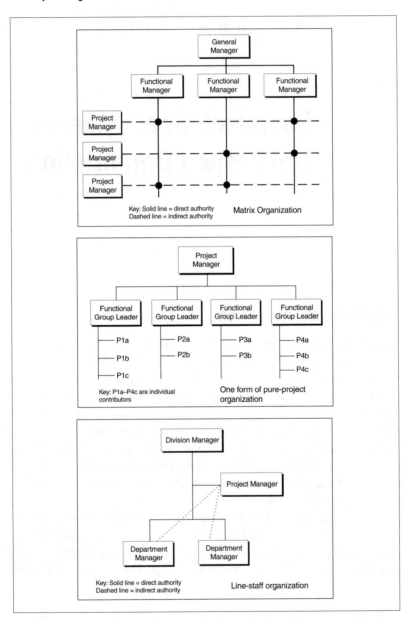

Key: Solid line = direct authority
Dashed line = indirect authority   Matrix Organization

Key: P1a–P4c are individual
contributors   One form of pure-project
                                                    organization

Key: Solid line = direct authority
Dashed line = indirect authority   Line-staff organization

some observations and recommendations for organizing large projects on the basis of those principles.

The recommendations offered are not the cookbook type, however. That is, no step-by-step, how-to-do-it approach has been worked out. What is recommended is more in the nature of experiment, experiment, experiment!

That is not very comforting to those who want nice, tidy prescriptions, but it is the best that can be recommended, given the state of the art in organization design. My primary purpose in offering this chapter is to make readers think about the issues, so that they can at least heighten their *awareness* of the complexity of the problem. The approach used to be called *consciousness-raising*. It is my belief that, by being aware of the issues involved, project managers will be able to avoid some of the problems of traditional forms of organization and perhaps invent some solutions.

WHAT IS A SOCIOTECHNICAL SYSTEM?

The term "sociotechnical system" was coined by Eric Trist (Weisbord, 1987) to identify systems that are combinations of human (social) and technical components. A system is characterized by four basic elements, as shown in Figure 18.2. It has *inputs, outputs,* a *process* that converts those inputs to outputs, and a *feedback* mechanism to regulate the transformation process. A system may be open or closed. An *open system* interacts with its external environment, which of course suggests that the external environment will affect system performance. A *closed system,* on the other hand, will not experience such effects.

In a sociotechnical system, the process, input, output, and feedback elements are all combinations of people and technical "things"—computers, manufacturing equipment, telephones, and so on. The gist of sociotechnical systems design is that there must be a joint optimization of the social and technical elements for the system to function at optimum levels. If only the technical components are optimized, then the social component may suffer.

F I G U R E   18.2

Feedback System

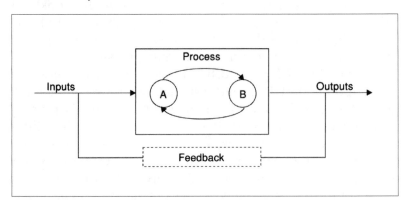

John Naisbett has referred to our society as a "high tech, low touch" system, because technology has become so dominant that human interaction at the "touch" level has been reduced. We interact by phone or computer, often not dealing with people face to face, a fact that causes some grief to individuals who need that human interaction.

A third component, which is actually a part of the social and technical systems and which every organization contains, is the *reward* system. This component is a major influence on organization performance. As shown in Figure 18.3, the three components interact, so that changes in one may affect the other two. For example, a change in technology will affect both the social and reward components. Introduction of computers changes the way people interact, which affects both the social system and the reward system, at least for those who derive significant rewards from interacting with others. In addition, some individuals will find working with the new computers to be rewarding, while others find it boring, threatening—in short, *un*rewarding.

A change in the reward system may affect the social system as well as the way in which the technical system is em-

F I G U R E 18.3

Reward, Technical, and Social System

ployed. If people are rewarded for making better use of the new technology, then it should affect that utilization. In short, there must be a joint optimization of all three components if an organization is to operate optimally, and that is the thrust of sociotechnical systems design.

WORKING PREMISES OF THIS CHAPTER

This chapter is based on a number of premises that may be argued. However, they are grounded in the current body of evidence from studies and real-world organization events.

Need for Continuous Improvement

The quality movement of the 1980s seems to have convinced most people of the need to continuously improve organizations. As Dr. Edwards Deming, one of the most widely respected gurus of quality, has said, there are two kinds of organizations—those that are improving and those that are dying. An organization that is standing still is dying—it is just that no one knows it yet. The reason is simple: The world is dynamic, and your competitors are certainly improving their performance, so if you stand still for long, pretty soon your competition has left you behind.

Interestingly, many people do not have a good understanding of what their competition is doing, and so become complacent. Several workers from a county sanitation department were once asked if they had any competition.

"Nope," was the positive answer.

"You better wake up," someone in the audience told them. "If a private garbage collection agency bids a lower price to the county than you guys cost them, you'll be out on the street."

I agree completely with that position.

Numerous organizations have failed to see the impact of critical events on themselves until it was too late. Some have only one customer—in most cases, the military—and when that customer quits buying, they are in trouble. Others fail to realize how a major development in new technology will affect them, again, until it is too late.

The American auto industry has had to make major changes as a result of Japanese competition. At one time it took U.S. companies a week or more to change over a production line to begin manufacturing a new-model car. The Japanese got it down to hours, and American industry was forced to do the same.

Likewise, it used to take six to eight years to develop a completely new automobile design. The Japanese got it down to three years. You can't compete with a company that brings out a new model in three years when it takes you six years.

In fact, speed is almost the "name of the game" today. In his documentary *Speed Is Life,* Tom Peters demonstrates how some companies have managed to shorten their development times considerably by using cross-functional teams and other approaches.

Another factor that enters into the equation is the current labor shortage. Early in the 1990s, demographics experts predicted that by the year 2000 the U.S. population would grow by 12 million, while 14 million new jobs would be created. The prediction was that we would have a shortfall of some 565,000 engineers. Those figures are coming very close to the mark, and one thing is certain: The growth of jobs will eventually outpace the growth of population, so that every organization must find ways to *do more with less.* Thus the need for improvement of processes.

During the past decade, much of the effort to improve organizations has been aimed at manufacturing. Only in the past few years have people begun to realize the importance of improving organizations *across the board.* In fact, we seem to have reached a point at which reducing labor costs through improvements in human productivity may not be all that useful. Peter Drucker has argued that we need to focus on the application of capital, since the largest portion of product costs are now in that area.

However, we still have a lot to gain through the improvement of performance in administration, support, engineering, and project teams. The costs to develop new products have reached staggering dimensions, with labor costs ranging from $40 to $100 per hour. Because of those high costs, companies must either charge high prices for products or sell large quantities of them just to recover their investment. Thus, the development of some products has become too expensive, and those markets have gone to companies that have lower hourly costs for development.

The Impact of Management on Projects

Whatever happens or doesn't happen in a project is because management either wants it to happen or *permits* it to happen. The first part of the premise will be accepted by most people. The second, that management permits (undesirable) things to happen in a project, may raise some defensiveness. Nevertheless, with the exception of acts of nature, it is management's responsibility to monitor project work closely enough to anticipate and address effects that might have a negative impact on a project, and failure to do so is to permit the impact through neglect.

Project Organization Is a Sociotechnical System

From the description of sociotechnical systems given at the beginning of this chapter, it is clear that all project organizations are sociotechnical systems. They employ technology and people, and have a reward component, all of which must be jointly optimized for the organization to function optimally. Sociotechnical systems design methods therefore should be applied to projects.

To date, the most visible applications of sociotechnical systems design have been in self-directed work teams and other job designs. As was mentioned earlier, the application has largely been restricted to manufacturing, but I believe that it can just as readily serve project organization.

This chapter, then, examines what sociotechnical systems design principles have to offer in the organization of projects—especially product development projects—even though the principles can be applied to any kind of project team.

SOCIOTECHNICAL SYSTEMS DESIGN OF PROJECT ORGANIZATIONS

Involvement of All Members of the Organization

One of the tenets of the quality movement is that the person closest to a job is likely to be the most competent person to improve it. Whether this principle comes from sociotechnical systems theory, its validity is evident. Many organizations have found that employees who are closest to the operational processes must be involved in the organizational design process. The consequences of lack of involvement are low employee commitment to the job, incorrect work estimates (of time, cost, and other factors), omissions of work, and other errors. This happens when the design process involves only technical specialists and senior managers. It is seen most frequently in projects, which typically are planned by people *other* than those who actually have to carry out the work. (See Chapter 4.)

Managers often complain that people in their organizations resist change. I don't believe this is true. In my view, people don't resist change, but they *resist being changed*. That is a significant difference. If we make people a part of the change process, then we do not get such resistance.

Another point here is that *people don't argue with their own data.* If you make them part of the change process, then they get data firsthand that validate the need for change, so they don't argue with it. Further, the fact that they develop the change process means they do not resist it. These are important facts for managers to remember in trying to bring about improvements in organizational performance.

Assessment of Strengths and Weaknesses of the Organization

One of the recommended practices of project planning, noted in Chapter 6, is for the team to analyze its strengths, weaknesses, opportunities, and threats, with threats and risks being more or less synonymous. The SWOT analysis should be conducted through a review of objective data whenever possible. When the analysis is dependent only on individual perceptions and general ideas, it is suspect, partly because managers often are too optimistic at the beginning of a project, tend to minimize weaknesses and threats, and fail to take risks seriously enough. Further, their optimism sometimes causes them to underestimate the number of resources or time required to do the work.

There is, in fact, a macho notion prevalent among some managers that one should never admit any weakness—whether organizational or personal. Clearly, failure to admit weakness means that such weakness is not accessible to correction. Chris Argyris (1990) has discussed the processes that prevent organizations from learning from SWOT analyses and postmortems of previous projects. The two key processes are defensive routines and fancy footwork.

Defensive routines are attempts by members of the organization to avoid embarrassing anyone, so they hide *from* the truth as well as hide the truth from other members of the organization, and therefore the truth cannot be used to signal the need for change.

Fancy footwork often involves reinterpretation of the data so that it has a favorable meaning. A recurrent example is the "interpretation" of unemployment statistics released by the Department of Labor. When unemployment rates fall off slightly, it is often because some people simply give up looking for jobs; they are therefore dropped from the list of unemployed. This means, of course, that the situation really has not improved. Nevertheless, the President may appear on television saying that the decline is a very positive sign, especially since it is the third consecutive month in which a drop has occurred.

The Need for Joint Optimization

As has been stated previously, optimum performance of any organization can be achieved only through joint optimization of the social and technical systems. In the past, we have seen organizations falter because they came under the influence of managers who optimized only the social component. These individuals may have been heavily influenced by the human relations movement of the 1950s and 1960s. Their bias was that what was important in organizations was promoting job satisfaction, good relations, low levels of interpersonal conflict, and so on. In other words, they tried to create a "country club" environment in the workplace. Unfortunately,

Optimum performance of any organization can only be achieved through joint-optimization of the social and technical systems.

making people happy does not always correlate with good organizational performance—improved quality, productivity, and profitability—and such country-club companies soon found themselves in trouble.

At the opposite extreme are those organizations that try to optimize only the technical component. They invest in state-of-the-art equipment, streamline the work processes, employ statistical process control methodology, and ignore the social system except for the minimum requirements. People are allowed to atrophy through lack of training and development. Rewards are dispensed only in the form of money. Conflicts are allowed to reach the boiling level before any attempt is made to resolve them. Even then, resolution may take the form of warning the parties involved that the conflict will not be tolerated, rather than trying to get at the root cause so that the conflict is eliminated.

Unfortunately, joint optimization is much more difficult to achieve than it is to prescribe. Part of the difficulty lies in the fact that the systems are not independent. We talk about them separately for convenience, but they are in most cases interrelated. Therefore, as has been pointed out above, a change in one component affects the others. In fact, it may well be that the *interaction* effects are more important than the *first-order* effects.

For example, giving Tom a computer is a first-order effect in the technical component of the system. Whereas Tom previously had to do his calculations manually, he now has new technology, making it possible for him to carry out the calculations considerably faster than before.

However, he now finds that he is not as free to talk with Charlie as he used to be. Before the computer came along, he and Charlie often met together to work up weekly reports, helping each other with the calculations. Now each has a computer and is expected to perform the calculations individually. This is an *interaction* effect. The change made to the technical system has caused a change in the social system, and this change may have more severe consequences than the first-order effect. The reason: Tom and Charlie both miss their social inter-action so much that their morale declines. They begin com-plaining to their coworkers that the organization is becoming too cold and impersonal for their tastes, and they do so much "rabble-rousing" that soon the decline in morale spreads.

Their manager notices the rabble-rousing and warns Tom and Charlie that it must stop. This further confirms that the organization (represented by their boss) has become cold and uncaring about them as human beings. They protest more. The boss finally dismisses them because she cannot live with their *attitudes!*

Another example: One of my client organizations de-cided to eliminate a piece of equipment that had become obso-lete. The word got out that this was the plan. Unfortunately, the fellow who had operated the equipment for years saw the handwriting on the wall. If there was no need for his machine, what would happen to him?

He became despondent, believing that he would go out the door with the machine. His performance declined. His boss thought he was trying to retire on the job, and became concerned. Ultimately the employee was forced out of the company—his belief about the company's intentions became a *self-fulfilling prophecy.*

The sad thing is, the company fully intended to move him to another position after his machine was eliminated. He was always considered a valuable employee. Yet no one took the time to tell him what was going on (thereby attending to the social system component). Unfortunately, this is not an isolated incident.

Reactive versus Proactive Management

Much has been written about the tendency of American man-agement to focus on the short term rather than the long term, and to be reactive rather than proactive. This same problem afflicts project management. Project managers become so in-volved in solving today's problems that they fail to look ahead or to interpret the problems as symptoms of a greater "illness" that afflicts the project. This is understandable, since people usually respond most strongly to that which is most salient in their experience, and it is the *immediate problems* that clearly are most salient. Tomorrow is "out there" somewhere in never-never land. It is not tangible.

It takes real discipline and the ability to back away from today and look at the "big picture" to get out of this short-term focus. It may even require the help of an outside reviewer. Indeed, periodic project reviews (covered in Chapter 11) are recommended as a safeguard against this tendency.

Goal Selection and Orientation

Organizations tend to select goals in an either/or manner. *Either* we can have quality *or* we can have it finished on time, but we can't have both! This sometimes leads to our seeing the customer as the enemy.

I got into a cab at O'Hare Airport once and asked the driver to take me to a hotel on the outskirts of Chicago. As he started to drive away, he said aloud, "The other cabs get to go downtown. Me, I get to go to (my destination)."

I said to him, "Look, if you don't want to take me there, let me out, and I'll get another cab."

"No, it's too late," he said. What he meant was that he had lost his place in the queue and would lose even more if he had to start over.

I must admit to being more than a little steamed. Finally I said to him, "It seems to me you have forgotten who pays your salary. Your customers are not the enemy. If you don't want to take them wherever they want to go, then you should hang a sign on your window saying 'downtown only.'

The driver didn't say anything, but I know that he was thinking only about profits. If he went downtown, he had a good chance of picking up someone at a hotel who wanted to go back to the airport. Taking me to a suburban hotel meant that he would probably have to return to the airport empty, thus losing money.

I understand his concern, but for him to dump on me, the customer, was inappropriate.

On any project mission, it is necessary that the project team understand its primary reason for existence, which is *to satisfy the needs of its customers.* Failure to keep that in mind is certain to lead to failure overall. As I have said in a previous chapter, the prime *motive* of a business (or project) is to make a profit, but its *mission* must be customer satisfaction. This is not an either/or choice. The two goals must be achieved simultaneously.

Limits of the "Old Standbys"

As has been stated previously, project organization largely falls into two categories: hierarchical and matrix. These are the standbys with which we are all familiar. The problem is, when they are viewed as the only choices, they limit our ability to achieve more optimum solutions. Often we limit ourselves by working from a constraint orientation that emphasizes what cannot be changed, rather than from an innovative orientation that looks for what *can* be changed.

We must constantly search for organization forms that solve some of the problems of matrix and hierarchical structure. A recent trend is cross-function management, which is neither matrix nor hierarchical. Dimancescu (1992) described the development of this form of organization at Boeing. Design-build teams were assembled to construct the 777 aircraft. Nearly 215 teams, of as many as 15 members each, were assembled. Many were colocated, to avoid the problems typically encountered with matrix structure, in which members are spread out physically so that communication occurs haphazardly, if at all.

This form of organization created a unique situation. Matrix results in a "one person, two bosses" form, which has long been deplored, yet deemed necessary to get complex jobs done. The Boeing organization created a situation of two bosses, one hat.

Cross-function management is probably here to stay, for the foreseeable future. Multidisciplinary teams are essential to deal with complex engineering projects, and the old matrix structure has proved to have numerous problems. No doubt cross-function management will as well.

Regarding the Organization Design as "Finished"

To expect that the design of an organization is finished "once-and-for-all," is to limit ourselves to new possibilities and also to freeze our response capability in the face of changes that make the old design obsolete. It is better to regard design work as a part of regular operations and not a separate front-end activity. This requires setting goals for people development so that appropriate skills and flexibility are generated to respond to the changing environment.

A FINAL CAUTION

Although this chapter has suggested that principles from sociotechnical systems design might be applied to project organization, a word of caution is in order. Sociotechnical systems principles have been applied primarily to manufacturing environments, where jobs tend to be simplified, boring, and nonchallenging. In those cases, cross-training of workers tends to enlarge and enrich their jobs, making them more motivating.

To apply the same ideas to knowledge workers can be risky. For example, one practitioner suggested to me that engineers be cross-trained in project teams. My response was that this was like trying to teach a brain surgeon to do heart surgery, or vice versa. You wind up with two surgeons who are no good at either specialty. The reason is simple—it is very nearly impossible to keep up with one's specialty now, much less try to learn the skills of another!

Marvin Weisbord (1987), who is regarded by his colleagues as one of the nation's foremost practitioners of organization development, observes:

> Anyone who tries to clone this procedure for project management, product development, or planning quickly discovers that knowledge work happens differently from repetitive production work (a continuing source of irritation between scientists and cost accountants). The flow chart spills out in all directions. People already have multiskilled jobs, with considerable decision latitude. (p. 324)

In my opinion, the answer to improving project team performance is in applying the ideas of cross-function management, as discussed above. To that approach, we might apply sociotechnical systems design principles and come up with the project organization of the twenty-first century.

19

C H A P T E R

Profiling the World-Class Project Management Organization[1]

By Robert K. Wysocki*

*Robert K. Wysocki, Ph.D., has been an information systems man-
ager, systems and management consultant, author, training devel-
oper and provider, and professor of information systems. He is
coauthor of five books on project management and information systems management. He is a frequent chairperson and speaker at con-
ferences and professional society meetings.

He is cofounder and president of Enterprise Information Insights, Inc., a management consulting practice specializing in the
development of the Information Technology organization, its managers and professional staff, through the design and integration of
project management methods and tools into the processes that drive
the contemporary IT organization. In this capacity EII has completed engagements in project management methodology design
and integration, project management training program design and
delivery, project office establishment, and process quality management.

He also serves as Curriculum Coordinator for the Boston University Corporate Education Center. In that capacity he advises

them on project management training programs and their 20 course curriculum. He is a member of the ASTD, the PMI, the IAHRIM, SHRM, and the ISPI. He earned a B.A. in Mathematics from the University of Dallas and an M.S. and Ph.D. in Mathematical Statistics from Southern Methodist University.

CHAPTER SUMMARY

First, let us understand that there are very few world-class project management organizations. After surveying more than 200 organizations, Harold Kerzner (1999) came to the conclusion that the number who could claim such honors were very few. In his book *In Search of Excellence in Project Management,* he concludes: "Unfortunately, there are not many companies that have actually achieved excellence." In fact, from among those surveyed, he includes only 29 companies as having achieved excellence or being on the right track. They are:

Armstrong World Industries	Kinetico, Inc.
Battelle	Lincoln Electric
Bellcore	MCI
BellSouth	Mason & Hanger Corporation
BTR Sealing	Motorola
Centerior Energy	National City Corporation
ChoiceCare	Nortel
Ericsson	OEC Medical Systems
General Electric	Radian International
General Motors	Roadway Express
B. F. Goodrich	Sprint
Hewlett-Packard	Standard Products
ISK Biosciences	United Technologies
Johnson Controls	Automotive
Key Services Corporation	USAA

Although several other organizations would undoubt-edly like to achieve world-class status, they have not. The first question such organizations should ask is: "How are we doing with respect to becoming a world-class project man-agement organization?" The answer to that question can be determined by taking the one-minute survey discussed in this chapter.

Assuming the one-minute survey shows that the con-tender is not a world-class project management organization, the next question to be answered is: "Is our organization ready to move toward world-class project management?" Wanting to be world class is certainly a necessary condition but desire is not enough. "Can we become world class?" is an equally important question. The organizational readiness as-sessment presented in this chapter will help senior manage-ment make this determination.

Another part of the investigation of an organization's readiness for project management is an assessment of the competencies and skills of those who are or would like to function as project managers. Some will have the required ex-periences and skills to be *full-time project managers*; others will be *occasional project managers* with some training and experi-ence; still others will be *accidental project managers* with no training or preparation. The remainder are *wanna-be project managers* who are simply drawn to the profession. In what follows we discuss the competencies and skills needed for all types of project managers.

For our purposes, projects can be classified according to their technical and business characteristics. Because all pro-jects are inherently different, we would expect them to re-quire different skills from those who would manage them. That is in fact the case, and so we associate a project manager type with each project type. The project types have a natural ordering from least complex to most complex, and the project manager types associated with them also have a natural or-dering. Using this construct, we will then have defined a ca-reer path for project managers. Movement along that career path will be equivalent to acquiring the skills needed to manage projects of increasing complexity.

In this chapter we will present the profiles of project managers in terms of the skills needed to successfully manage projects of the type to which they are assigned. Using these profiles as a reference point, individual managers can compare their skills with those required to manage projects of a given type. The difference between the skills they possess and the skills required is defined as their "skill gap." The greater the "gap" between the competencies and skills needed and the actual competencies and skills possessed, the bigger the challenge posed to the organization. Knowing their skill gap, individuals can begin to build a plan to address it and hence prepare themselves to manage projects of increasing complexity.

WHAT IS A WORLD-CLASS PROJECT MANAGEMENT ORGANIZATION?

A quick way to assess your organization's position relative to being a world-class project management organization is through the one-minute survey presented in Figure 19.1. Take a minute to answer the seven questions and compute your organization's score. How close are you to world-class status? Were you surprised at the results?

ORGANIZATIONAL READINESS

Given that the results indicate that world-class status is still a goal to be attained, the next question is: "Are we ready to become a world-class project management organization?" To answer that question we can use a readiness assessment tool developed by Enterprise Information Insights, Inc., a project management consulting organization headquartered in Worcester, MA. The EII assessment tool measures an organization's readiness for adopting an enterprisewide project management process.

F I G U R E 19.1

One-Minute Survey

☑ Take This One-Minute Survey

	YES	MAYBE	NO
Our organization successfully completes more than 70 percent of its projects.	❏	❏	❏
Our project portfolio is always aligned with our business goals and objectives.	❏	❏	❏
Our senior managers know the business value and status of all active projects.	❏	❏	❏
Our managers visibly support our enterprise-wide project management process.	❏	❏	❏
Our managers have the skills to deliver business value from projects.	❏	❏	❏
Our project managers are achieving their professional development goals.	❏	❏	❏
Our managers proactively address the training needs of their project teams.	❏	❏	❏

To compute your score count
the number of checked boxes

☑ Yes   x 5 = _____
☑ Maybe x 3 = _____
☑ No   x 1 = _____
TOTAL SCORE = _____

How did you do?

Score   What does it mean?

31-35   Your project management environment is world class!
22-30   Performance is acceptable. There is room for improvement.
13-21   Corrective action is required. Get a team to work at once.
 7-12   Immediate action is required. Outside help will be needed.

Through a survey consisting of 66 questions (see Figure 19.2 for a sample) the assessment tool produces a report that measures 20 dimensions of organizational readiness for an enterprisewide project management methodology. The report also assesses the current management of the organization's project portfolio, the extent to which the professional staff are aware of and have implemented effective project management practices, and the relationship of project managers and teams to their customers.[2] Figure 19.3 provides a summary sample of the readiness assessment, and Figure 19.4 gives an interpretation of the data. Several conclusions that can be drawn from the report are listed in Figure 19.5.

Analysis of the organizational readiness data will help the organization formulate a plan for attaining world-class project management status. We are assuming that the data support that effort. The organization should develop a strategy for addressing the areas needing improvement before it commissions a team to design, develop, and implement an enterprisewide project management methodology. For example, the conclusions given in Figure 19.5 suggest the following corrective action as a prerequisite to any further steps toward achieving world-class project management status:

1. Determine the reasons for some managers' reluctance to support an enterprisewide methodology and put a program in place to address their concerns.
2. The lack of understanding of current project management practices is easily addressed through documentation, communications, and training initiatives.
3. Task forces should be charged with developing and implementing problem resolution and changing management processes.
4. There is a widespread and consistent lack of project management knowledge, which has resulted in poor practices. Training can address this problem.

F I G U R E 19.2

Sample of Organizational Readiness Questions

A Sample of Questions from the Organizational Readiness Assessment Survey

 SA (Strongly Agree)   A (Agree)   N (Neutral)
D (Disagree)   SD (Strongly Disagree)
If you have no experience or observation that pertains to the question, respond with an "N", the neutral response.
Try to answer as many questions as possible with a non-neutral response. Circle the correct response to each question.

1. I know when the project manager understanding what I have requested.   SA A N D SD

2. My staff feels like they are really part of the project team.   SA A N D SD

3. Executives have communicated the importance of project management.   SA A N D SD

4. I often participate in problem resolution for projects in my area.   SA A N D SD

5. Project managers are handling scope changes in a professional manner.   SA A N D SD

6. We have a formal change management process.   SA A N D SD

7. Turnover on project teams is comparable to turnover in other departments.   SA A N D SD

8. We do a good job managing resources that are allocated to projects.   SA A N D SD

9. Project managers are genuinely concerned about customer satisfaction.   SA A N D SD

10. Project managers display a positive "can do" attitude.   SA A N D SD

11. I understand why certain project priority decisions have been made.   SA A N D SD

12. Project managers read project management publications.   SA A N D SD

copyright (c) 1999, Enterprise Information Insights, Inc.

F I G U R E 19.3

Typical Project Management Organizational Readiness Assessment

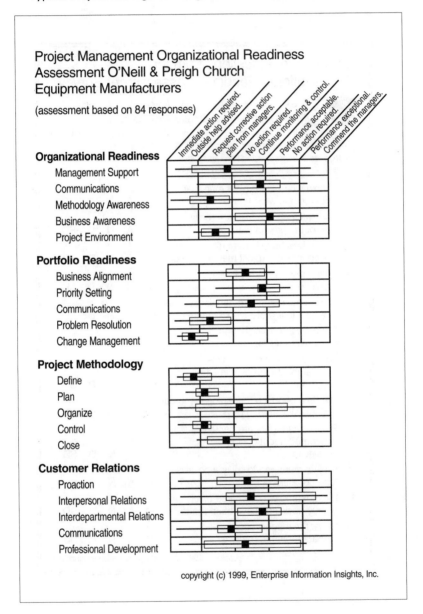

Project Management Organizational Readiness
Assessment O'Neill & Preigh Church
Equipment Manufacturers

(assessment based on 84 responses)

copyright (c) 1999, Enterprise Information Insights, Inc.

F I G U R E 19.4

How to Interpret the Organizational Readiness Assessment

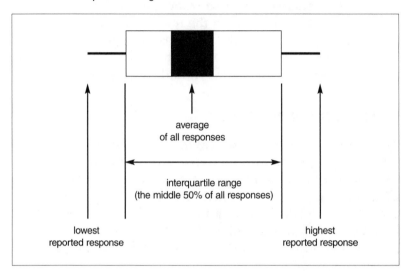

F I G U R E 19.5

Conclusions from the Organizational Readiness Assessment

❏ Management support for an enterprisewide management methodology varies widely.

❏ The current project management methodology is not widely understood nor is the corporate environment supportive of current project management practices.

❏ Problem resolution and change management processes are not meeting management expectations.

❏ Overall the lack of understanding of project management practices has resulted in poor practices especially in the definition, planning, control, and closing phases of projects.

❏ Customer relations vary widely which indicates that some business units' expectations are being met while others are not. This may be indicative of varying business awareness on the part of project managers and team members as evidenced by the wide range of responses in the business awareness dimension.

5. Interpersonal skills are generally lacking and must
be addressed. Furthermore, this problem is not consistent across the organization, as evidenced by the
large variance among the responses. There are probably areas where the relationship is good and others
where it has sadly deteriorated. The reason for these
differing relationships should be investigated.

A TAXONOMY OF PROJECTS

There are various criteria we could use to classify projects: by
total budget, project duration, risk, business value, team size,
or some combination of them. For the purpose of matching
project manager and team members with the type of project
team they are qualified to join, we will use a classification
based on the technical and business environments that char-
acterize the project. Figure 19.6 graphically displays the classification scheme.

Given a project, the process summarized in the complexity assessment matrix measures as many as 40 characteristics to map the project into two dimensions: business
environment and technical environment. At least conceptu-
ally a typical project can then be plotted as a data point on
the complexity assessment matrix. The data point will fall
into one of four regions on the matrix. Starting from the
simplest situation, Type IV projects have low business value
and use well-established technology. In fact, they are projects that may have repeated themselves several times and
have become rather routine. Type II projects, on the other
hand, may be using new or complex technologies even
though the business value may be low or moderate. Type III
projects are characterized by high business value even
though they may have low or moderate technical complexity. These projects are therefore distinguished from the
other two by their high business content. Type I projects
bear all the characteristics of Type II and Type III projects.
That is, they use complex technologies and have high busi-

F I G U R E 19.6

Project Complexity Assessment Matrix

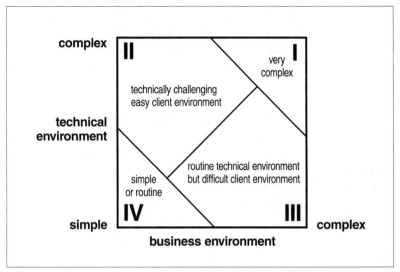

Source: Adapted from the Project Complexity Assessment Matrix developed by the Center for Project Management.

ness value. They are the most demanding of the four types and are often mission-critical as well.

A CLASSIFICATION OF PROJECT MANAGERS

Just as projects come in several flavors, so do project managers. The more seasoned project managers are qualified to manage the most complex and mission-critical (Type I) projects. On the other hand, those who have just been anointed project managers may be limited to less complex and noncritical (Type IV) projects. Additional training eventually lead to promotions and the opportunity to work on more complex projects.

We can relate project manager classifications to project classifications. We define four classes of project manager:

Team Leader, Project Manager, Senior Project Manager, and Program Manager. They relate to the complexity assessment matrix in the following way. Type IV projects can be managed by any one of the four classes of project manager but will most frequently be managed by those who have demonstrated Team Leader qualifications. By choosing the appropriate Type IV project, the project manager and project team can learn and practice new skills. Type II and Type III projects can be managed by anyone who has demonstrated Project Manager or above qualifications, but will most likely be managed by someone who has reached Project Manager status. Depending on the mix of technical and business skills they possess, they will be assigned to either Type II or Type III projects. Type I projects are the domain of the Program Manager or Senior Project Manager classes. The most critical of the large Type I projects may be treated as programs and be staffed by a Program Manager and several Senior Project Managers or Project Managers.

F I G U R E   19.7

Project Manager Type by Project Classification

Project Complexity	Team Leader	Project Manager	Senior Project Manager	Program Manager
I			X	X
II		X	X	X
III		X	X	X
IV	X	X	X	X

Later in this chapter we will profile each type of project manager according to the competencies and skills needed to be effective at that class. To each of the four types of projects we will then assign types of project managers as shown in Figure 19.7. This matching of project manager type to project classification will facilitate our discussion of skill profiles of project managers as a function of the type of project they are assigned to manage. In preparation for that discussion, later in this chapter, let us first look at the functions and tasks that any one of our four project manager types may be called upon to perform.

Job Functions and Tasks for Project Management

Project managers are called upon to perform a variety of functions and tasks. Many of these may seem to be removed from the direct management of the project. In order to set the stage for our discussion of competencies and skills, we provide the following list, which was developed by the Boston University Corporate Education Center in partnership with several of its clients and is used with permission here.

I.   **Planning the Project (Strategic and Tactical)**
 a. Develops preliminary study with project team, identifying business problem, requirements, project scope, and benefits.
 b. Identifies key project results and milestones.
 c. Develops project plan and work breakdown structure and communicates to team and client.
 d. Determines needed resources, including client involvement.
 e. Estimates timelines and phases.
 f. Influences selection of project team members.
 g. Assigns project responsibilities from an assessment of individual skills and development needs.

    h. Defines clear individual roles and performance
       expectations.

    i. Establishes acceptance criteria.

    j. Determines appropriate technological approach.

II. Managing the Project

    a. Continually reviews project status.

    b. Reviews work against key results criteria.

    c. Uses systematic method for logging project
       status—checking against schedule.

    d. Uses change management/request procedure.

    e. Uses project meetings to measure progress
       against plan and to communicate changes and
       issues.

    f. Assesses skill-needed documentation of meetings,
       work, conversations, and decisions.

    g. Measures quality through testing against
       requirements.

    h. Conducts project reviews and walk-throughs (with
       appropriate client involvement).

III. Leading the Project Team

    a. Involves team in planning.

    b. Uses both formal and informal methods to track
       project status.

    c. Recognizes individual and team accomplishments or
       results.

    d. Manages performance issues in a timely manner.

    e. Delegates tasks effectively through understanding
       individual strengths and weaknesses.

    f. Maintains open door for staff ideas and
       concerns.

    g. Sets performance and development objectives for
       staff.

    h. Schedules and holds regular team meetings.

IV. Building Client Partnerships

a. Involves working jointly with client in defining project goals and key results.

b. Works with client to ensure alignment of project with overall business goals.

c. Listens and responds actively and documents client needs, changes, and demands.

d. Implements procedures for controlling and handling change.

e. Develops client understanding of the system and trains client in systems use.

f. Presents and reports periodically to client.

g. Establishes lines of responsibility and accountability to client.

V. Targeting to the Business

a. Manages in accordance with visions and values.

b. Links overall architecture principles.

c. Interfaces effectively with business systems and processes.

d. Plans for impacts on related systems/departments to achieve maximum efficiency.

e. Understands business needs as well as time and cost pressures.

f. Keeps current with business and technology developments in competitors.

g. Aligns project with corporate and business priorities and direction.

Competencies and Skills of the World-Class Project Manager

If you know of a foolproof method for identifying a professional who will make a competent project manager, please let me know. We can show you how to make a lot of money. In fact, it is very difficult to identify someone with the requisite competencies. Figure 19.8 demonstrates the reason why. There

F I G U R E 19.8

Project Manager Competencies and Skills

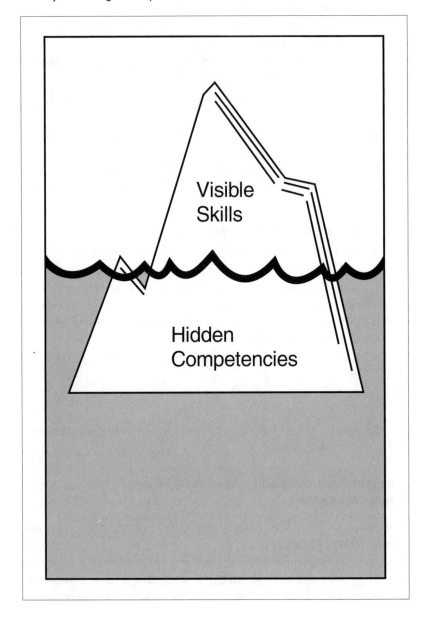

are two levels of characteristics that determine success or failure as a project manager. At the visible level are skills, which can be measured in terms of mastery and which a person can acquire through training. That is the easy part. More difficult are those traits (competencies) that lie below the surface, out of the range of the visible. We can see them in practice but we cannot directly measure them in the sense of determining whether a particular person has them and, if so, to what degree. They are also the traits that are more difficult to develop through training. Some of them may, in fact, be hereditary.

Enterprise Information Insights uses an assessment tool to measure competency in 18 different areas, using a set of observable behaviors that are related to the competencies. To establish an individual's competency level, EII recommends that the candidate perform a self-assessment and that several coworkers also provide their assessment of the individual. These coworkers may be managers, peer professionals, subordinates, or customers. The individual's self-assessment can then be compared with coworkers' assessments. Although this approach may seem simplistic, it has practical value and has surfaced rather insightful conclusions on individual performance.

Effective project managers must have competencies and skills that are specific to the discipline in which the project they manage lies. They also need a set of competencies and skills that are not discipline-specific and that fall into one of the five categories described below:

1. **Business**. These competencies relate to the business and business processes in general and do not involve specific business function knowledge.
2. **Personal**. Competencies in this category relate to the individual. They do not require another party in order to be practiced.
3. **Interpersonal**. Competencies in this category relate to the individual. They involve at least two people, neither of whom is the manager of the other.

4. **Management**. These competencies relate to all aspects of management, whether people management or work management. Also included are competencies related to the performance of strategic and tactical management functions not specific to any individual.

5. **Project management**. Project management skills span the five phases of project management: initiation, planning, organizing, controlling, and closing. Unlike the first four categories, the skills covered here are visible and can be measured.

COMPETENCY PROFILE OF THE WORLD-CLASS PROJECT MANAGER

We turn now to the competencies common to all levels of project manager. The profile generated here is meant to give you a general sense of what is required to be an effective project manager. It will help you match your current competencies against those required of world-class project managers. What results from this examination is a gap between the competencies you have and those you will need to add to your profile as you progress through the ranks of project management responsibility. This assessment will form the core of your personal learning contract.

Figures 19.9 through 19.12 provide a capsule description of the business, personal, interpersonal, and management competencies required to be an effective project manager. The list was originally developed by the Boston University Corporate Education Center in cooperation with several of its major corporate accounts. It has since been revised through experience with several other clients and has been adapted here with permission.

The competencies are presented in a survey format so that you can evaluate the extent to which you practice each one. As an exercise, review the list and personally assess how your competencies measure up. The rating scale is 5 = Strongly Agree, 4 = Agree, 3 = Neutral, 2 = Disagree, and 1 =

F I G U R E   19.9

Business Competencies

Business Competencies

Business Awareness
Ensures that the project is linked to the organization's
business plan and satisfies a business objective
by solving a business problem.   5 4 3 2 1

Evaluates the impact of industry and
technology developments.   5 4 3 2 1

Balances ideal technical approaches and project
scope against business deadlines and priorities
to find the best compromise.   5 4 3 2 1

Quickly adapts to changing business conditions.   5 4 3 2 1

TOTAL BUSINESS AWARENESS SCORE [   ]

Business Partnership
Follows up with business partners, throughout
the cycle of the project, to ensure full understanding
of the business partners' needs and concerns.   5 4 3 2 1

Seeks meaningful business area participation
during the design process.   5 4 3 2 1

Conducts business-oriented walk-throughs.   5 4 3 2 1

Structures the activities of the project team, so that
systems staff work closely with a business partner.   5 4 3 2 1

TOTAL BUSINESS PARTNERSHIP SCORE [   ]

Commitment to Quality
Pushes for more efficient ways to do things.   5 4 3 2 1

Sets and enforces high standards of quality
for self and others.   5 4 3 2 1

Develops a quality plan coordinated with
the project plan.   5 4 3 2 1

Monitors performance against quality plan
and objectives.   5 4 3 2 1

TOTAL COMMITMENT TO QUALITY SCORE [   ]

F I G U R E   19.10

Personal Competencies

Personal Competencies

Initiative

Develops innovative and creative approaches to
problems when faced with obstacles or limitations.   5 4 3 2 1

Takes calculated risks.   5 4 3 2 1

Takes persistent action to overcome obstacles
and achieve solutions.   5 4 3 2 1

Puts in whatever effort is needed to get job done.   5 4 3 2 1

TOTAL INITIATIVE SCORE [   ]

Information Gathering

Actively solicits input from all groups that may
be affected by the project.   5 4 3 2 1

Seeks information or data from various
sources to clarify a problem.   5 4 3 2 1

Identifies and consults individuals and groups
that can expedite project activities or provide
assistance.   5 4 3 2 1

Gets enough information to support design and
implementation decisions.   5 4 3 2 1

TOTAL INFORMATION GATHERING SCORE [   ]

Analytic Thinking

Develops an overall project plan including
resources, budget, and time.   5 4 3 2 1

Translates business goals into project goals
and project goals into detailed work breakdown
structures.   5 4 3 2 1

Uses project management software to develop
plans and track status.   5 4 3 2 1

Generates and presents logical, clearly
reasoned alternatives.   5 4 3 2 1

TOTAL ANALYTIC THINKING SCORE [   ]

Continued

F I G U R E   19.10 (Concluded)

Personal Competencies

Personal Competencies (continued)

Conceptual Thinking

Considers the project within the context of a
broader view of how the business and technology
will be changing over the next several years.   5 4 3 2 1

Uses understanding of business and technical
objectives to prioritize effectively (for example:
project tasks, test cases, issues to be resolved).   5 4 3 2 1

Anticipates and plans for the impact of the
project on other systems.   5 4 3 2 1

Develops a clear vision or conceptual model of
the deliverables.   5 4 3 2 1

TOTAL CONCEPTUAL THINKING SCORE [   ]

Self-Confidence

Presents a confident and positive attitude
to set the tone for the team.   5 4 3 2 1

Confronts problems with others quickly and directly.   5 4 3 2 1

Controls own feelings and behavior in stressful situations. 5 4 3 2 1

Works effectively under pressure.   5 4 3 2 1

TOTAL SELF-CONFIDENCE SCORE [   ]

Concern for Credibility

Maintains credibility by consistently delivering
what has been promised.   5 4 3 2 1

Stays on top of the details of the project effort, to be able to
answer questions authoritatively and maintain credibility. 5 4 3 2 1

Answers questions honestly, even if awkward to do so. 5 4 3 2 1

Promptly informs management and the customer
about any difficulties.   5 4 3 2 1

TOTAL CONCERN FOR CREDIBILITY SCORE [   ]

Flexibility

Adjusts readily to changes in the work environment.   5 4 3 2 1

Adjusts own managerial style, depending on
the people and situation.   5 4 3 2 1

Uses or shares resources to best accomplish
organizational goals.   5 4 3 2 1

Delegates tasks and activities to others.   5 4 3 2 1

TOTAL FLEXIBILITY SCORE [   ]

F I G U R E 19.11

Interpersonal Competencies

Interpersonal Competencies

Interpersonal Awareness

Tries to know team members, to understand
what motivates them.   5 4 3 2 1

Understands the issues and concerns of other
individuals and groups.   5 4 3 2 1

Notices and interprets non-verbal behavior.   5 4 3 2 1

Is objective when mediating conflicting positions of
team members.   5 4 3 2 1

TOTAL INTERPERSONAL AWARENESS SCORE [   ]

Organizational Awareness

Identifies and seeks the support of key stakeholders.   5 4 3 2 1

Proactively engages groups and individuals with
technical and/or financial overseeing responsibilities.   5 4 3 2 1

Takes the time to understand and consider the political
dynamics among groups involved in the project.   5 4 3 2 1

Uses relationships with people from other units within the
organization to resolve issues or provide assistance.   5 4 3 2 1

TOTAL ORGANIZATIONAL AWARENESS SCORE [   ]

Anticipation of Impact

Adapts style or approach to achieve a particular impact. 5 4 3 2 1

Manages expectations by ensuring that what is
promised can be delivered.   5 4 3 2 1

Arranges for a senior manager to attend the initial project
meeting and explain the project's mission and objectives. 5 4 3 2 1

Considers the short- and long-term implications of
project decisions.   5 4 3 2 1

TOTAL ANTICIPATION OF IMPACT SCORE [   ]

Resourceful use of Influence

Develops strategies that address other people's
most important concerns.   5 4 3 2 1

Enlists the support of his/her management to
influence other managers.   5 4 3 2 1

Enlists cooperation by appealing to people's unique expertise. 5 4 3 2 1

Involves project team members in the detail planning
of the project, so they will have ownership of the plan.   5 4 3 2 1

TOTAL RESOURCEFUL USE OF INFLUENCE SCORE [   ]

F I G U R E 19.12

Management Competencies

Management Competencies

Motivating Others

Ensures that team members understand the project's goals and purpose.	5 4 3 2 1
Provides rewards and recognition to people as milestones are reached.	5 4 3 2 1
Initiates informal events to promote team work.	5 4 3 2 1
Takes appropriate action to assist and counsel marginal performers.	5 4 3 2 1

TOTAL MOTIVATING OTHERS SCORE [ ]

Communications

Organizes and meets regularly with a management team composed of representatives from all areas affected by the project.	5 4 3 2 1
Plans and holds regular, frequent meetings with the project team to discuss status, resolve issues and share information.	5 4 3 2 1
Ensures that presentations are well-organized.	5 4 3 2 1
Tailors his/her language to the level of the audience.	5 4 3 2 1

TOTAL COMMUNICATIONS SCORE [ ]

Developing Others

Gives team members assignments or training to provide opportunities for growth and development.	5 4 3 2 1
Provides direct, specific, constructive feedback and guidance to others regarding their performance.	5 4 3 2 1
Empowers team members to create challenge and stretch their abilities.	5 4 3 2 1
Provides closer supervision for inexperienced people.	5 4 3 2 1

TOTAL DEVELOPING OTHERS SCORE [ ]

Continued

copyright (c) 1999, Enterprise Information Insights, Inc.

F I G U R E   19.12 (Concluded)

Management Competencies

Management Competencies (continued)

Planning

Develops and maintains a detailed master plan that
shows resource needs, budget, time schedules, and
work to be done.   5 4 3 2 1

Assesses project design and implementation approach
often to ensure that the project properly addresses the
business problem to be solved.   5 4 3 2 1

Ensures a common understanding and agreement
on the project scope and objectives and on any
subsequent changes.   5 4 3 2 1

Maintains control of accepted changes to the project
plan and ensures that any changes are communicated
to all team members.   5 4 3 2 1

TOTAL PLANNING SCORE [   ]

Monitoring and Controlling

Regularly obtains status information from each project
team member on their assigned tasks, monitors
resource usage, schedule variances, and keeps the
project on schedule.   5 4 3 2 1

Identifies the economic and schedule consequences of
requested and/or mandated scope changes and
communicates these to management.   5 4 3 2 1

Accepts responsibility for resolving project issues,
especially scope changes, focusing on solutions,
recommendations, and actions.   5 4 3 2 1

Conducts a post-project review to identify what went
well, what should have been done differently and what
lessons were learned.   5 4 3 2 1

TOTAL MONITORING AND CONTROLLING SCORE [   ]

Strongly Disagree. When you are done, add the score value for each of the 19 competency areas. The resulting scores are interpreted as follows:

Score Range	Project Manager Competency Level
4–7	Does not meet minimum competency level
8–10	Meets Team Leader minimum competency level
11–15	Meets Project Manager minimum competency level
16–18	Meets Senior Project Manager minimum competency level
19–20	Meets Program Manager minimum competency level

Knowing your score on each of the competencies will give you a rough guide as to where you should concentrate your development activities. You may want to ask coworkers to assess your competencies so you can compare their responses with yours. You will discover that others do not perceive you as you perceive yourself. Their perceptions are reality regardless of how closely they agree with reality as you see it. Figure 19.13 presents a typical competency assessment report.[3] The narrow, filled rectangle is the individual's self-assessment; otherwise the report follows the presentation in Figure 19.4.

SKILL PROFILE OF THE WORLD-CLASS PROJECT MANAGER

We turn our attention to skills of the project manager. Unlike competencies, skills are visible and can be assessed. The following assessment of skill levels is based on Bloom's Taxonomy of Educational Objectives—Cognitive Domain. This six-level taxonomy measures cognitive abilities according to observable and verifiable events as they relate to each of the skills.

Explanation of Bloom's Taxonomy

1.0   Knowledge (I can define it)

Knowledge, as defined here, involves *the remembering or recalling* of ideas, materials, or phenomena. For measurement

F I G U R E 19.13

Competency Assessment Report

O'Neill & Preigh Church
Equipment Manufacturers
(assessment based on 8 responses)
Competency Assessment Report
for Sy Yonra

Business Competencies

Business Awareness
Business Partnership
Commitment to Quality

Personal Competencies
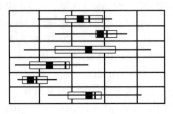
Initiative
Information Gathering
Conceptual Thinking
Self-Confidence
Concern for Credibility
Flexibility

**Interpersonal
Competencies**

Interpersonal Awareness
Organizational Awareness
Anticipation of Impact
Resourceful Use of Influence

**Management
Competencies**
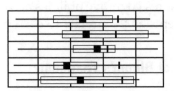
Motivating Others
Communication Skills
Developing Others
Planning
Monitoring & Controlling

purposes, the recall situations involve little more than bringing to mind the appropriate material. Although some alteration of the material may be required, this is a relatively minor part of the task.

2.0   Comprehension (I can explain how it works)

Comprehension encompasses those objectives, behaviors, or responses that represent an understanding of the literal message contained in a communication. In reaching such understanding, you may change the communication in your mind or in your overt responses to some parallel form that is more meaningful to you. You may also have responses that represent simple extensions beyond what is given in the communication itself.

3.0   Application (I have limited experience using it in simple situations)

Application involves the use of abstractions in particular and concrete situations. The abstractions may be in the form of general ideas, rules of procedures, or generalized methods. The abstractions may also be technical principles, ideas, and theories that must be remembered and applied. Examples include:

- The ability to use an abstraction correctly, given an appropriate situation in which no mode of solution is specified.
- The ability to apply generalizations and conclusions to real-life problems.
- The ability to apply scientific principles, postulates, theorems, or other abstractions to new situations.

4.0   Analysis (I have extensive experience using it in complex situations)

Analysis breaks a communication down into its constituent elements or parts such that the relative hierarchy of ideas is made clear and/or the relations between the ideas are made explicit. Such analysis is intended to indicate how the communication is organized and to clarify the way in which it manages to convey its effects, as well as its basis and arrangement. Analysis deals with both the content and form of material.

5.0   Synthesis (I can adapt it to other uses)

Synthesis is the putting together of elements and parts so as to form a whole. It involves arranging and combining pieces, parts, elements, and so forth in such a way as to constitute a pattern or structure not clearly there before.

6.0   Evaluation (I am recognized as an expert by my peers)

Evaluation involves judging the value of material and methods for given purposes, or making quantitative and qualitative judgments about the extent to which material and methods satisfy criteria. A standard appraisal may be used. The evaluation may be based on criteria you devise or on criteria given to you.

Application of Bloom's Taxonomy

Figures 19.14 through 19.18 give the attainment levels for each set of competencies or skills—project management, management, business, personal, and interpersonal—as a function of project manager class. The material is presented in matrix form. At the intersection of a row (competency or skill) with a column (project manager class) a value from 1 to 6 indicates the attainment level that is required for a project manager of that class. Note how the levels change for each class of project manager. Project managers can identify skills development needs as they consider progression through the ranks of project management.[4]

F I G U R E 19.14

Project Management Skills of Project Managers

PROJECT MANAGEMENT SKILLS	IV	III	II	I
Charter Development	3	4	4	4
Complexity Assessment	-	3	3	4
Cost Estimating	3	4	4	5
Cost Management	3	4	4	5
Critical Path Management	3	4	4	4
Detailed Estimating	3	4	4	5
Project Planning (WBS, network, PERT, etc.)	3	4	4	4
Project Closeout	3	4	4	5
Project Management Software Expertise	4	4	4	4
Project Notebook Construction & Maintenance	3	4	4	4
Project Organization	-	3	3	5
Project Progress Assessment	2	3	3	4
Resource Acquisition	2	4	4	5
Resource Levelling	2	4	4	5
Resource Requirements	2	4	4	5
Schedule Development	3	3	3	4
Scope Management	3	4	4	5
Size Estimating	3	4	4	5

copyright (c) 1999, Enterprise Information Insights, Inc.

Management Competencies of Project Managers

MANAGEMENT SKILLS	IV	III	II	I
Delegation	3	4	4	5
Leadership	-	-	-	4
Managing Change	-	4	4	4
Managing Multiple Priorities	3	4	4	5
Meeting Management	3	4	4	5
Performance Management	-	3	3	4
Quality Management	3	3	3	4
Staff and Career Development	-	-	-	4
Staffing, Hiring, Selection	-	4	4	4

Business Competencies of Project Managers

BUSINESS SKILLS	IV	III	II	I
Budgeting	-	3	3	4
Business Assessment	-	4	4	4
Business Case Justification	-	-	-	4
Business Functions	3	3	3	4
Business Process Design	-	3	3	3
Company Products/Services	-	3	3	3
Core Application Systems	3	3	3	3
Customer Service	-	-	-	3
Implementation	4	5	5	5
Planning: Strategic and Tactical	-	3	3	3
Product/Vendor Evaluation	-	-	-	4
Standards, Procedures, Policies	3	4	4	4
Systems and Technology Integration	-	4	4	4
Testing	4	4	4	4

F I G U R E 19.17

Interpersonal Competencies of Project Managers

INTERPERSONAL SKILLS	IV	III	II	I
Conflict Management	3	4	4	4
Flexibility	3	4	4	4
Influencing	-	3	3	4
Interpersonal Relations	3	4	4	4
Negotiating	-	3	3	4
Relationship Management	-	4	4	5
Team Management/Building	3	4	4	4

copyright (c) 1999, Enterprise Information Insights, Inc.

N O T E S

1. For a more expansive treatment of the material presented in this chapter, see Robert K. Wysocki and James P. Lewis, *Achieving World-Class Project Management: A Career Development Guide* (Reading, MA: Perseus Publications, forthcoming).

2. Enterprise Information Insights, Inc. offers a Web-enabled version of the Organizational Readiness Assessment. For more information or to arrange for an assessment of your organization, contact EII at 508-791-2062 or by e-mail at rkw@eiiinc.com.

3. Enterprise Information Insights, Inc. offers a Web-enabled version of the Individual Competency Assessment. To get more information or to arrange to have the assessment

F I G U R E 19.18

Personal Competencies of Project Managers

PERSONAL SKILLS	IV	III	II	I
Creativity	3	4	4	5
Decision Making/Critical Thinking	-	4	4	5
Presentations	-	4	4	4
Problem Solving/Trouble Shooting	4	4	4	5
Verbal Communications	3	4	4	4
Written Communications	3	3	3	4

copyright (c) 1999, Enterprise Information Insights, Inc.

conducted at your organization, contact EII at 508-791-2062 or by e-mail at rkw@eiiinc.com.

4. Enterprise Information Insights, Inc. offers a Web-enabled service to assess skills and skill gaps of individuals and groups using self-assessments and user-defined 360 assessments. For more information or to arrange to have a skill assessment for your staff, contact EII at 508-791-2062 or by e-mail at rkw@eiiinc.com.

20 CHAPTER

Improving Your Communication Skills

It is a fact of life that when you survey people in organizations, they always bring up communication problems. This is probably the most widespread issue an organization faces. In spite of all the talk about information overload, people are hungry for information, and if they don't get the information they need, they make things up. So, often, begins the rumor mill.

There is, of course, a lot of talking going on in most organizations. There just isn't much communication taking place. The problem exists on both sides of the fence—the talker isn't being effective and the listener isn't practicing good listening skills.

Communicating is not just talking—it is both talking and listening. Thus, to teach a person good talking skills without also dealing with listening is to deal with only part of the problem. Project managers (in fact, all managers) have problems with both aspects of communicating. They don't

listen well when team members talk, and they don't talk in ways that their team members understand. Add to this that team members also don't communicate well and you have a standard formula for miscommunication.

The question is: Can you solve the problem yourself? If others don't listen well, can you do anything about it? Perhaps not completely, but you can improve the "hit rate" by improving your own speaking and listening skills.

There are five factors that affect whether a person is a good or poor communicator: *self-concept, listening, clarity of expression, coping with angry feelings,* and *self-disclosure* (Bienvenu, 1969).

SELF-CONCEPT

The most important factor affecting our communications with others is our self-concept. This is how we see ourselves. The self-concept is composed of many parts: who we are, what we stand for, what we do and do not do, what we value, what we believe, and so on. For most of us, some of these parts are very clear while other parts are vague or fuzzy. The Johari window, as shown in Figure 20.1, illustrates the point.

F I G U R E 20.1

The Johari Window

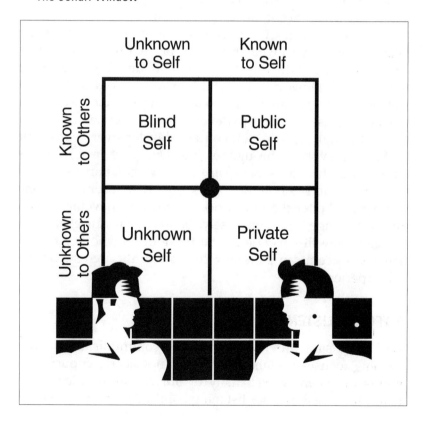

The Johari window shows that there are things that we know about ourselves and that others know about us. This is called our *public self*. There are also things about ourselves that we know, but that no one else knows. This is called our *private self*. Then there is the *unknown self*—those aspects of ourselves that neither we nor anyone else knows about. Finally, there is the part that we don't know but that everyone else knows. We are *blind* to this part of ourselves.

The core of our self-concept is formed early in childhood and is based on what family members tell us about ourselves. The "telling" is not necessarily verbal, of course. As children, we receive messages about who we are that are both verbal and nonverbal. There is evidence that just the amount of holding, nurturing, and "baby talk" that parents provide will affect our self-concept and chances of survival.

If the messages we receive as children say that we are okay—that we are loved and cared for, that we can do whatever we set out to do—then we will develop a positive self-concept. However, if as children we are told that we are *not* okay—that we are not loved and wanted, that we can't do a lot of things—we tend to develop low self-esteem.

Although the core self-concept develops very early, our self-image evolves throughout life. One way in which this happens is through *social comparison*. We compare ourselves with others to see how we "stack up." If we seem about the same as or better than most people, then we develop a positive self-image, and conversely. Self-concept can change as we gain new life experience. So those of us who begin with low self-esteem can gain new confidence through successful life experiences.

EFFECTIVE LISTENING

As I have said previously, much of communications skills training focuses on talking. There is not nearly enough emphasis on listening, yet many of our communication problems are caused by poor listening habits. An effective listener listens not only to the words but to the *meaning* of the words. This includes understanding what the speaker is *feeling*. Not attending to the speaker's feelings can cause that person to feel unappreciated and misunderstood.

It is for this reason that we should practice *active* listening, as opposed to passive listening. Passive listening occurs when we respond to the speaker by saying "Uh-huh," nodding affirmatively, or repeating, "I understand." The speaker has no way of knowing whether we really understand, or whether we simply think we understand.

> An effective listener listens not only to the words but to the *meaning* of the words.

In active listening, we repeat back to the speaker what we have heard, but we rephrase it in our own words. If we simply parrot the words used by the speaker, it will seem that we understand even when we don't. For example:

> *Speaker:* "There is a problem with this schedule. I don't think you have as many resources to do the work as you are showing."
>
> *Listener:* "You don't think I have enough resources to do the work?"
>
> *Speaker:* "Right."

Now this may seem almost trivial, and if we do it with every comment made by the speaker, we will be accused of being deaf or playing games. But it is a useful way to check our understanding when an issue is difficult—especially if it is emotional.

When people are upset with us, they almost always feel that we do not understand them and their position on an issue. Active listening is a way of assuring them that we have heard and understood.

Consider this exchange:

John: "I don't think you appreciate how hard I have been working to get this job finished on time. All you want is more, more, more!"

Jane: "You don't think I appreciate your hard work, John? Is that true?"

John: "You bet!"

Now John may still be upset with Jane, but at least he knows that Jane is listening to understand his viewpoint. With that, it is possible for them to resolve their conflict. Otherwise, they will arrive at an impasse.

Listening actively when you are presented with data or factual information is a very useful approach to understanding a situation. Problem solving involves understanding the problem, and unless you are careful to listen for the proper data, you may define the problem incorrectly.

There are two major reasons that people do not listen effectively. One is that they simply don't care what the speaker is saying. The other is that they are trying to think of a response to what the speaker just said, so they miss what the speaker is currently saying. Other causes of ineffective listening include being distracted by noises, activities nearby, or previous concerns. When it is important to listen, these distractions should be eliminated. Get away from the noise or nearby activity, if possible. If preoccupations with previous concerns are keeping you from listening, then ask the speaker to meet with you later, after you have had a chance to deal with your concerns.

SPEAKING CLEARLY

Some people seem oblivious to the fact that others do not understand them. They reason that, because what they are saying is clear to them, it must be clear to their listeners. A student raises a question in class. The instructor responds by going back through the original explanation in the very same words that were used the first time. The frustrated student may be tempted to say, "If those words had been any good, I wouldn't have had a question. Change the way you say it this time!"

To communicate effectively, follow these rules:

1. Know what *outcome* you want. Are you trying to inform? Get information? Give advice? Get the person to do something, change a behavior, or stop doing something? Are you trying to punish or shame the person verbally? Unless you are clear on your desired outcome, you may not communicate effectively.

2. Decide to *whom* you need to communicate. Is it the entire group? One person? It has always been a pet peeve of mine to see managers respond to undesirable behavior in one team member by writing a memo (or developing a written policy) to all group members telling them not to do what the offender did. In the first place, they probably had no intention of doing so, and in the second place, the memo to the group probably won't affect the behavior of the offender if she decides to misbehave again. The memo or policy is just a cop-out to avoid dealing face-to- face with the offender, and a manager who is afraid to confront employees who behave inappropriately should rethink his role.

3. Determine the best *mode* in which to communicate. Is it written, verbal, both? Putting things on paper can lead to problems, especially when you get angry and blast someone in writing. However, if you want to be sure that someone is clear on your instructions, you may want to write them out.

4. Use *nonverbal* clues to determine if you are getting the response that you want. Many students seem completely unaware that people in their classes are totally lost. I have often thought that it would make no difference to them if the room were empty—they

would give their lecture, pack up, and go home. Clearly, you need to pay attention to your listeners when you talk, and try to determine from their non-verbal responses if they are with you or not.

5. Acquire *flexibility*. Be willing and able to vary your communication until you manage to get through to the other person. If you continue to repeat yourself, using the same words, you are deadlocked.

DEALING WITH ANGER

Sometimes we deal with anger inappropriately and thus block communication with others. When I first entered the workforce, I had a manager who liked to say, "Leave your feelings outside when you come to work." Yet he wanted his people to be motivated. It never occurred to him that motivation and emotion have the same root—that is, feelings and motivation are both emotions. The real reason the manager wanted people to leave their anger outside was that he felt uncomfortable dealing with it.

The result of such a rule is that some people learn to suppress their anger, for fear that others will think their behavior is inappropriate. The problem is, this is saving up "brown stamps"—to use a term from transactional analysis (TA)—and eventually you "fill up your book" and "cash them in." Of course, the way you cash them in is to have an explosion. It may be an emotional explosion or it may be a physical explosion, in which your body literally "explodes" into a serious illness. Neither outcome is desirable.

Being able to express feelings appropriately is necessary if we are going to have healthy relationships with others. Bienvenu (1969) offers the following suggestions for dealing with your emotions:

1. Be *aware* of your feelings. When we are afraid of our emotions, we sometimes create a blind spot that keeps us from even knowing that we are feeling

anything. If you have done this, it may take some time for you to regain your awareness.

2. Admit that you have feelings—especially those considered "bad" or undesirable. We all have negative feelings sometimes. It is not human to be feelingless, or to have only positive feelings. We aren't robots.

3. Accept responsibility for what you do with your emotions. If you lash out at someone when you are angry, you must accept the consequences of that behavior.

4. Tell people how you are feeling. Congruent communication requires that there be an accurate match between what you are experiencing and what you are saying.

5. Learn from understanding your emotions. Ask yourself what caused you to feel as you did. Do this even with positive emotions.

SELF-DISCLOSURE

If you want to have really good relationships and good communications with others, you must be willing to disclose things about yourself that help them get to know you. This must be a mutual process, of course. If your associates are closed off, it will be hard to get to know them. The more you know about others, and others know about you, the more effective your communications can be. In terms of the Johari window, you are disclosing more of your private self to your associates.

It is virtually impossible to know and relate to people who never let you know anything about themselves except that which is superficial. Unfortunately, some companies foster such a climate of suspicion and fear that employees do not want you to know them, and any attempt to do so is met with resentment. These people see your attempt to get to know them as a way of taking advantage.

In one company, a manager wanted to enroll his children in a private school. He heard that a woman on the assembly line had her children in the school he was interested in, so he went to talk to her. When he asked if it was true that her children went to that school, her reaction shocked him. "It's none of your business," she said angrily, so he backed off. The next thing he knew, she went to human resources and complained about this invasion of her privacy. In such settings, it is nearly impossible to get to know members of your team.

CONTENT AND RELATIONSHIP

Every communication carries two components: (1) a message conveying your content and (2) a definition of relationship with the person or group you are addressing. Suppose I say to someone, "Let's go." The content is clear. I want to leave. The definition of relationship being expressed is one in which I feel it is okay to tell the person to leave with me, and can expect her to do so.

Contrast this with, "Shall we go?" The content is the same, but the definition of relationship is different. We would say that in the first instance the relationship is one of unequal status, whereas the second suggests a more equal status. If both parties see the relationship the same way (either equal or unequal), then the definition offered will be accepted. However, if the other person sees the relationship as equal and you define it as unequal, then your definition will most likely be rejected.

> Every communication carries two components: (1) a message conveying your content and (2) a definition of relationship with the person or group you are addressing.

All of us constantly have to deal with definition of relationship, whether we are conscious of it or not. Furthermore, it is impossible to communicate without offering a definition of relationship. How many times, on a plane or bus, have you sat next to people who stare out the window for the whole trip and never say a word? What did their silence convey to you about the way they viewed the relationship? Clearly, they did not want to engage you at all. They saw the relationship as nonexistent. So even silence communicates.

In technical terms, there are two types of relationships: *complementary* and *symmetrical.* A complementary relationship is one of unequal status, whereas a symmetrical relationship is one of equal status. It is interesting to note that symmetrical relationships can be stable over the long term (on average, we might say), but they are unstable from minute to minute. For example, my relationship with my wife may be symmetrical on average, but at any given moment she may "call the shots" and at another time I may do so. When either one of us is calling the shots, the relationship is momentarily complementary—unequal in status.

METACOMMUNICATION

Not only do we define relationships when we communicate: we also convey the true meaning of a remark through the *manner* in which we communicate. This is called metacommunication. It is communication *about* the communication. As an example, suppose someone comes into my office and I say, "Get out of my office," in an obviously joking way. The person knows not to take me seriously. This is the meta-aspect. The fact that I have jokingly told her to get out of my office also defines our relationship as one in which we are very comfortable with each other. We like to kid around.

Suppose, however, that I say, "Get out of my office," in a way that sounds serious, and therefore really means that the words are to be understood at face value. The person turns around to leave. If I really mean for the person to leave, then the communication and metacommunication are congruent. However, if I really don't mean for her to leave—if I am joking but she thinks I am serious—then the communication and metacommunication are incongruent, and she will be totally confused.

The other person always has to interpret the true meaning of a communication, and this is where the difficulty comes in. If she misinterprets my meaning and gets angry, then I am going to have to repair the damage to our relationship. Sometimes the mending is close to impossible, because she is convinced that she understood my meaning, and that I was serious.

PUNCTUATION

Consider the following exchange between me and my friend Celia, who thinks I have thrown her out of my office.

"Celia, I need to talk to you. When you came into my office earlier I was just joking when I told you to get out."

"Sure you were. You were serious, and you know it. I've never been so insulted in my life!"

"Come on, Celia, you know I was just joking. I would never throw you out of my office. You're welcome any time."

"Well, you sure sounded serious to me, and I think you're just trying to get out of it now."

"You're being silly, Celia. You know very well I wasn't serious."

"Well! Now you're calling me silly! I guess you don't want silly people in your office!"

"Well, if that's how you see it, I sure don't!"

"Fine!"

"Fine!"

Now note what happened. Ask Celia why she behaved as she did, and she'll tell you that she was only responding to my behavior. Ask me why I behaved as I did, and I'll tell you that I was only responding to Celia's behavior. After all, I complain. She's the one who misunderstood and overreacted.

Thus, I see my behavior as a response to Celia's behavior, and she sees her behavior as a response to mine. In fact, there is a sense in which I see her behavior as *causing* mine, and she will say the same, that my behavior caused her to behave as she did. This will be discussed in more detail in Chapter 22.

CONDITIONS REQUIRED FOR EFFECTIVE COMMUNICATION

Communication depends on the following conditions:

- ◆ **A common culture**. When technical and nontechnical people interact, there is no common culture. Using jargon and failing to explain technical points will result in failed communication. The engineering manager serves a translation role between nontechnical personnel and the engineering staff.

+ **Common expectations**. When expectations differ, communication suffers.

+ **Motivation to communicate**. You will have a hard time "getting through" to people who have decided they don't want to hear what you have to say.

SENSORY PREFERENCES AND COMMUNICATIONS

We gain knowledge about the world in which we live through the five senses. Most of us, in fact, prefer one of the five senses over the others, and find that we gain knowledge and understanding most easily through that sense. In our society, the primary system for communication are visual, then auditory, then kinesthetic (feelings).

Our language reflects the use of the sensory systems, as shown by the following examples:

1. VISUAL: I don't *see* how you got such a distorted *picture* of things.
2. AUDITORY: I *hear* what you are saying, but it still doesn't *sound* right.
3. KINESTHETIC: That doesn't *feel* right to me! I still can't get a *handle* on it.
4. SMELL: This proposal *smells* fishy to me!
5. TASTE: The whole affair left a bad *taste* in my mouth!

Note that, although smell and taste are seldom primary representational systems, they can be powerful memory joggers. When you smell a certain fragrance, you may be reminded of a former flame. Table 20.1 lists some of the more common expressions used in visual, auditory, and kinesthetic modalities.

T A B L E 20.1

Primary Representational Systems

Meaning	Kinesthetic	Visual	Auditory
I (don't) understand you.	What you are saying feels (doesn't feel) right to me.	I see (don't see) what you mean.	I hear (don't hear) what you are saying.
I want to communicate something.	I want to put you in touch with something.	I want to show you something.	I want to tell you something.
What do you mean?	I can't get a handle on that.	I don't see what you are saying.	What are you saying?
Do you understand me?	Does that feel okay to you?	Do you see what I mean?	Do you hear what I'm saying?

Since people process information most efficiently when it is presented in the sensory system of their choice, you will find it helpful to notice which system they use and communicate accordingly. Auditory people, for example, are turned off by long reports. A quick verbal summary is adequate. Visual people, on the other hand, want pictures, diagrams, and more, in order to process information efficiently. And kinesthetic individuals want to *experience* it firsthand. They like walk-throughs and other experiential ways of dealing with information. They prefer a hands-on approach.

21

CHAPTER

Managing Business-to-Business Marketing and Communication Projects Successfully

By Julian Stubbs*

*Julian Stubbs has worked in advertising and marketing his whole career, on both the consultancy side and the client side. Today he is CEO of The Strategy Works, a specialist marketing and communications company with offices in London, England, and Stockholm, Sweden. BASE-UP is a trademark of The Strategy Works.

INTRODUCTION: THE BASE-UP™ SYSTEM

This chapter is about how to manage business-to-business marketing and communications projects successfully from a client's perspective. It is written for people relatively new to the area who want to broaden their understanding of what marketing campaign planning is all about. Typical projects include the creation of campaigns involving such areas as advertising, literature, direct mail, public relations, and graphic design. The chapter also provides some insight into what third-party suppliers such as advertising agencies, public relations consultants, and designers will expect from you as a client.

The chapter does not go into the actual mechanics of setting-up a project flow-chart, since the topic is well covered in Section Three of this book. Rather, it focuses on the major topics and phases that you will go through in running such projects as well as on the composition and handling of the project team.

At The Strategy Works we have developed a structured five-step program to help us manage a client's project successfully. This program is called BASE-UP™. The acronym stands for Brief, Audit, Strategy, Execution, and follow-UP. The model very much fits the Lewis Method presented in Chapter 2. This proven marketing

BASE-UP: A structured approach to handling marketing and communications projects.

management tool will help you set out the main steps of any marketing project and show you how to approach each of the tasks to be considered within those steps.

A number of years ago, while working for a large London-based advertising agency, I noticed how unstructured the majority of marketing communication projects were, on the client side as well as the agency side. Disorganization seemed to breed disorganization. It wasn't that things didn't get done—they did. And they were highly creative. But the waste, subsequent cost, and chaos caused en route were immense, to say nothing of the stress levels that are inherent in the business.

I promised myself from that moment that if I ever was in a position to work in a more organized way, I would.

A number of years later I moved to Sweden, where structure and orderliness are inbred—a matter of course to most Swedes. It is the ultimate planned society. In fact, the

Swedish social system is managed as one large project with, amazingly, most people generally sticking to the stated goals and rules.

In working with a number of large Swedish clients, I realized quickly that I still needed to deliver creative excellence while doing so in an organized way. The result was the BASE-UP program—a structured approach to managing creative marketing communications effectively. The steps in the BASE-UP system are shown in Figure 21.1.

STEP 1: THE BRIEF

The starting point for managing any marketing communications project successfully has to be the brief. This is the method of detailing all of the relevant information regarding the marketing task you are undertaking. It will give outside vendors the information they need to create the right results for you. The brief is without doubt the single most important step in any marketing and communications project. Simply put, if the brief is correct, the work and creative approach will be correct nine times out of ten. (Note that the brief is equivalent to step 2 of the Lewis Method presented in Chapter 2. As was pointed out in that chapter, it is where projects often fail.)

Too often, however, the brief is poorly managed with too little time spent on it, and in the enthusiasm to get to the fun part (working on the creative execution), the brief is ill-defined.

Agencies and outside vendors can be guilty themselves of shortening the briefing stage and then hoping the creative types will produce "stunning" ideas to put right a flimsy brief.

Even worse, in some instances the clients do not really have a clear idea of their goal or objective—what they need to produce. As a result, they wait until the creative work is presented as visuals or scamps[1] before deciding what they really want to say with their communication! "The client loves the advertisements but thinks there're wrong" is a phrase heard too often in any agency and does not count as any

F I G U R E 21.1

The Base-Up System

B STEP ONE – BRIEF The correct parameters are defined with the client to help build the brief. This important document will be the benchmark against which all elements of the work will be judged.

A STEP TWO – AUDIT At this stage existing research is studied or new research, internal or external as required, is carried out. The Strategy Works gets intimately involved in the research and analysis phase to provide the right context for the brief to be truly evaluated.

S STEP THREE – STRATEGY Based on the brief and using the research as a foundation, The Strategy Works will give a playback strategy brief to the client detailing the strategy to be undertaken, its execution plan and timing.

E STEP FOUR – EXECUTION The Strategy Works will then work alongside existing advertising or PR agencies if required, or can work with another partner company in the Matrix network. The Strategy Works stays with the project at this vital stage ensuring that the strategic goals are being met in the actual execution of the work. An important point to note here is that we specialise in working with clients' overseas partner or subsidiary companies, ensuring they are fully part of the implementation, planning and execution process.

U
P STEP FIVE – FOLLOW-UP The project is not finished until a full follow-up and evaluation is performed. This is all documented and presented back to the client for final sign-off and discussion of any subsequent actions that are needed.

measure of success. And this is not only a little frustrating for the creative folks but very wasteful of time and money.

Function of the Brief

The main function of the brief is to give direction to the work and, most important, to answer the question "What do we want to achieve?" The brief is the opportunity for you to put down all the relevant facts as you see them. Any existing research data should be handed over at the same time to help support the brief. It could well be that additional research is needed and will be carried out during the audit stage (see below) to help substantiate the whole campaign. The next section shows the format of a briefing form as used by one of Europe's leading business-to-business advertising and communications companies: MMC International, based in London and Stockholm. As you work through the main headings, you will start to understand the main function of the brief. You will also learn what the agency or consultant wants from you and what it takes to produce the right creative solution. Although the format can vary a little, most good agency briefs cover the same ground.

Information Obtained in the Brief

Following is an explanation of the information asked for by the brief.

1. Background Information

The first task is to give all relevant background information that will be of value to the agency or consultant. It's a good idea to give a general overview or synopsis of information you plan to cover later on in more detail. Identify the main goal of the campaign and provide product information, pricing details, other linked promotional activities, sales force information, and so on—whatever is relevant and will assist the understanding of the campaign or marketing project goals.

If the brief relates to a specific product, explain how the product will be used, describe the alternative, and detail the specific benefits the user will derive.

2. Market Information

Here is the place to give background market information. Describe the conditions of the marketplace you are or will be competing in. Is it growing, declining, or segmenting? If relevant, outline the history of the market and the major forces within it. What are the main market drivers? Technology, price, delivery systems? Try to be as specific, straightforward, and jargon-free as you can so people from outside your own business area can understand the information.

3. Competitor Information

What are your competitors up to? What products do they have that compete in this sector? How are their products positioned against yours? Be as realistic here as you can be. Be honest about the reasons why customers buy competitive products. Your competitors must be doing something right, and understanding them will help you create an approach that will work successfully against them.

4. Target Audience

Who are you trying to reach with your campaign? Is it just the user of the product? Is it more than one group? Are senior managers as well as purchasing agents important in the decision as well? Describe them as best you can and give a realistic profile of the people you will be targeting.

5. Campaign Goal

Put simply, what result do you want from your target audience? Do you want people to pick up the phone and call you? Are you expecting them to buy a product or service off the page? Do you want to alter their opinions about your product or service and help them start to view it in a different way? Do you want people to see your company as younger and more dynamic than they presently do? Be specific. Remember, goals involving the changing of attitudes and opinions will normally take a good while to achieve—so don't expect miracles from one advertisement. It is the cumulative effect over a period of time that will have the desired result.

6. Essential Message

Now we come to the heart of the brief. The essential message is the single most important part of the brief for the creative people working on the marketing communications project. Keep the essential message very realistic and don't waffle. The shorter the better. One way to view the essential message is to pretend that you have key customers in front of you and need to explain, in just 15 words, the one thing about your product or service that will convince people to buy your product instead of a competitor's.

7. Supporting Evidence

If the essential message is the most important part of a brief, then the supporting evidence is a close second. Here you need to provide the hard proof that your claim in the essential message is fact and not fiction. Market research data, customer studies, and independent assessments can all help in supporting the claim made in the essential message.

Too often, clients make claims about their products that are not justified. The biggest problem is that the clients are just kidding themselves, and their claims will probably not produce the most effective promotion.

As an example, if a competitor really has the quickest "gizmo" on the market, don't make a claim that your gizmo is just as quick. The customers will know the truth if this claim is not substantiated. Look instead to reposition the competitor by perhaps showing (if it is supportable with facts) that your own product is much easier to use. In fact, it has a much higher overall speed of use over X number of operations.

The message is: *Don't try to copy but look to reposition.*

8. Mandatory Details

Use this section to furnish all details and mandatory items. These include instructions on use of trade names, corporate identity comments, typeface specifications, length of body copy, pictures or graphics to be used, and so on.

9. Timing

Finally, when does all this have to happen? What happens when? In the case of advertisements, the deadlines are normally very "fixed" since you will have booked media space and the publication will be waiting for your copy. Otherwise you will be paying for a large piece of white space with nothing in it! In the case of an overall campaign brief, decide on presentation: When will the various elements in the campaign appear?

Again, be realistic with timing. Things can be done extremely quickly under abnormal time constraints, but this is no way to organize a solid campaign. It will cost you more in stress and mistakes and much more in vendor costs, since everything will be on a rush charge.

STEP 2: THE AUDIT

The audit stage is really the chance to validate a lot of the information contained within the brief. If the supporting information or analysis is in the brief itself, all the better. This is not always the case, however. As noted earlier, a common pitfall of many briefs is the unsubstantiated claim. The client simply asserts that its product is faster/more economic/more recognized/more advanced than a competitor's.

The client will also tell you, with authority, that customers love the product and are quite happy paying more for it!

The audit stage is there to provide the proof and evidence that may still be lacking. Many a brief has been amended in light of some research "facts" that the client omitted from the original analysis. Finally, the audit stage can provide excellent benchmarking opportunities for judging the future success of any marketing campaign.

Secondary versus Primary Research

Information that is already available to you is called secondary research data. It is based on accessing and digesting research that has already been carried out. Primary research is that which is carried out in a new study, often for the specific purpose of bringing new information to an understanding of a client's situation.

Secondary Research: Internal Sources

Much vital information can be found simply by accessing existing records. The company's own operating records can often throw a huge amount of light on a marketing situation. Records may show customer groups and segments, geographic sales, advertising costs and returns, distribution costs, customer complaints, and sales patterns.

Secondary Research: External Sources

Secondary data accessed from external sources offer a potentially enormous area of research. State and federal governments publish a large amount of "official" data on many markets. To this can be added the vast store of information published by banks, stockbrokers, trade and professional associations, and media organizations.

Secondary data can also be purchased through a variety of research companies, many with distinct specialty areas. Finally, the company itself may have an archive of commissioned or purchased external research reports that can be accessed for additional reference.

Primary Research

Conducting primary or original research can involve many different areas of focus. In the consumer arena, highly professional and targeted research is often critical in helping determine the correct approach for a marketing or advertising campaign. Sophisticated and proven techniques, developed over many years, can provide valuable information.

In the business-to-business or industrial market, research is used far less and there are additional complications to be aware of. Who makes the purchase decision, for example? In industrial marketing a number of different individuals can influence the purchase decision, and all these views should be taken into consideration at the audit stage.

Qualitative versus Quantitative Research

In general, research can be divided between qualitative and quantitative.

Qualitative research gives us an in-depth view on a subject, often through focus groups, personal interviews, and one-on-one phone interviews. This form of interviewing means that the relative cost of qualitative research can be high.

What we are really seeking here is high-quality, in-depth information on the subject being researched. This is without doubt one of the most demanding areas of research, since so many variable factors are involved. The form of questioning, the moderator's ability, and the data analysis are all important considerations that can dramatically influence the result.

The art of conducting good qualitative research is to elicit the information you need without asking for it directly.

Too many industrial marketing managers assume that the solution to all their marketing problems is to conduct research and simply ask customers what they want. "What would you like to see in an advertisement?" "What color should our product be?" "When would you like us to send you direct mail?"

This approach is not only supremely naïve, it is also a total delegation of the responsibility of any manager. If your customers know the answers better than you do, they should be doing your job!

If qualitative research gives us an in-depth view, then quantitative research gives us some numbers and scale. *Quantitative* research is focused on producing reliable statistics to support a proposition. The sample size should be sufficiently large to allow us to draw conclusions as to how many and what sorts of customers think about products and services in a given way.

Typical techniques employed include mass teleresearch, mail questionnaires, Internet-based research, and short one-on-one questionnaire surveys—all conducted with a *statistically significant and representative* sample size.

Finally, when the two types of research are employed together, they can be very insightful. First conduct qualitative research to reveal in-depth views and attitudes, then use quantitative research to add some scale and support.

STEP 3: STRATEGY

The brief has been taken and examined. The audit has brought further relevant facts to the brief to inform our thinking and add substance and benchmarking possibilities. We now move to the strategy stage, where all the thinking and evaluation come together in a plan of action to meet our goals.

> Never let strategy get in the way of tactics.

Making the Strategy Really Work

At The Strategy Works, devising strategies that really work is looked upon as a mix of art and science. Many comparisons have been made between business strategies and military strategies, and the analogy is worthwhile. On the battlefield or in the boardroom, the same principles apply.

To begin with, a strategy must be responsive. Far too many strategies are set in stone, steel, and concrete and are not adjusted for any reasons: "Our strategy must be carried out as planned!" This approach will result in missing the very real possibilities and opportunities that usually present themselves enroute to achieving most strategic goals. And at the end of the day achieving the goal *is* the objective, not just playing out the strategy for its own sake.

In a military context, when two opposing armies prepare to meet on the field of battle, the opposing generals look to their strategic plans for victory. What happens, however, when the day of battle arrives and predicted "good weather" turns into a downpour, making a solid field into a quagmire? The winning general is the one who can amend his strategy to take account of very real "tactical" considerations. Business strategies work in exactly the same way. Things happen that are not always foreseen. A competitor brings out a new product line; another competitor radically lowers its price. On the positive side, a competitor pulls out of a market segment you had both been fighting over. The lesson is "Never let the strategy get in the way of tactics."

A second point to bear in mind is that strategies, military or business, must be dosed with a good measure of "reality-based thinking." They must take into account the reality of the organization through which the plan of action will be carried out.

The general, in his bunker putting forward grand plans and sophisticated ideas and strategies, will not succeed if his troops are not in tune with his thinking and capable of carrying out the plan of action. Specifically, his immediate commanders must be the champions of the plan and make that plan a reality. They must also be the ones to inject a good dose of realism into any strategy.

Plans can get bogged down or even derailed by the *inertia effect* of large organizations. A marketing and communications plan can fail at this vital step. So the simple messages are:

- Keep the strategy flexible.
- Make a big reality check and find yourself some champions.

Project Planning and the Strategy Stage

How do we apply this knowledge to managing a project at the vital strategic stage? There are some immediate rules we should keep in mind:

1. Let everyone in the project group know at the outset that the objective is to achieve the project goal, not to rigidly carry out the strategy.
2. Allow the strategy to change in response to tactical considerations and opportunities. Make sure everyone in the project group is aware of the change and why as soon as possible.
3. Remember that a strategy change is bound to affect critical original objectives and criteria, such as timing, costs, and execution. Make sure all these steps are amended, and all affected parties are aware of the implications to the project.
4. On any marketing and communications project, the project team itself is often the critical factor in solving any organizational problems you may face. The project team must become the immediate project champions. Otherwise the inertia effect sets in. If a certain segment of the organization will be most affected by a project or is most opposed to it, the wise approach is to invite the most critical people in that segment to be project members themselves. Even if you cannot always win them over to the project completely, having them on the inside is safer than having them on the outside.

STEP 4: EXECUTION

One simple rule applies to the execution phase: The devil is in the detail. Staying on top of that detail is *everything* in a marketing project. I have seen wonderful concepts and ideas turn into very average campaigns through lack of attention to detail.

As noted in the strategy section, we must never lose sight of tactical considerations and opportunities when executing a marketing project. Such opportunities

> The devil is in the detail.

will occur and can often add enormous value when fully taken.

The Marketing Project Team

Making sure the project team is set up correctly at the beginning of the project is always a vital consideration. There are some points worth noting with project teams:

1. **Project sponsor.**   One person alone should be appointed project sponsor. This is the person who, at the end of the day, takes responsibility for the success or failure of the project. This is the person who, when called upon to make big decisions, is capable of doing so. The role of adjudicator also falls to the project sponsor.

2. **Project manager.**   There should then be a separate project manager for the hands-on management of the project. This person is responsible for running the project, ensuring that time schedules and budgets are met and keeping all group members fully informed as to what is happening as the project progresses.

3. **Project group members.**   I have always believed that having good representation, from all interested parties, is vital to any marketing project. Not only does it give a wider spread of experience to the project, but having all parties adequately represented, even those who might not fundamentally agree with overall marketing project goals, is better than ex-

cluding them from the project altogether. By working with them in the project, you might well be able
to bring them around. At worst, at least they cannot
say they did not know what was going on!

4. **Consultants.** Your marketing project may need to
employ consultants. Indeed, for a typical campaign
you may end up using several different consultants.
Coordination is the key here, and the task should
fall to the project manager. Whenever consultants
take part in an action or attend a meeting, they
should confirm what happened in a written contact
report. At The Strategy Works we send a contact report after every main contact with the client, con-
firming what was said or what happened. All
marketing projects should employ them.

Visuals or Roughs

Often in a marketing project you will be working with consultants or agencies that need to present visual ideas to you
at an early stage. These are most often called "visuals" or
"roughs" or sometimes "scamps."[2] The visual is an artistic interpretation of what the final piece will look like. Often the
visual is filled in with dummy text to represent where the final copy will be placed and how much copy there will be.

Remember the visual is just that. Don't be intimated by
the agency or consultant who presents it as a "work of art"! It
is, after all, just a working document that will need enhance-
ments and changes. Still, if the brief has been well written,
the visual should provide you with a good starting point for
what the finished piece will look like.

Photography

You might well need to commission photography in your
marketing project. A very simple rule applies here. Hire the

best photographer you can afford. A picture does speak a thousand words.

> Hire the best photographer you can afford.

Whenever I have tried to cut corners by hiring a cheaper photographer, I have always regretted it. Get the best you can afford.

Signing Off

As a project progresses, text or copy will have to be approved, visuals amended, and graphics refined. If you are the client, try to make the consultant's job easier by coordinating the sign-off process. If you are the project manager on a marketing project, have the consultant send you the piece of work needing "approval" only. Make your own comments and changes, then pass the work on to relevant members of the project team. Ask for their sign-off approval or amendments and comments. This way the consultant or agency will have to deal with just one "set" of changes or comments, and the process will work a lot more smoothly, to say nothing of being cheaper!

Strong Creative Work

Rarely, if ever, have I seen a good promotional campaign that everybody in a company agrees with or endorses. We all have different opinions about approach, writing style, and so on. So remember you cannot please everyone and you are bound to ruffle a few feathers if the creative work on a campaign is strong and stands out. If you are using an agency or consulting firm to produce the work, remember you are not paying people to produce wallpaper. The first rule of a promotional piece is that it has to stand out from the crowd. (The second rule is that it must make a relevant statement about the uniqueness of your product.)

So, be brave and don't water down great creative work.

STEP 5: FOLLOW-UP

Of all the neglected areas in marketing, I would rate follow-up as the most important area that everybody forgets. In
the Lewis model, this is Step 15: the lessons-learned review.
So much can be learned at this stage and applied to future
planning, campaigns, and promotions. So much can be
learned too from the dreaded topic of failure, no matter how
sensitive marketing people are to it. There is value even in
failure—the value of learning *what went wrong* and being able
to apply that knowledge to future campaign plans.

But many people fail to take this final step.

The Marketing Project Scorecard

At The Strategy Works we like to conduct a formal project
sign-off, asking the client to complete a marketing project
scorecard of how successful a particular project has been.
This is simply a way of reviewing and recording the facts of
the project. A generic project scorecard is shown in Figure
21.2. Using it as a guide, you can easily shape a more specific
scorecard for your own marketing project needs.

The Importance of Following Up

Public relations consultants, Makovsky & Company, based in
New York, have really set the standard in the area of client
quality control and follow-up programs. *Inc.* magazine and
the *PR Strategist* both ran stories on their approach.
Makovsky clients are asked to complete an assessment form
similar to the marketing project scorecard in Figure 21.2. Clients rate how well the consulting firm is doing on their be-
half on projects. Their assessment goes pretty deep, even
extending into details on how sensitive the firm is to the client company's culture.

Too few PR companies or advertising agencies take
enough time with follow-up. In my opinion, the task is crucial.

F I G U R E 21.2

Marketing Project Scorecard

When a weighted answer is requested on a scale of 1 to 5, 5 denotes that the project met expectations completely and 1 denotes that the result was far from expectations. Circle the number that best reflects the outcome.

1. How closely did the project meet the original objectives?

    1   2   3   4   5

    Please give some commentary.

    _____

    _____

    _____

    _____

2. If the project objectives were changed en route, how closely did the project meet the new objectives?

    1   2   3   4   5

    Please give some commentary.

    _____

    _____

    _____

    _____

3. Did the project meet the original time plan objectives?

    1   2   3   4   5

    Please give some commentary.

    _____

    _____

    _____

    _____

Continued

F I G U R E 21.2 (Continued)

Marketing Project Scorecard

---

4.   Were the budgetary and financial <u>costs</u> of the project met?

                          1   2   3   4   5

     Please give some commentary.

     _____

     _____

     _____

     _____

5.   Were the budgetary and financial sales/income objectives of the
     project met?

                          1   2   3   4   5

     Please give some commentary.

     _____

     _____

     _____

     _____

6.   If the projects goals were not short-term sales or financially
     driven, were these other objectives measurably met?

                          1   2   3   4   5

     Please give some commentary.

     _____

     _____

     _____

     _____

                                                          Continued

F I G U R E 21.2 (Concluded)

Marketing Project Scorecard

7. Give a review of how well the project team worked.

   _____

   _____

   _____

   _____

   _____

8. What worked best about this project?

   _____

   _____

   _____

   _____

9. What did not work well in the project and what would you change next time?

   _____

   _____

   _____

   _____

   _____

10. Any thoughts about what we could do better next time?

   _____

   _____

   _____

   _____

   _____

CONCLUSION

We conclude with the most difficult question of all: How do you make your marketing campaign convince, persuade, or influence the mindset of those you are communicating with?

Remember this. Telling people something is not the same as helping them understand it. Advertisements that shout "We are the best" will probably only elicit the response, "Well they would say that, wouldn't they?"

Don't shout. But whisper loudly.

The secret is that well-executed campaigns encourage people to do some thinking. Once they themselves understand a clever proposition, they can make their own judgments as to whether to believe you or not.

So don't shout. But whisper loudly.

N O T E S

1. "Scamp" is the name given to outline visual ideas presented by an agency or consultant.

22
CHAPTER

The Need for Systems Thinking in Project Management

LINEAR VERSUS SYSTEMS THINKING

Unless you are very young or in some way exceptional, you almost undoubtedly learned to think in linear causal terms. I say this because a few schools are beginning to teach systems thinking, some at the urging of Dr. Jay Forrester, one of the pioneers of the discipline.

For most of us, however, the proposition that cause-effect relationships can be described as "A causes B" seems reasonable, and perhaps irrefutable. This has been so often our experience of the world that we seldom stop to think that things do not always operate in this manner. When an accident happens, we ask, "What caused it?" If two children get into a fight, we ask, "Who started it?" More often than not, the children point at each other, adamantly claiming, "He did!"

Adults tend to get frustrated at that response. When my sister and I fought as children, my father would ask, "Who started it?" We would both accuse the other. He would get annoyed at this parry and threaten to punish both of us if the *guilty party* didn't confess. In his mind, A causes B. It could not be possible that A causes B causes A, but that is exactly how it works in systems terms.

You might say that, at the microsecond level, one party made the first move. However, there is communication at both the verbal and nonverbal levels, and the nonverbal channel is operating continuously in both directions. Since some, if not most, of the influence between humans is a function of the nonverbal channel, that influence is operating simultaneously. Again, the process is circular, not linear.

> In human interaction, A causes B causes A.

In systems thinking, you must abandon linear causality and talk in terms of circular causal effects. This is because systems involve *feedback*, which introduces circularity. The concept is illustrated in Figure 22.1. When you heat your home in the winter, the thermostat senses the room temperature and tells the furnace to turn on when the temperature drops below a preset level. As the heat causes the room to warm up, the thermostat sends another signal to the furnace, telling it to shut down.

We can say, then, that as the temperature drops the furnace comes on and causes the temperature to rise, which causes the furnace to stop, which causes the temperature to drop—and so on, in a limitless number of cycles. Notice how convoluted our language becomes when we try to describe circularity. Our language itself is inherently linear. For example:

Johnny hit the ball.

Johnny is the subject, hit is the action, and ball is the object. Johnny is A in the equation "A causes B," and the ball is B. The causal link is *hit*. Notice that the verb *hit* can be re-

F I G U R E 22.1

Heating System

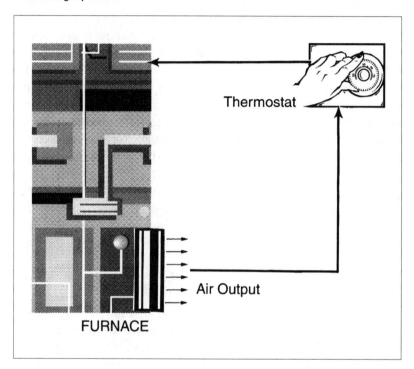

placed with all kinds of action descriptors: stole, dropped, held, threw, saw, accepted, liked, and so on.

It would be just as accurate to say that the ball hit Johnny's bat, as the bat swung through an arc, and rebounded at almost the same velocity at which it hit the bat. It would be just as accurate. But it would take forever to say.

Consider this sentence: "Johnny cried until his mother gave him some cake and then he smiled." It is a linear flow, but it does involve a reciprocal action. The action goes from A to B and back to A. Johnny cries, which causes his mother to give him some cake, which causes him to smile. A causes B causes A.

THE LANGUAGE OF MANAGING

This same linear causal thinking carries over into managing. Managers are supposed to "make things happen." One common definition of managing is that "a manager gets work done through other people." This suggests that the manager is a causal agent and that she does no work herself. A causes B.

Now suppose the employee does not do what the manager has directed should be done? Then the manager will respond. She may give the directive again, probably in more forceful terms. If there is still no response, she may take disciplinary action. How do we understand this exchange in systems terms? The manager is A and the employee is B. A causes B causes A causes B causes A. The employee's response to the first directive causes the manager to give another directive, which elicits another response from the employee, which causes another directive (or discipline) from the manager, and so on.

Causality in human relations, then, is circular, and must be drawn as shown in Figure 22.2.

There are times when the action of one person causes the other person to do more of what he was doing and other times when the action causes him to do less. For example, behavioral reinforcement theory suggests that rewarding a person for performing well on the job will usually make him try to perform even better in the future. Thus, positive reinforcement (sometimes called "strokes") increases desired performance. The relationship is plotted in Figure 22.3.

Conversely, negative reinforcement should cause a behavior to diminish. If the behavior being displayed is undesired, then negative reinforcement should extinguish it. Unfortunately, there are times when desired behavior is also extinguished because it is negatively reinforced. Figure 22.4 presents the outcome.

It is interesting to consider the interaction between a manager and employee in terms of behavioral reinforcement. If a manager strokes an employee for good performance and the employee performs even better in the future, what effect

F I G U R E 22.2

Circularity in Human Relations

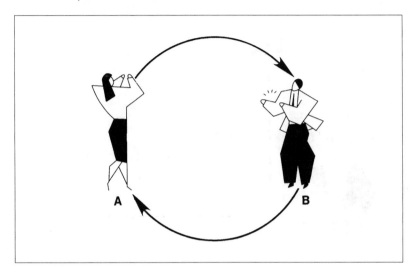

F I G U R E 22.3

Positive Reinforcement Increases Desired Behavior

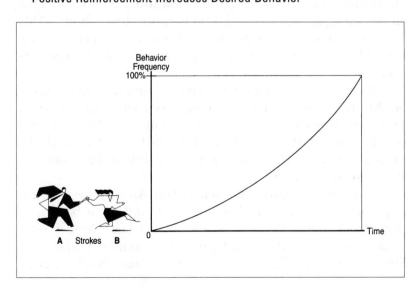

F I G U R E 22.4

Negative Reinforcement Extinguishes Behavior

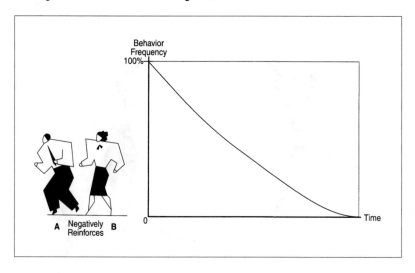

does this have on the manager? She is rewarded for stroking the employee. What does she do? She strokes him even more. His performance improves. She is rewarded. She strokes the employee again, and so on. (Who is controlling whom?) This is called a positive feedback loop, in which each action is followed by a reaction of increasing strength. Can it go on forever? No.

Eventually the employee becomes satiated with strokes or the manager becomes fatigued from so much stroking. There are limits to growth in any system. Note that as a person becomes satiated with strokes, each additional stroke loses some value. Thus, there is nonlinearity in the system, as shown in Figure 22.5.

The opposite effect is also possible. An employee suffering from Stroke Deficit Disorder, a term I have borrowed from organization development specialist Lee Kleese (1996), values strokes much more highly than someone who is in Stroke Overload. People tend to suffer from Stroke Deficit

The Value of Strokes Diminishes as the Quantity Increases

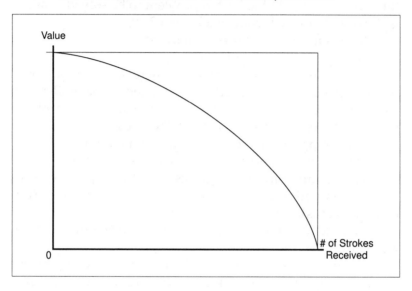

Disorder at the left side of the curve in Figure 22.5 and to suffer Stroke Overload on the right side of the curve.

Control in Relationships

In all human interaction there is a constant struggle to define the relationship. There are basically two kinds of relationships, as defined by status. Symmetrical relationships are based on equal status; complementary relationships are based on unequal status. Every communication between two individuals carries a proposed definition of the relationship, as defined by status. Note that the communication can be verbal or nonverbal. Nonverbal aspects of a communication include body gestures and/or posture, tone of voice, inflections, phrasing, and so on. Verbal communication is strictly the words themselves.

Consider the following question:

"Can you *solve* the problem?"

When the word *"solve"* is stressed, the meaning is something like, "Is it possible for the problem to be solved at all, or is it likely that it will come back again?"

Now suppose the stress is changed:

"Can *you* solve the problem?"

The meaning is very different. There seems to be doubt that this particular individual can solve the problem. Perhaps someone else can, but not this person. The meaning of the words has changed just by shifting the stress.

Now suppose a supervisor says to an employee:

"Have your report to me by 3 o'clock tomorrow."

This communication suggests that the supervisor sees the relation with this employee as very complementary (unequal in status). Compare this with:

"Would you please get your report to me by 3 o'clock tomorrow?"

In both cases, the message is the same: The supervisor wants the report by 3 o'clock tomorrow. However, in the second case the relationship definition offered by the supervisor is more equal in status or symmetrical.

Does it matter?

Sometimes it does. In American culture, we recognize that there are status differentials between supervisors and employees, but we do not like them to be emphasized too strongly. If the employee feels that the supervisor is "coming on too strong," then he may get angry. A conflict can result in which the two try to define the relationship in mutually acceptable terms.

It is bad enough when people have to interpret relationship definitions from the nonverbal component of a communication. It is even worse when one of them offers a definition opposite to the one he really wants.

Let's Go out for Dinner

Lee Kleese, whom I cited previously, has a wonderful example. You come home from work dead tired. Your significant other says, "Dear, I've had a really hard day and obviously you have too, so why don't we go out for dinner?"

"That's a great idea," you say. "What would you like to eat?"

"I don't care. What would you like to eat?"

Now you say, "I don't care," but inside you're thinking, "If you loved me as much as I love you, you'd say steak."

"Well, if it really doesn't matter, I'd like to try that new Chinese restaurant. Everyone says it's really good."

There may be a momentary flash of disappointment on your face, but this quickly changes to a forced smile and you say, "Okay. Let's go."

Inside you're thinking, "Chinese! That doesn't have *anything* to do with steak. I'll go, but you owe me one."

Some time goes by. You come home from work again, dead tired, and your significant other says, "Dear, I'm really tired, and you seem to be also. Why don't we go out to dinner?"

"Great idea," you say. "What would you like to eat?"

"I don't care."

"Me either." But the little voice inside is saying, "If you loved me as much as I love you, you'd say *steak*."

"Well, if you really don't care, I'd like to try that Italian place on Vine Avenue. Margie says it's really good."

"Italian!" the little voice screams. "That doesn't have anything to do with steak."

This time, the little voice wins. "I don't want to eat Italian," you say. "I want to eat steak."

"Well, why didn't you say so?" says your significant other politely. "Let's go."

So you go eat steak.

Do you think you're going to enjoy it?

Not a chance!

Now the problem here is that you have offered a definition of your relationship with your significant other that is symmetrical. What you really would like to do, of course, is call the shots and choose steak. When your significant other chooses something else, you get upset. It would be much clearer if you had said, "Well, I'd like to have a steak. Maybe we can have steak this time and Chinese the next (or vice versa)." When you agree that one person chooses this time and the other chooses the next, that says the relationship is symmetrical over the long run but complementary for the specific choice. When both parties agree to this, there is no problem.

You notice that, in systems terms, the system is trying to adjust itself for stability. It turns out, though, that the most unstable system is one that is symmetrical. A tiny shift causes it to become complementary. A system that is inherently complementary, however, can experience shifts in either direction and will remain stable. This is why people who are highly concerned that they be treated as equal in status with everyone else are always frustrated. They constantly see signs that the relationship is unequal, and they attempt to restore balance. That attempt may be met with a counter-response aimed at keeping the system unbalanced, and thus a conflict develops.

This is not to suggest that all relationships would be better if they involved unequal status. It is important to recognize that no relationship can ever be totally equal all the time for every situation. The only thing we can achieve is equal status on the average.

Conflict in Management

Inevitably there are conflicts in human relations. Conflict occurs when one person frustrates the concerns of another person. Those concerns include goals, values, self-interests, status, and control. This is one area in which systems thinking is essential if we are to understand and deal with conflict.

Remember the example of two children arguing? When asked who started it, each blames the other. This is because *each sees his own behavior as a response to the behavior of the other child!* The way this works is shown in Figure 22.6.

F I G U R E 22.6

Punctuation in Human Relationships

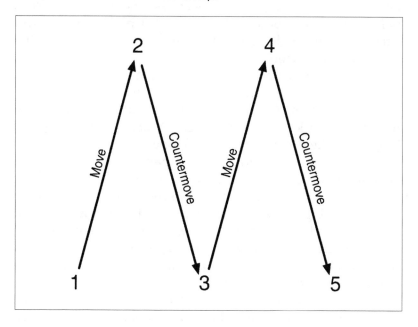

Person A behaves. This is the arrow 1-2. Person B responds, as sequence 2-3. Person A responds to that behavior as 3-4. This goes on as a long series of interactions that we can call *move-countermove, move-countermove*. Now, as I have said previously, if you ask each person why she behaved as she did, she will tell you that she was only responding to the other person's behavior. Person A sees the exchange as sequence 2-3-4, while person B sees it as 1-2-3. This is called *punctuation* in communication (Watzlawick, Beavin, and Jackson, 1967).

In some cases, once such an interaction begins, it becomes almost impossible to stop. Each side sees his behavior as a response to that of the other. As noted in Chapter 20, such a sequence is called a *game without end*, and naturally, it is dead serious. Examples of such games without end are the

Middle East conflict and the religious conflict that has gone on in Northern Ireland for so long. There have been many attempts to resolve those controversies, and they have been only temporarily successful. The conflict breaks out all over again when one side makes a move that is seen by the other as similar to previous moves.

There is only one way to end a game without end, and that is to break the pattern. This is an important lesson for project managers. When conflicts break out in project teams, it is often unproductive to try to get at causes. Each party will just blame the other. When this happens, it is more productive to find some way to break the pattern. This means you have to get at least one party to the conflict to abandon the normal behavioral response and do the opposite of what he has been doing. Here I am suggesting what you would do if you were mediating a conflict between two members of your team. If it is conflict between yourself as project manager and someone else, and you want to resolve it, then you will have to break the pattern yourself by behaving differently.

Here is a simple example: I made a point in class one day and a woman in the audience exclaimed, "That's a bunch of bull!" I must admit being surprised. The normal response would have been to counterattack. Instead, I said, "Tell me why you say that."

You could almost see relief spread across her face. She expected me to hit her back. When I didn't, she said, "Well, because. . . ." We were then able to resolve the difference without further conflict. I interrupted this pattern even before it could get started.

THINKING IN SYSTEMS TERMS

The examples throughout this chapter suggest that we must abandon linear thinking if we are to understand the dynamics of human affairs in general and project teams in particular. In the next chapter, we will expand our understanding of systems thinking and introduce some tools that will demonstrate how certain actions on our part can make projects better and how some can actually make them worse.

23

CHAPTER

Understanding
Systems Thinking

For several hundred years scientists have tried to understand the world through reductionist thinking. They initially believed that you could understand a "thing" by taking it apart and studying the components individually. After all, they reasoned, a machine is the sum of its parts, and

> A house is not the same as a pile of building materials.

Newtonian physics had led them to believe that the universe was a big clockwork mechanism.

At first glance, this sounds okay, until you begin to realize that a house is not the same as a pile of building materials. Further, you cannot understand the qualities of a house by analyzing a single brick or an individual board that goes into it. The difficulty is compounded when you try to analyze more complex aggregates of parts, such as biological organisms and sophisticated machines.

WHAT IS A SYSTEM?

Often enough, even after you put all the parts of the thing together, you still don't have a system. There is no active quality to a house. It just sits there. It may be cozy, comfortable, and great to live in, but it doesn't do anything! A system, on the other hand, is active. It does do something. In fact, a system is defined as: a collection of parts that *interact with each other* to function as a whole.

The parts of a system, taken separately, are often useless. To be of value, they must be present and arranged correctly. If the arrangement and interaction of parts do not matter, then you are dealing not with a system, but with a "heap." Further, the definition of a system leads to an interesting conclusion: A system is actually *greater* than the sum of its parts. This principle, known as *synergy*, is one of the things that differentiates systems from nonsystems.

Many systems are actually subsystems of a larger construct. Thus, the earth is part of the solar system, which is part of our galaxy, which is part of the collection of galaxies known as the universe. The human body is a large system, and it in turn contains a number of subsystems. The nervous system is a subsystem of the body. So is the circulatory system.

Note that each individual is a complex system in his or her own right. Put that person with a number of other individuals, and have them work together to achieve a certain result, and you have a larger system called a team. It is true that you can study the various members of the team individually, and you can describe their personalities, motivations, neuroses, and other characteristics. However, this understanding will not tell you a great deal about how individuals will function in the team, nor will it tell you a lot about the team as a system. Notice that I am not saying you will know nothing about the team. I am just saying that understanding will be limited.

Part of the reason is that people are different in different settings. The attributes of a gear might not change when you assemble it into a clock. The attributes of human beings, however, are not so stable. I am a different person when I am teaching a seminar than when I am interacting with my family. Naturally, some characteristics are constant, but the differences make it hard to predict group behavior by observing individual behavior. Also, I am not the same in all teams. Individual attributes are very context-sensitive.

As a project manager, you have to be careful making predictions about what kind of project team you will have by looking only at individual team member qualities. As a simple example, you like working with Jane. You have found her to be reliable, hard-working, intelligent, cheerful, and resilient. You also like working with Bob. He is extremely knowledgeable about a certain technology that you intend to employ, and he has very desirable work habits. You are certain that if you put these two on your team, you will have a dynamite combination!

The only thing is, Jane and Bob can't stand the sight of each other. There is an intense jealousy that manifests itself as sniping, competitiveness, and other acts of sabotage. Individually, they may be great. They may even be great for *you* to work with. It is just that the two of them can't work together.

Again, the key to understanding systems is in that word *interact*. Jane and Bob interact with each other in a dysfunctional way. Naturally, for a team to be a good team, the members

> The key to understanding systems is in the word *interact*.

must interact in a harmonious, cooperative manner. So Jane and Bob together turn out to be a bad combination for your team.

Now consider a simple interaction that most of us experience every day. You are driving a car. This forms a simple human–machine system. As you drive along, you approach a hill that you must climb. The car begins to slow down, so you press down on the accelerator, and the car speeds up. When you have regained your original speed, you relax the pressure a bit and the car resumes a constant speed. When it reaches the top of the hill, you have to back off on the accelerator even more, or else the car will begin to speed up. This interaction between you and the car is called negative feedback.[1] It is negative because the feedback negates the change in system behavior. As the car slows down, your pressing the accelerator negates the change in speed. As the car speeds up, your letting up on the pedal negates the change in speed again. The system is diagramed in Figure 23.1.

Some drivers are able to maintain very good speed control going up and down hills. Others seem not to notice the feedback that tells them their speed is varying, so they speed up and slow down (even on level ground). When there is a lot of variation in a system, we say it is a *loose* system. Note that a self-stabilizing system does not prevent change; it just

F I G U R E 23.1

Simple Feedback System for Driving a Car

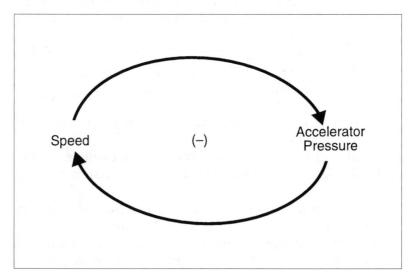

responds to change to try to minimize its effect on the system. The thermostat that turns your furnace on and off has a certain amount of looseness. The room temperature may vary by several degrees. The typical home thermostat costs only a few dollars. A system that maintained temperature within a degree would cost many times more, and probably wouldn't be worth the expense to most people. It is important to know the limits of a system.

Another characteristic of systems is reaction time. This is the amount of time it takes a signal to go around the loop. If it is too slow, the system can be damaged. An example is touching a hot surface. If you don't feel it instantly, you can be seriously burned. This is, in fact, the problem with sunburn. It takes so long for you to realize you are being burned that when you finally do, it is too late. The damage has been done. This is analogous to placing a frog in a pot of water and slowly heating it up. The frog doesn't react. He just feels warmer, until the temperature is too hot. He lets himself be boiled. If you were to drop the frog into very hot water, however, he would jump out.

Anticipation

What if you can't afford the delay of even a fast-response system? For example, it is best not to get burned in the first place, rather than to react to being burned. Systems cope with this problem by reacting to *warnings*. Avoiding a growling dog is better than taking a chance that the dog might bite. Countries that wait until they are attacked to arm themselves may never get the chance. It is more prudent to pay attention to intelligence reports that indicate imminent danger and prepare in advance. Figure 23.2 shows the difference between avoiding danger and simply responding to it.

When a system only responds to problems, rather than anticipating them, it may be too late to deal with the problem, and the system is destroyed. The lesson for managers is to anticipate problems and deal with them ahead of time,

F I G U R E 23.2

Avoiding Danger versus Simply Responding to It

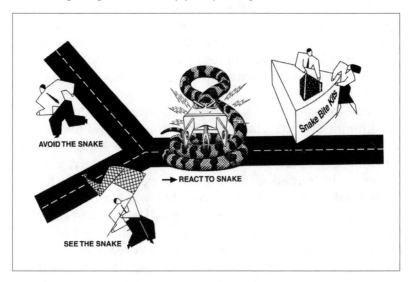

rather than simply react to them. This is the difference between reactive and proactive management. It is also called
risk management, and is covered in Chapter 17.

POSITIVE FEEDBACK

So far we have discussed systems that contain negative feedback loops. Negative feedback loops keep systems stable.
They *resist* change. We often encounter such feedback systems when we try to change organizations. The French have
a saying that can be applied to such systems: "The more
things change, the more they stay the same." In fact, it seems
that most systems employ negative feedback to protect themselves from being affected by outside influences. How then
do systems change, develop, or grow?

They contain some kind of positive feedback loop—
positive in the sense that a small perturbation introduced

into the system leads to a large system effect. Examples include the growth of compound interest, rabbit populations, knowledge, personal power, and audio systems that howl.

The audio system is diagramed in Figure 23.3. When you speak into the microphone, the sound of your voice is amplified and fed to the speakers. The microphone picks up the sound from the speakers, amplifies it, and a positive loop

F I G U R E 23.3

An Audio System That Howls

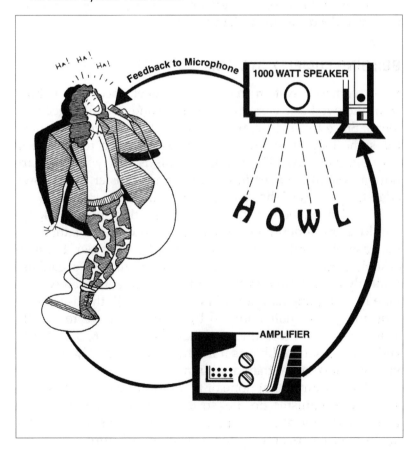

is created. You might ask why the system does not get louder and louder. There are always limits to growth. In the case of an electronic system, the amplifier can produce only so much power, so when the sound reaches that level, it can go no higher. Rabbit populations can grow only so far. They reach a point at which there is not enough food to feed all of them. They either have to move to new areas or begin to starve. Even compound interest may reach a limit. Banks can pay interest on deposits only if they can lend the money out at higher interest. So if they reach a point at which no one wants to borrow, they will no longer be able to pay interest to depositors. Of course, you would have to be a very large depositor indeed for this to happen.

BUILDING COMPLEX SYSTEMS

Every complex system that you will ever encounter is built from the two basic elements—positive and negative feedback loops. Since this is true, when you see two systems that have the same loop structure, you can expect them to behave in very similar ways. The beauty of this is that you can learn how a system behaves in one area and transfer that knowledge to systems of the same structure in other areas.

As I explained in the previous section, positive loops would grow indefinitely if something didn't limit them. In the case of rabbits, it is the food supply. Consider a similar system composed of bacteria. These single-cell organisms multiply by dividing. In the right environment, a cell will divide in about one half hour. The two cells will themselves divide in another half hour, so by then, you have four cells. This progression continues, so that you get 8, 16, 32, 64, 128, and so on. As incredible as it might seem, after only 10 hours, you will have more than a million cells!

This assumes that none of them die, of course. However, all living organisms do die, so to know how many bacteria you would have after a certain period, you must factor in the death rate. The overall system is shown in Figure 23.4.

F I G U R E 23.4

System for Bacteria Population Growth

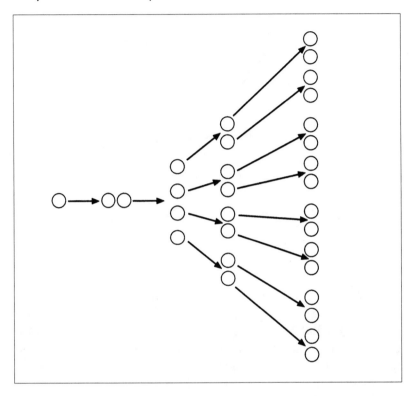

As you can see, the two loops work against each other. If 10 bacteria are "born" and 6 die, the net increase in population is 4. However, if 12 die for every 10 that are born, the population will gradually decline. The overall system behavior is determined by which loop is stronger or dominant.

This basic model can be applied to other populations. A city grows or declines in the same way that bacteria do. However, in addition to being born and dying, people move into and away from cities, so the situation is more complicated. In this case, you may have four loops, as shown in Figure 23.5.

F I G U R E 23.5

Growth of a City

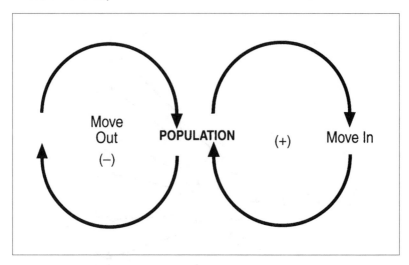

We might also ask what controls the rate at which loops operate. For example, in the case of population growth, we would ask what affects the birth and death rates. If the population is one of animals, death would be affected by the food supply, predators, and disease. For simplicity, we can begin by adding the effect of food alone, to get the diagram in Figure 23.6.

In the same way, we can add the effects of predators and disease, to arrive at the system shown in Figure 23.7.

Is this everything? Not really. For animal populations, overcrowding introduces a significant factor. (The same may be true of human populations, too.) For example, when rabbits get too crowded, they may go into shock and die at the slightest stimulus—a loud noise, the sight of an enemy, even the sight of another friendly rabbit. They literally die of fright or excitement. This means that, if the other negative loops fail to control the population, the overcrowding loop takes over.

F I G U R E 23.6

Effect of Food Supply on Death Rates

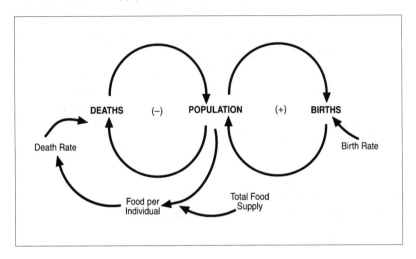

F I G U R E 23.7

Effects of Food, Predators, and Disease on Death Rates

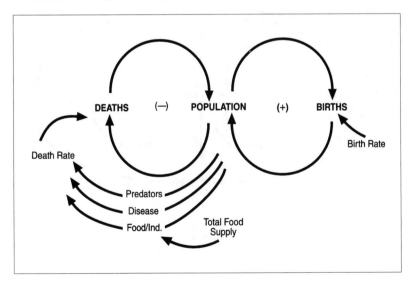

In addition, some animals use the amount of food or space to control population by moderating the actual birth rate. Considering all these factors together, we can construct a diagram like the one in Figure 23.8. In this system, the loop that will eventually stop population growth depends on the particular situation. In some cases the loops all work together to control the positive loop. Sometimes a few do the major job and others are kept in reserve in case these fail.

One problem is that people sometimes intervene in a system to eliminate a negative feedback loop that they don't like. The next thing they know, a worse one takes its place.

F I G U R E 23.8

Major Factors Affecting Animal Populations

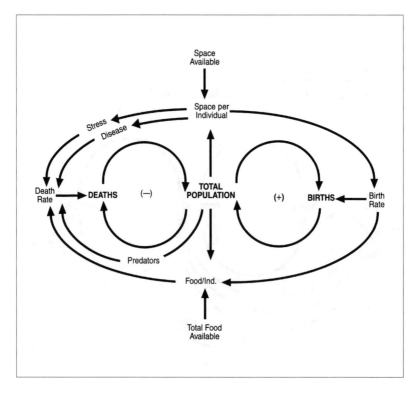

For example, if medical science eliminates disease and nothing is done to limit the birth rate, the population may grow to the point where not enough food is available. The resulting famine kills even more people. Even if the food supply is not a factor, there are other consequences. We can already see the effects of people living longer through improved health care. They may wind up in nursing homes or may suffer Alzheimer's, which would not have struck them had they died younger.

Most systems will balance themselves if left alone, and will return to the balance point if disturbed. It is important to look for the balance point in complex systems. By understanding the nature of the positive and negative feedback loops, you can also differentiate between things that are going to affect

> Any change that affects the relationship between the positive and negative loops is going to alter the long-term behavior of the system.

the system only temporarily and things that will have a lasting effect. Any change, no matter how big, that does not change the important positive or negative loops of a system will be only temporary. Conversely, any change—no matter how small—that does affect the relationship between the positive and negative loops is going to alter the long-term behavior of the system.

From a practical point of view, this says that if we want to change a complex system, we must find a way to change the relationship between the loops that keep the system balanced. Otherwise, every change we try to make will end up being "resisted" by the system, which will just return to the status quo.

That is a brief introduction to systems thinking. In the next chapter, we will look at ways to apply these ideas to projects.

N O T E S

1. Feedback here does not have the connotations associated with organizational feedback. People in organizations often talk about giving each other positive feedback (compliments) and negative feedback (criticism). Positive systems feedback is not necessarily favorable, nor is negative systems feedback necessarily unfavorable.

24
CHAPTER

How to Apply Systems Thinking in Managing Projects

In previous chapters, I showed how systems thinking can help us understand the dynamics of human interactions. Since project work is generally performed by people, it should be possible to apply systems concepts to the understanding and management of projects.

FIXES THAT FAIL

Let's begin by considering a fairly common problem in projects. The work is falling behind schedule. It seems that the only thing you can do is ask Sherry, a key member of the team, to increase her working hours each day—that is, to work a few hours of overtime to get back on track. She agrees. The first week, Sherry works 12 hours a day, and is making progress. The amount of work being done is definitely greater than what was previously accomplished. However, after a couple of weeks, you discover that Sherry is making a lot of mistakes, and these must be corrected. Furthermore, her output is down from what it was the first week. In fact, you find that the amount of work she is turning out is just about equal to what she was doing in a normal 40-hour week before! You are actually losing, because Sherry now has to spend time correcting the errors she has made, and her output drops even more.

Something must be done.

You decide that, if overtime is not the answer, then extra resources must be obtained. You convince your boss to assign a new person to help. To your amazement, the work accomplished by the two workers is barely the same as for one person working alone, and considerably more errors are being made. What is going on?

You bring this up to Sherry, who explains: "It's very simple. The guy you gave me knows nothing about what I'm doing, so I spent most of Monday getting him on board. Then I found that he's making a lot of mistakes, so I had to help correct those, and I'm still having to work overtime to take care of training him and to correct all the errors. I would be better off with no help at all!"

This is an example of *fixes that fail.* Having Sherry work overtime initially worked, until the long-term effect of fatigue kicked in. Then Sherry started making more errors, which had to be corrected, which caused her to fall further behind, which required her to work harder, which caused more fatigue and more errors, and on and on it goes. Then a helper was assigned to the project. Sherry had to train the helper, which dropped her productivity further, which caused her to work harder, which made her more fatigued. Plus the helper made errors, which had to be corrected, which made Sherry even more tired, and so on.

Another example: ABC Electronics makes components that go in products manufactured by other companies. Occasionally, a customer has a problem with one of the components, and ABC design engineers are sent to the field to see if they can correct the problem. Since they are currently working on designing new components, that work comes to a standstill. They manage to correct the problem for the customer, and return to work.

Unfortunately, the deadline for completing the current component design has not changed, but they have fallen behind. The only solution is to work hard to try to catch up. The result: They do poor-quality work, which is not caught. The new component is released. The customer again has problems with the new part. The engineers are sent to the field to correct the problem. Current work comes to a standstill. They work hard to catch up, turn out another bad design, and the cycle begins all over again.

The common expression that describes this situation is firefighting. The engineers are doing a reasonable job of firefighting, but nothing is being done to prevent future fires.

LEVELS OF UNDERSTANDING

There are numerous levels from which we can understand the world around us. Systems thinkers are concerned with four of these, as shown in Figure 24.1. At the level of *events* are things that occur on a day-to-day basis. Accidents happen, people go to work, eat lunch, perform a work task, or write a memo. In the case of our engineers, they correct a problem with a component—they put out a fire. This level is called *reactive*, because we are always reacting to the event, rather than trying to control its occurrence.

At the next level are *patterns of events*. In the case of our engineers, we begin to notice that the same pattern keeps appearing. Note that patterns become evident only over a period of time. This level is called *adaptive*, because we try to adjust to the patterns that we see developing. We give the engineers training in firefighting, so that when they have a fire, they can extinguish it quickly. This still does nothing to prevent fires.

At the *systemic structure* level we begin to ask what causes the patterns of events to occur. This level is called *cre-*

F I G U R E 24.1

Levels of Understanding

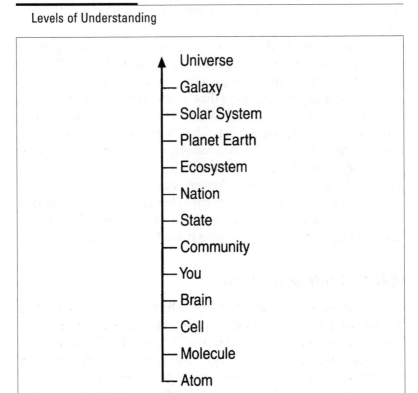

ative, because we might be able to prevent fires if we can understand the patterns. This level is future-oriented. By preventing fires, we create a different future from the one that would have occurred normally. At this level, we might decide to set up a firefighting group separate from the design engineers. This would free the engineers from any firefighting, so that they could concentrate on doing new designs really well, which over the long run should reduce the number of fires that break out.

The next tier is called the *shared-vision* level. Here we look to the structures that form patterns. This level is called *generative,* and is truly future-oriented. At this level, we ask questions like, "What is the real role of design engineers?" "How should firefighting be handled?" "What trade-offs are we willing to make between resources devoted to design and those dedicated to firefighting?"

THE TRAGEDY OF THE COMMONS

Complex systems have a lot of strengths, but they come at a price—you don't get anything for free. So complex systems create their own set of problems. One of these is called the tragedy of the commons. In medieval England and later colonial America there were commons, or common pasture areas, where all members of a community were entitled to graze their livestock. Common here means open to public use. The individual livestock owner soon begins to think, "The more cows I have, the better off I'll be, and since the grazing is free, I will increase my herd as fast as I can." This creates a positive feedback loop.

It also creates a situation that each individual is powerless to avoid. Each person tends to think the same way, so herds start growing. Soon they reach a point where the cows eat the grass faster than it can grow. Faced with nothing to eat, the animals crop the grass down to the roots, killing it, so that there is nothing at all to eat. Soon the cows are all starving and the entire village is faced with disaster.

Notice that it does no good for a single villager to voluntarily keep down the size of his herd. That just leaves more pasture for the others, who then have more incentive to add more cattle. Thus, the unselfish action will not prevent the disaster, and the person will just be poorer in the meantime, while his neighbors are prospering. The significant thing about this situation is that, if every person makes the best decision from his own point of view, everyone winds up worse off!

Enlightened self-interest would call for every villager to do what is best for the village—not himself individually. In doing so, the villager knows that he will benefit himself over the long run. Of course, it is very hard to enlighten a village. People tend to look out for number 1, never realizing that their actions will eventually destroy them. Such is the dilemma posed by many of the environmental problems we face today.

What does this have to do with project management? One of the significant aspects of project management is that we are always competing for scarce resources to get our jobs done. If we realized that our real self-interest lies in cooperation, rather than competition, our project teams would function better. Instead, we sometimes get locked into win-lose conflicts over resources—each of us wants to optimize our project "herd," with no regard for the impact on other teams. From a systems point of view, anything that I do to help my organization in one area tends to help the entire system, and conversely, anything I do to hurt it hurts everyone.

I showed in Chapter 20 how we sometimes get locked into games without end, because we set up a move-countermove interaction. Now that you understand negative feedback loops, you can see that such a system not only resists change but tends to return to the balance point if disturbed. So if you try to reduce the conflict, it just comes back after a while. Unless you can interrupt the pattern—that is, disturb the negative feedback loop—the interaction will continue, unabated, forever! (Or until both parties get tired of it.)

LIMITS TO GROWTH

In his book *The Fifth Discipline*, Peter Senge (1990) presents a number of systems archetypes that occur in organizations, groups, and even individual performance. One of these is the limits-to-growth model. This archetype is almost always found in situations where "growth bumps up against limits" (Senge, 1990, p. 96). Organizations grow for a while, then stop growing. Teams get better for a while, then stop getting better. The same happens to individuals. Attempts to im-

F I G U R E 24.2

Limits-to-Growth System Structure

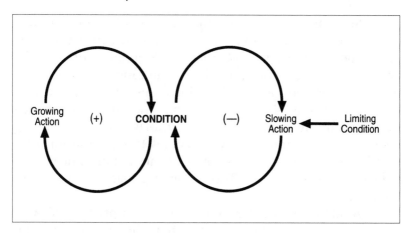

prove organizations through reengineering might succeed for a while and then reach a limit.

This model certainly applies to project teams. When trying to improve processes in project teams, we often come up against limits to the improvements we can achieve. We try to solve deadline problems by working longer hours, but, as I showed at the beginning of this chapter, the stress and fatigue begin to slow our work speed and undercut quality, thus reducing the benefit of the longer hours.

A limits-to-growth system has a structure like the one shown in Figure 24.2.

SHIFTING THE BURDEN

The shifting-the-burden pattern is prevalent throughout government and corporate organizations. There is a problem that causes symptoms that demand attention, but the underlying problem is difficult for people to address, because it is either obscure or costly to confront. So people shift the burden of the problem to other solutions. These are well intentioned, easy fixes that seem efficient. However, the fixes just deal with the symptoms and leave the underlying problem unchanged.

One example at the personal level is shifting the burden of overwork. An employee may be overworked because the department is understaffed. She tries to juggle work, family, and her ongoing education, always running from one thing to another. When the workload increases beyond her capacity, the only real solution is to limit the workload. It may mean declining a promotion or prioritizing and making choices. Instead, the employee decides to juggle faster, tries to relieve her stress with alcohol or meditation, but neither provides a real solution. The problem persists, and so does the need for drinking.

We also shift the burden in our attempts to deal with problem members of teams. Rather than dealing directly with the problem employee, we try to develop our human relations skills. Perhaps we call on the HR people to intervene. They talk to the person, coach, counsel, and maybe "write him up." However, the employee persists in his problematic behavior. The real solution is to remove him from the group (and probably the company), but no one wants to take that *hard medicine*, so the problem persists.

A systems model for shifting the burden is shown in Figure 24.3.

I hope these examples show how systems thinking can be useful to project managers. For an in-depth treatment of systems in organizations, I know of no better source than Senge's book *The Fifth Discipline* and a companion book entitled *The Fifth Discipline Fieldbook* (Senge et al., 1994). You might also want to subscribe to *The Systems Thinker Newsletter*. See the listing for Pegasus Communications in the Resources for information.

F I G U R E 24.3

Shifting-the-Burden System Structure

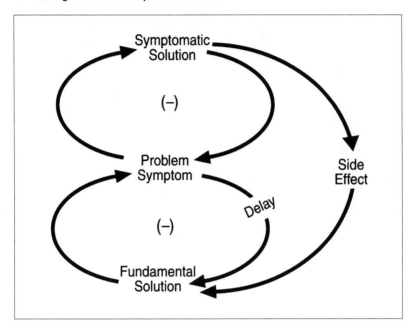

25

CHAPTER

Problem Solving
in Projects

FUNDAMENTAL CONCEPTS OF PROBLEM SOLVING

J. M. Juran (1989) defines a project as a problem scheduled
for solution. Expanding on that definition, we can view a
project as a job designed to solve a problem on a large scale.
Furthermore, the way a problem is defined affects how it is
solved, so it is important that a proper definition be established before any work is done. In addition, it is safe to say
that many small problems exist to be solved in any large project, so it is impossible to separate problem solving from project management.

Another, related issue, is that many decisions must be
made throughout the life of a project, and how these are handled can well determine whether a project is successful. For
that reason, we need to hone our skills in problem solving
and decision making if we are to be successful in managing
projects.

DECISIONS VERSUS PROBLEMS

Making a decision means trying to select the best alternative from a list that might be large or small. We often feel frustrated either because the list is so large that it is overwhelming or because only one choice seems to be available, and it is not very desirable.

A decision may be one step in solving a problem, or it may just be a choice that we must make. An example is selecting from a menu in a restaurant. It could be argued that making this choice is part of solving a problem, which is that we must eat to live. However, we usually don't call eating a problem, so we can say that our choice involves pure decision making.

On the other hand, when the decision is part of solving a problem, it is one of several steps. The first step is to define the problem; the next is to generate alternative courses of action that might be taken to solve it. Once this list is made, a

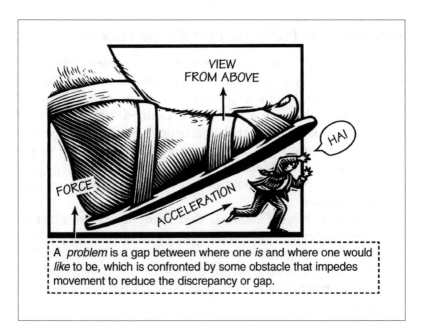

A *problem* is a gap between where one *is* and where one would *like* to be, which is confronted by some obstacle that impedes movement to reduce the discrepancy or gap.

choice from the alternatives can be made. This is the decision-making step. In other words, problem solving always involves decision making, but not the other way around.

Problems are often stated in terms of a desired goal. Lack of a desired goal is not a problem. An obstacle to attaining a desired goal constitutes a problem. Searching for ways to get around the obstacle constitutes problem solving. The proper statement of a problem is one that stimulates searching behavior.

Creativity consists in shifting our thinking from one obstacle to another that can be more easily overcome, rather than staying focused on finding a way to overcome a single obstacle.

OPEN- AND CLOSE-ENDED PROBLEMS

It turns out that there are two kinds of problems, called open-ended and close-ended (Grammatically, we should say closed-ended, but it is common in the literature to use *close* instead.) An open-ended problem is one that has no single correct answer, and that has boundaries that can be challenged. A close-ended problem, on the other hand, has a single right answer. Most

> A *close-ended* problem is one that has a unique solution.
>
> An *open-ended* problem is one that may have a number of solutions.

close-ended problems are typified by math problems or situations in which something once worked and has quit.

Our educational system teaches us to find the *one right answer* to problems presented, implying, perhaps, that most problems are close-ended. Actually, it is very likely that *most* of the problems we encounter in life are open-ended, yet our educational bias makes us reluctant to challenge the boundaries of real-world problems. One way out of this dilemma is to always insist on finding the *second right answer!*

Problems encountered in projects may involve both open- and close-ended types. For example, if the process once worked but has become dysfunctional, we are dealing with a close-ended problem, since finding the cause of the dysfunction and fixing it involves a single solution. On the other hand, if the process is functioning correctly, but is to be improved, we may engage open-ended problem solving.

Figure 25.1 should help you determine whether you are dealing with an open- or close-ended problem. Table 25.1 details the differences between close- and open-ended problems.

F I G U R E 25.1

Open- or Close-Ended Problems

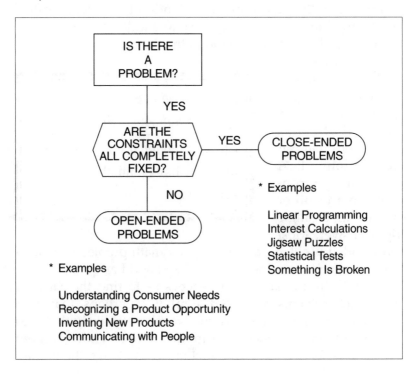

T A B L E   25.1

Differences between Open-Ended and Close-Ended Problems

Open-Ended Problems	Close-Ended Problems
Boundaries may change during problem solving.	Boundaries are fixed.
Problem solving often involves production of novel and unexpected ideas.	The process has a predictable final solution.
The process may involve creative thinking of an unpredictable kind.	The process is usually conscious, controllable, and logically reconstructible.
Solutions are often outside the bounds of logic—they can neither be proved nor disproved.	Solutions are often provable and can be shown to be logically correct.
Direct, conscious efforts at stimulation of creative process may be difficult.	Procedures are known that directly aid in problem solving.

26

CHAPTER

Solving Close-Ended Problems

USING THE SCIENTIFIC METHOD TO DEFINE PROBLEMS

Before a problem can be solved, it must be defined. This seems clear enough, yet the educational system in the United States inadvertently produces students who are *solution-minded*, rather than *problem-minded*. Throughout our schooling, we are given problems to solve, and our teachers will generally accept only one right answer.

Then, when we leave school, we find that no one gives us the definition of the problem, and in many cases there is more than one right answer. For that reason, Americans tend to have difficulty with defining problems, and sometimes make the mistake of finding the right solution to the wrong problem.

> The way a problem is defined determines its solution possibilities.

As was stated in Chapter 3, the first major step in managing a project is to define the problem to be solved by the project. Since most projects involve solving open-ended problems, the material in this chapter will be of limited usefulness at the problem definition stage. However, during implementation of the project, there will be many opportunities to apply the methods of solving close-ended problems.

The following story illustrates the importance of defining problems. I was having breakfast in a hotel one morning, and overheard two men talking at the table next to me. It soon became clear that one of them was a district sales manager for a large corporation and the other was one of his young salesmen. The sales manager was clearly unhappy with his staff, and was giving his salesman a lecture. It went like this:

"The company has spent a great deal of money developing product X," he said, "and none of you are selling it. If you guys don't get busy and start selling the product, I'm going to get myself some salesmen who can sell!"

Well, it is pretty obvious how he has defined the problem, isn't it? He has himself a group of poor salesmen. So if they don't get busy and start selling, he is going to get rid of them and get some who can sell.

Now I don't know about anyone else, but I don't think his problem is with his salespeople. After all, how can he have *all* bad ones? Doesn't it seem reasonable that he should have hired at least one good one—even by accident?

But he claims to have all bad ones.

Let's give him the benefit of the doubt for a moment and assume that he is correct, and that he has indeed hired all bad ones. Suppose he gets rid of all of them and hires new ones. What do you suppose he will have?

You bet! He'll end up with all bad ones again.

But the fact is, I suspect there is something wrong with the product, or the market has changed, or the pricing is wrong. If *none* of his salesmen can sell the product, it isn't likely to be the product. Nevertheless, he has defined the problem as people, and so the only solution open to him is to deal with the people.

This situation is more common than might be imagined: People simply make up their minds what the problem is and go about solving it, without conducting a proper problem analysis to be sure that their definition is correct. For close-ended problems, the best approach to defining the problem is to use what is commonly called the scientific method, which consists of the following steps:

- ◆ Ask questions.
- ◆ Develop a plan of inquiry.
- ◆ Formulate hypotheses.
- ◆ Gather data to test those hypotheses.
- ◆ Draw conclusions from hypothesis testing.
- ◆ Test the conclusions.

Attributes of a Good Problem Statement

A good problem statement should:

- Reflect shared values and a clear purpose.

- Mention neither causes nor remedies.

- Define problems and processes of manageable size.

- List measurable characteristics whenever possible.

- Be refined (if appropriate) as knowledge is gained.

SOLVING CLOSE-ENDED PROBLEMS WITH PROBLEM ANALYSIS

As was previously stated, close-ended problems have single solutions. Something used to work and is now broken. The remedy is to determine what has broken and repair it—a single solution. To solve close-ended problems, we use a general approach called *problem analysis.* The steps in analyzing a close-ended problem are presented in Figure 26.1.

Identification

The first step in the problem analysis process is identification. "How do I know I have a problem?" As was previously stated, a problem is a gap between a desired state and a present state—confronted by an obstacle that prevents easy closure of the gap. When a process is involved, as in monitoring progress on a project, that gap can be a *deviation* from standard performance. When the critical ratio falls outside acceptable limits, it is a signal that a potential problem exists with the task in question. This is where problem analysis begins.

When dealing with deviations, we have to know the *norm.* How is the process supposed to behave? Some project

F I G U R E 26.1

Problem Analysis Steps

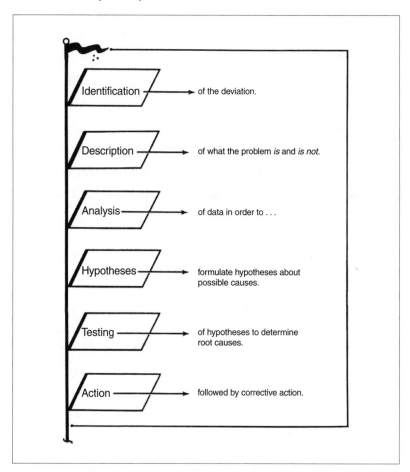

work will have a great deal more variability than others. For that reason, critical ratio limits for some tasks might be set tighter than others. Once the normal variability is known, we can determine if the deviation is significant, whether it is positive (performance is better than the norm) or negative (performance is worse than the norm).

Making Glass

Making glass is a nifty process. You melt sand to turn it into glass. Unfortunately, the process seems to be somewhat unreliable. Yields are often poor. A quality consultant went into a plant that had just achieved a yield of 85 percent. The people were ecstatic!

"How did you do it?" he asked.

"We don't know."

"Then how are you going to replicate it?" he asked.

In a more general sense, a problem is recognized because the *effects* produced are different from the normal outcomes expected in the process. Those effects might be a change in scrap level, higher or lower production, or a shift in customer purchases.

In order to correct for the deviation, we need to find its *cause*. For a desirable deviation, we must know the cause so it can be replicated. For an undesirable deviation, the cause must be remedied.

To determine the cause of the deviation, we move to the next step: *description* of the problem.

Description Using Is/Is-Not Analysis and Stratification

Stratification and is/is-not analysis are ways to localize a problem by exposing underlying patterns. This analysis is done both before collecting data (so the team will know what kinds of differences to look for) and afterward (so the team can determine which factors actually represent the root cause).

To stratify data, examine the process to see what characteristics could lead to biases in the data. For example, could different shifts account for differences in the results? Are mistakes made by new employees very different from those made by experienced individuals? Does output from one machine have fewer defects than that from another?

Begin by brainstorming a list of the characteristics that could cause differences in results. Make data collection forms that incorporate those factors, and collect the

Stra • tum: a layer.

data. Next look for patterns related to time or sequence. Then check for systematic differences between days of the week, shifts, operators, and so on.

The is/is-not matrix in Figure 26.2 is a structured form of stratification. It is based on the ideas of Charles Kepner and Benjamin Tregoe (1965).

Analysis

Once stratified data have been collected, we need to analyze the differences to set the stage for formulating hypotheses about causes of the problem. The following questions are designed to help identify differences:

- ◆ What is different, distinctive, or unique between what the problem is and what it is not?
- ◆ What is different, distinctive, or unique between where the problem is and where it is not?
- ◆ What is different, distinctive, or unique between when the problem is seen and when it is not?

These questions are structured to help us determine what has changed about the process. If nothing had changed, there would be no problem. Our search should be limited to changes within the differences identified above. The following question can help keep us focused:

- ◆ What has changed about each of these differences?

F I G U R E 26.2

The Is/Is-Not Matrix

	Is Where, when, to what extent, or regarding whom does this situation occur?	Is Not Where does this situation NOT occur, though it reasonably might have?	Therefore What might explain the pattern of occurrence and nonoccurrence?
Where The physical or geographical location of the event or situation. Where it occurs or is noticed.			
When The hour/time of day/ day of week, month/ time of year of the event or situation. Its relationship (before, during, after) other events.			
What Kind or How Much The type or category of event or situation. The extent, degree, dimensions, or duration of occurrence.			
Who What relationships do various individuals or groups have to the situation/event? To whom, by whom, near whom, etc., does this occur? (Do not use these questions to place blame.)			

Instructions: Identify the problem to be analyzed. Use this matrix to organize your knowledge and information. The answers will assist you in pinpointing the occurrence of the problem and in verifying conclusions or suspicions.

Noting the date of each change may also help us relate the start of the problem to some specific change that was made to the process.

Formulation of Hypotheses

At the heart of the scientific method is the testing of hypotheses formulated on the basis of our data collection and analysis. A hypothesis is a guess or conjecture about the cause of the problem. At this point *all* reasonable hypotheses should be listed.

One of the most commonly used tools for formulating hypotheses is the Ishikawa or cause-effect diagram (Figure 26.3). It can be used separately or in conjunction with is/is-not analysis to help formulate hypotheses. The group technique employed will usually be brainstorming.

F I G U R E 26.3

Ishikawa Diagram

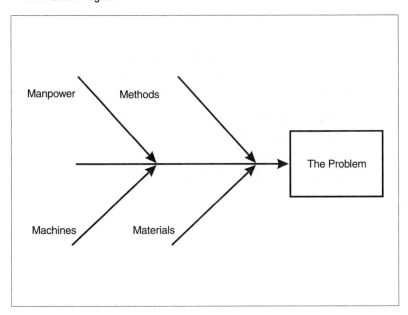

Testing of Hypotheses

To test hypotheses, we first ask if the suspected cause can explain both sides of the problem description. That is, does the cause account for both the *is* and the *is-not* effects? If it cannot explain both, it is unlikely to be a real cause.

The testing method follows:

- Test each possible cause through the description, especially the sharp contrast areas.
- Note all "only if" assumptions.

The most likely cause will be the one that best explains the description or the one with the fewest assumptions. To be certain, you must now verify the hypothesis quickly and cheaply. One test is whether you can make the effects come and go by manipulating the factor that is supposedly causing the deviation. If you can, you have probably found the root cause.

Action

At this point, there are three possible actions that might be taken. These are:

- **Interim action.** You buy time while the root cause of the problem is sought. This action is only a Band-aid™ to cover symptoms.
- **Adaptive action.** You decide to live with the problem or adapt yourself to it.
- **Corrective action.** You correct the actual cause. This is the only action that will truly solve the problem.

27

Solving Open-Ended Problems

PROBLEM SOLVING THROUGH CREATIVE ANALYSIS

In solving project problems, it may be necessary to employ creative techniques to develop definitions, ideas, and so on. In particular, the problem being solved by the project itself is likely to be open-ended, requiring different methods than those presented in Chapter 26 for defining and solving close-ended problems. For close-ended problems, the scientific approach to analyzing data can be used. For open-ended problems, however, we need different methods. The techniques presented in this chapter are intended to help problem solvers develop good definitions of open-ended problems and apply a variety of idea-generating aids to solve it.

I should mention here that Edward de Bono (1992) is considered by many to be a leading expert on creative problem solving, and his book *Serious Creativity* covers the subject in more detail than this chapter can possibly do. I heartily recommend that the interested reader consult Dr. de Bono's works.

In solving project problems, it may be necessary to employ creative techniques to develop definitions, ideas, and solutions.

C.R.E.A.T.I.V.I.T.Y

REDEFINITIONAL PROCEDURES

The procedure outlined in Table 27.1 is designed to help you develop a good definition for an open-ended problem. However, it is only one approach, and others are presented below.

THE GOAL ORIENTATION TECHNIQUE

Goal orientation is first of all an attitude and second, a technique to encourage that attitude. Open-ended problems are situations for which the boundaries are unclear, but in which there may be fairly well-defined needs and obstacles to progress.

T A B L E   27.1

Exercise to Develop a Good Problem Definition

---

1. Write down an open-ended problem which is important to you and for
    which you would like some answers that could lead to action. Take as
    long as you wish.

2. Complete the following statements about the problem you have chosen.
    Again, take your time. If you cannot think of anything to write for a par-
    ticular statement, move on to the next one.

    ◆ There is usually more than one way of looking at problems. I could
       also define this one as . . .

    ◆ . . . but the main point of the problem is . . .

    ◆ What I would really like to do is . . .

    ◆ If I could break all laws of reality (physical, social, etc.) I would try
       to solve it by . . .

    ◆ The problem, put another way, could be likened to . . .

    ◆ Another, even stranger, way of looking at it might be . . .

3. Now return to your original definition (step 1). Write down whether any
    of the redefinitions have helped you see the problem in a different way.

The goal-oriented person tries to recognize the desired
end state ("what I want") and obstacles ("what's stopping me
from getting the result I want"). To illustrate the goal-orienta-
tion technique, consider the problem outlined in Table 27.2.
Note that each redefined goal has a different target audience:
adults, kids, parents, schools. Each goal may solve a different
facet of the problem. Note that, for problems with many
causes, many solutions may be required.

THE SUCCESSIVE ABSTRACTIONS TECHNIQUE

Suppose a company that makes lawn mowers is looking for
new business ideas. The first definition of the problem is to
"develop a new lawn mower." A higher level of abstraction
is to define the problem as "develop new grass-cutting machines." An even higher level of abstraction yields "get rid of

T A B L E 27.2

Goal Orientation Technique

Original problem statement
Adult illiteracy has reached alarming proportions. Ford Motor Company
reports that it is having to train almost 25 percent of its workforce in basic
reading, writing, and arithmetic, at considerable cost.

Redefinitions
1. (How to) efficiently and effectively teach adults to read.
2. (How to) keep kids from getting through school without being able to
    read.
3. (How to) get parents to take an interest in their kids so they will learn to
    read in school.
4. (How to) eliminate the influences that cause kids to take no interest in
    school.

T A B L E 27.3

Successive Abstractions

Level	Example
Higher	Get rid of unwanted grass
Intermediate	Develop new grass-cutting machines
Lower	Develop new lawn mower

---

unwanted grass." The successive abstractions are shown in
Table 27.3.

Another definition of the problem, of course, might be
to "develop grass that grows to a height of only x inches
above the ground." Such a definition would eliminate the

need for the lawn mower and put the company in a different business.

ANALOGY AND METAPHOR PROCEDURES

One of the really interesting approaches to describing problems is through analogy and metaphor. Such definitions increase the ways of looking at a problem and thus improve the chances of finding a solution. In brainstorming and other group settings, they are actually preferable to literal statements, since they tend to be extremely effective in stimulating creative thinking. For example:

+ "How to improve the efficiency of a factory" is a down-to-earth statement.
+ "How to make a factory run as smoothly as a well-oiled machine" is an analogical redefinition.
+ "How to reduce organizational friction or viscosity" is a metaphoric definition.

WISHFUL THINKING

Many left-brained, rational people do not appreciate the value of wishful thinking. However, wishful thinking can provide a rich source of new ideas. Edward de Bono, in his work on lateral thinking (1971), talks about an "intermediate impossible"—a concept that can be used as a steppingstone between conventional thinking and realistic new insights. Wishful thinking is a great device for producing such "intermediate impossibles."

Rickards (1975) cites an example of a food technologist working on new methods of preparing artificial protein. As a fantasy, she considers the problem to be "how to build an artificial cow." Although the metaphor is wishful, it suggests that she might look closely at biological systems and perhaps look for a way of converting cellulose into protein, which is what takes place in nature.

Remember the statements from Table 27.1: "What I would really like to do is . . ." "If I could break all laws of reality, I would . . ." This too is thinking "out of the box."

NONLOGICAL STIMULI

One good way of generating ideas is through forced comparisons. Such comparisons are called nonlogical stimuli, and can be used for developing ways to solve a problem or as an aid to redefinition. The dictionary is often a companion tool in this exercise. Table 27.4 illustrates the procedure.

T A B L E 27.4

Exercise in Nonlogical Stimuli

For this exercise, you will need paper, pencil, and a dictionary

1. Write down as many uses as you can think of for a piece of chalk.
2. When you can think of no more ideas, let your eyes wander to some object in your range of vision, which has no immediate connection to a piece of chalk.
3. Try to develop new ideas stimulated by the object.
4. Now repeat steps 2 and 3 with a second randomly selected object.
5. Open the dictionary and jot down the first three nouns or verbs that you see.
6. Try to develop new ideas stimulated by these words in turn.
7. Examine your ideas produced with and without stimuli for differences in variety (flexibility) and total numbers (fluency).

BOUNDARY EXAMINATION

When a problem is defined, the statement establishes the boundaries as one sees them. If we accept that these are open to modification, then the definition is only a starting point. Unfortunately, many problem solvers tend to treat boundaries as unchangeable. One way to demonstrate that boundaries can be changed is to examine a problem statement phrase-by-phrase for hidden assumptions. The following is an example:

How to <u>improve</u> the performance of our <u>current engineering staff</u> in <u>managing projects.</u>

The underlined words can all be examined. Should we try to improve the performance of our staff, or should we perhaps appoint project managers who are separate from the engineering staff? Is it our staff who are not performing (through some innate problem), or is the system the cause of difficulty? Should the engineering staff be managing projects at all? Is it the management of projects that is the problem, or are we doing the wrong projects in the first place?

REVERSALS

Sometimes the best way to do something is to not do it. By turning a problem upside down and examining the paradox that is created, we can sometimes see new approaches. For example, if a product has a weakness, try to make it a strength. The problem with many cold remedies is that they make the patient sleepy. Why not turn that *disadvantage* into an advantage? Thus, NyQuil™ was born. It was marketed as a *nighttime* remedy that could actually help the cold-sufferer get some sleep.

A food low in nutritive value becomes a diet food. A glue that won't stick permanently becomes the selling point for Post-it™ note paper. (The idea was rejected initially. Who needs such a thing? It was a number of years before 3-M decided to market the product, and it is hard to imagine the world without Post-it paper now. In fact, in conjunction with a white marker board, Post-it paper is a great tool for project planning.)

Matrix Analysis

Matrix analysis is ideal for developing new product ideas. Suppose you wanted to investigate all possibilities for marketing training programs. You might then have a grid (matrix) that looks like Figure 27.1

> Nothing is more dangerous than an idea when it is the only one you have.
>
> —Emile Chartier

Each box (called an intersection) in the matrix represents a place to look for innovations. Thus, at the intersection "Retirees–Home Study" you might consider retirement activities that benefit from being taught in the home. At the intersection of Trainer and Computer, you might develop a computer-based training program.

F I G U R E 27.1

Matrix Analysis

	Client Groups			
Delivery Method	**Managers**	**Engineers**	**Trainers**	**Retirees**
Seminars				
Cassettes				
Videos				
Films				
Home study				
Workshops				
Computer				

Morphological Analysis

If you want to consider more than one or two variables, the matrix is not a very effective approach. Morphological analysis is probably better. As Miller (1986) says, this is a fancy title for a simple way to generate solutions to problems that have many variables. For example, to continue with our training programs, we might have to consider:

- ◆ Delivery method
- ◆ Course content
- ◆ Audience
- ◆ Location

Some of the topics that may fit into these categories are shown in Table 27.5.

T A B L E 27.5

Morphology for Product Development

Delivery Method	Content	Audience	Location
video	technical	college student	local
audio	behavioral	factory workers	foreign
workbooks	reading	managers	diff. state
films	writing	farmers	traveling
seminars	coping	housewives	same state
satellite	agriculture	school children	shipboard
computer	computer science	professionals	nationwide
mail	medical	paramedics	

Once the list is prepared, a single variable in each column is circled and the possibilities are considered. For example, suppose we circled *seminars, coping, factory workers,* and *nationwide.* The immediate ideas that come to mind are seminars designed to help workers cope with being laid off during the recession. They might need help with the feelings of frustration and self-doubt that invariably accompany such situations, as well as training in how to prepare a résumé, conduct themselves in an interview, and conduct a job search.

Attribute Listing

If you want to improve a procedure, product, or process, you might write down all the attributes or components and look for ways to improve any one or all of them.

For example, suppose you want to improve the project management process itself. It has the following attributes:

- ◆ Schedule
- ◆ Overall plan
- ◆ Project team
- ◆ Form of organization
- ◆ Control system
- ◆ Project manager

If you examine each of these attributes, you might ask how it can be improved. For example, how do you improve your scheduling methodology? Is our form of organization optimum? Is the control system functioning to keep the project on track?

Alternative Scenarios

The two primary ways of exploring possibilities for the future are hypothetical situations and alternative scenarios. With hypothetical situations, you make up something and develop a solution for it. For example: "If a certain set of conditions existed, what would I do? To which of these conditions am I most vulnerable? What can I do about those vulnerabilities?"

Alternate scenarios are more comprehensive than hypothetical situations. They are qualitatively different descriptions of plausible futures. When long-range planning is based on a single forecast of trends, there is a big risk of "betting the farm" on that single forecast. Thinking through several scenarios is less risky, and frees the problem solver to take more innovative actions.

Scenarios are developed for a particular problem. Your first task is to write a statement of the specific decision that must be made. Then, identify the major environmental forces that might influence the decision: technology, social values, economic growth, and so on. Next, build a scenario around the principal forces. Using information available to you, identify those plausible and qualitatively different possibilities for each force. Assemble the alternatives for each force into internally consistent "stories," with both a narrative and table of forces and scenarios.

Forced or Direct Association

This approach is similar to nonlogical stimuli, discussed earlier in the chapter. New ideas can be generated by putting together two concepts that seemingly have nothing in common.

For example, if we were trying to understand how to improve the performance of a work group, we might ask, "How is this group like a roller coaster?" The following list might result:

- **tracks** We stay on track, but the tracks just go up and down and around in a circle. All we seem to be doing is making ourselves sick.

- **cars** The cars are designed to keep us from falling out. Maybe we aren't taking enough risks.

- **speed** We aren't going anywhere, but we're getting there pretty fast.

- **control** The person controlling the roller coaster just started it going and went on a break. Who's in control here, anyway?

With these ideas, we might identify ways to respond to the situation.

Design Tree

Another term for design tree is "mind map." This approach has been used for many years to illustrate associations of ideas. For example, one author has a book on writing that makes use of mind maps. You begin by writing a single word—representing the issue you want to deal with—then draw a circle around it. Next you list all the ideas that come to mind, connect them to the first word with lines, and continue by examining each new word in turn for the ideas it might trigger. Figure 27.2 illustrates the approach with the word "transportation."

F I G U R E 27.2

Design Tree for Transportation

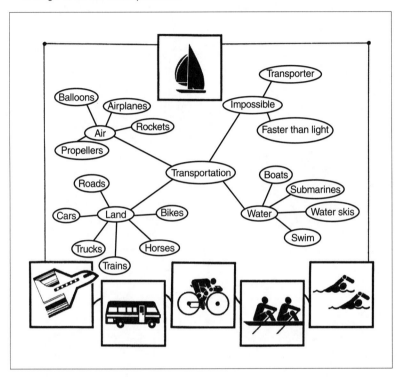

28

CHAPTER

Managing Decision Making in Project Teams

THE DILEMMA—INDIVIDUAL OR TEAM DECISION?

Every project manager occasionally must deal with the question, "When should decisions be made by the team and when by an individual?" If all decisions are made by consensus, you will spend all of your time making decisions and get very little work done. On the other hand, if you make an autonomous decision when the team should have been involved, you will spend your time regretting it. This chapter presents guidelines on when a decision should be autonomous and when it should be a consensus or team decision.

THE NATURE OF DECISIONS

Certainly there are times when consensus decision making is valid and other times when autonomous decisions should be made. The question is: When do you do which? To answer this question, you need to understand the characteristics of decisions. Potentially, every decision has two components or dimensions. One is whether there is some quantitative way in which one choice is better than another. We will call this the merit dimension.

> **de • ci • sion:** A choice made from among several alternatives.

The other is whether people affected by the decision will accept it. This is the acceptance dimension.

Of course, if you are making a decision that affects no one but yourself, then the acceptance dimension is automatically covered, since, presumably, if you make the decision, you accept it. This is clearly not the case if other people are involved.

It is possible for a decision to involve merit and/or acceptance. For example, if you are trying to choose a stock in which to invest, there is hardly any acceptance issue to deal with. The decision is almost entirely a merit issue.

> An effective decision is one that considers both merit and acceptance dimensions, when appropriate. This can be specified as:
>
> $$ED = f(M, A)$$
>
> which reads, "An effective decision is a function of merit and acceptance."

The situation changes, however, if you are picking restaurants rather than stocks. Suppose you assume that several restaurants have equally good food (merit). One restaurant is Thai, another is Chinese, and a third is American. If you want to take a group out for lunch, there are likely to be acceptance issues to deal with.

In practice, both issues affect most decisions. Someone who likes both Thai and Chinese food may very well say that the two restaurants are not really equal in quality. As a rule, she tells you, the Thai restaurant has better food. Since she likes both Thai and Chinese food, acceptance is not an issue, but merit is.

Another factor that influences how decisions are made is time. If a decision must be made in a hurry, you generally can't afford long, drawn-out group consensus. But you can't ignore the acceptance issue, either. What do you do? You might—in the case of choosing a restaurant—ask who would object to each one. The choice with the fewest objections would be the one you go to. It isn't perfect, but it might be the most satisfactory approach in this case.

DECISION-MAKING GUIDELINES

When Merit Is Most Important

One thing that should be clear at this point is that merit issues should be dealt with by those qualified to judge. If I know nothing about choosing good stocks, I had better get some expert advice. That is what financial advisers are for. Similarly, let us suppose that I am managing a project to design a nuclear reactor containment vessel. It turns out that a wide array of structural steels are available. The question is: Which one is best?

The question (a merit issue) concerns me, since a wrong choice could lead to disaster. How should this decision be made? Should I get the entire team to reach a consensus? Or should I make the decision myself, since the buck stops with me if there is a problem? Or should I delegate this choice to someone in the team who is an expert in properties of structural materials?

The answer is obvious, isn't it? An expert should make the decision. Why involve the entire team when most people know nothing about materials? What will they add to it?

Is there an acceptance issue involved? Only in the sense that the members of the team are probably concerned that the decision be a valid one, and if they know it has been made by an expert (and possibly reviewed by another expert), they are likely to be satisfied with it.

When Acceptance Is Most Important

Now consider the case in which my friends and I are trying to decide where to have a dinner party. Even though there are merit issues, this is largely an acceptance issue. The only way to maximize the probability that everyone will accept the final decision is if each person has input to it. This means a consensus.

When Merit and Acceptance Are Both Important

Finally, consider the situation in which both merit and acceptance are issues. This may, in fact, be the most typical case. Do we want a group to deal with expert issues that it knows nothing about? Certainly not. In this case, we want an expert to deal with the merit question. The expert should help people understand some of those issues and let them have input to implementation concerns. This is called the *consultative* approach.

Consider this example. A family wants to buy a new car. The wife is an automotive engineer, the husband is an artist, and the children are both boys, aged 15 and 17. Like their father, they tend to be artistic in their temperament, and what is important to them is that the car be *classy!* Their mother, on the other hand, wants to buy a car that has technical integrity, good economic performance, and serviceability, and she is much less concerned with the appearance of the car than they are.

Using the consultative approach, Mom selects several cars that she judges to be about equal, according to her technical merit criteria. The men can then choose the one that they like best, according to their artistic appearance criteria.

Of course, if they hate all of Mom's selections, then more negotiating may have to take place.

To summarize, then, here are the rules for handling group decision making:

When the issue is	The decision should be
M/A (largely merit)	Made by an expert
A/M (largely acceptance)	Made by consensus
A&M (combination of both)	Made by consultation

THE EFFECT OF TIME ON DECISION APPROACHES

If a decision must be made in a very short time, you can't afford long, drawn-out group discussions. For the M/A situation, there is no problem, as this is an autonomous decision anyway. It is the A/M and A&M cases that are the problem. For those decisions that would be normally made by consensus (A/M), the group would have to use some time-reducing strategy. Maybe people will all agree to flip a coin or draw choices from a hat or just vote, with majority rule being accepted. The same may be true for consultation (A&M), or the expert may make the choice and inform the group of the reasons for that choice.

WHAT IS CONSENSUS?

One dictionary that I consulted defines consensus as "general agreement or majority will." I don't like the "majority will" connotation, because majority vote leads to trouble when you need the full support of the group. On the other hand, "general agreement" may be taken to mean that the entire group agrees on an issue. Naturally, this is virtually impossible to achieve when the issues are tough. So why not just vote—use majority rule? After all, isn't that the democratic way?

It may be, but it has its drawbacks. In project teams, you want all members to support decisions that affect them (else there is no acceptance issue), and voting often does not achieve this result. In fact, it may have quite an opposite effect.

A school superintendent said to me once, "Now I understand why we always have problems. We regularly vote on important issues. Then I find, later in the school year, that some of my principals aren't supporting what was decided, and when I mention this, they say, 'Yes, but you remember, I didn't vote for it, either.'"

Exactly! When people don't vote *for* something, they feel no obligation to support it. Worse yet, they may continue to actively fight it, or look for opportunities to say, "I told you it was a dumb idea." Neither response is good for team camaraderie—or performance.

So if majority rule doesn't work, and it is impossible to get everyone to agree, then we're sunk. Is that it? Well, not necessarily. You just have to define consensus differently. What you want all team members to be able to say is, "While I don't entirely agree with the majority opinion, I hear you and understand your position. Furthermore, I think you've given me a fair hearing. And I can fully *support* the majority position." There is the key—the word *support*. If the person will support the majority position, that is often the best you can do.

Suppose, however, you have a team member who says, "Not only can I not agree with you, but I certainly am not willing to support you. I think it's a dumb idea." If you need this person's support, you definitely have a problem. What do you do?

There are four possibilities. One is to persuade the person that the majority position is correct. A second is to select another course of action that everyone can support. A third is to go the way the dissenter thinks is best. A fourth is to throw the person off the team. Each has a downside. Persuading the dissenter that the majority is correct may gain outward compliance without inner conviction. Or it may truly convince the person that the majority position is correct even when it is wrong. History is littered with examples of the majority being wrong. "Mob rule" is not a popular or positive term.

The second alternative is often a good one. Most of the problems that teams deal with have many possible solutions.

If a choice can be made that everyone can live with—even though it is not the one preferred by the majority—then the situation is resolved in a way that gains the support of all team members. I know the argument can be made that the majority solution is the optimum one, so why cave in and implement a less effective approach just because one person is against it? My answer is: A less-than-optimum solution that can be made to work is better than an optimum one that may never see the light of day. Clearly, there is no way to say that this is always the best approach. Every situation is different and must be handled in context.

The third option, which is to go the way of the dissenter, has merit when the dissenter is suggesting an approach that may be a paradigm shift. Any new paradigm is likely to seem strange to most people. So if the dissenter is presenting a different paradigm, it is worth considering with an open mind.

The final option, kicking the dissenter off the team, should be regarded as a last resort. If you remove too many people from your team because they resist majority opinion, no one is going to want to join up. Sometimes, however, people are assigned to a project team who simply do not fit. In that case, especially if their full support and contributions are vital to the success of the group, you may have no choice but to take them off the team. This is a soul-searching step, and one that should never be taken lightly. Instead, you must always "weigh the good of the many against the good of the one," as Spock said on Star Trek.

AVOIDING FALSE CONSENSUS AND GROUPTHINK

False Consensus

Remember the Abilene Paradox from Chapter 4? Jerry Harvey, a professor at George Washington University, told the story years ago to illustrate the false consensus effect (Harvey, 1988).

The story points out that the family drives 180 miles round-trip to Abilene for a mediocre lunch, when no one really wanted to go. They fell into the "silence-means-consent" trap.

Now for the important point. Harvey says it is tempting to see the situation as a failure to manage agreement, but *it is really a failure to manage* disagreement! If a poll had been taken on whether everyone really wanted to go, and if a climate existed in which people felt free to say no, then they would not have gone to Abilene.

> In *false consensus,* everyone agrees, because no one voices any dissent.

Note, however, that people operating in groups do not always feel free to express dissent. In some teams, a dissenter is called down for not being a *team player,* and is told "Don't *rock the boat.*" Under those conditions, people learn to be very tentative in their opinions, feeling out the group before being willing to say what they *really think.* When *everyone* is playing the same game, it becomes very difficult to find out what anyone really thinks.

Groupthink

Similar to false consensus is the phenomenon called *groupthink* by Irving Janis (Janis & Mann, 1977). This takes place when a group leader expresses a preference for a particular course of action and the group accepts it, regardless of its merits. Thomas Becket, Archbishop of Canterbury, was murdered in Canterbury Cathedral

> **group • think:** The acceptance by an entire group of a decision or course of action suggested by the leader, without questioning its merits.

on December 29, 1170, after King Henry II was heard to remark: "Who will rid me of this meddlesome priest?" Henry later claimed that it was simply a complaint, an expression of frustration—so the story goes—but those who heard him took it as something he wanted carried out. Leaders who deliberately "think out loud" are sometimes unaware of their power to manufacture consensus.

Numerous incidents of groupthink have been written about in modern times. A prime example is Admiral Kimmel's suggestion to his staff that an intelligence report on the Japanese plan to bomb Pearl Harbor was a smokescreen. By the time the bombs were falling, it was too late.

There is a standard way of dealing with groups that will reduce the probability of either false consensus or groupthink happening in a team. This procedure was originally recommended by Irving Janis and Leon Mann (Janis and Mann, 1977).

1. The leader should carefully avoid expressing a preferred course of action in the initial stages of a group's discussion.
2. The group should be asked to offer options in a brainstorming fashion—that is, with no evaluation during the idea-generation phase.
3. Once evaluation begins, *all* members should be encouraged to play the role of critical evaluator—looking at the potential risks and consequences of a particular option, no matter who offered it as a possibility. Such criticism as is offered should deal with issues, not personalities. That is, an idea should never be labeled "dumb," or any other derogatory term, since this tends to attack the person who suggested it. Rather, the person should say, "I have a concern with this option for this reason," and then state the reason.
4. An attempt should be made to reach a consensus decision, using the rule above that everyone should be willing to support the majority position even if they don't totally agree with it.

5. If time permits, a final check should be made a day later, so that people have time to "sleep on it." If concerns occur to them overnight, they should bring them back to the group to consider.

It is clear that this procedure takes a lot of time, and so is reserved for critical issues only. It should not be used for routine decisions.

SECTION SEVEN

RESOURCES AND REFERENCES

29

CHAPTER

Developing Project Managers

THE NEED FOR DEVELOPMENT

There seems to be a prevailing belief in the United States that if you are good at *doing* something, then you can manage other people doing that same work. Since 1981, when I entered the training and consulting business, I have talked to thousands of people who were put into management positions and given no training in how to manage. In fact, the same thing happened to me, and I know firsthand the fallacy of the implicit assumption.

I personally believe that this lack of skills is one of the major causes of project failure. So this chapter is intended to tell project managers what kinds of skills they need, and how to go about acquiring them.

SKILLS NEEDED BY PROJECT MANAGERS

Following is a list of the primary areas of knowledge and/or skills needed by project managers. There may be other skills specific to the job, but these are the broad-based areas. For example, if you are doing contracting, you need to know the details of how contracts work in your area and how to administer them.

Planning	Decision making
Problem solving	Conflict management
Goal setting	Data analysis
Negotiation skills	Leadership skills
Oral communications	Written communication
Interviewing	Coaching/counseling
Group dynamics	Team building
Quality function deployment	Listening skills
Total quality management	Scheduling methods
Concurrent engineering	Earned-value analysis
Time management	

WHAT IS MOST IMPORTANT?

I am frequently asked what skill is most important, and I have no hesitancy in answering, "People skills." A project manager who can't deal with people is going to have a lot of trouble. The director of a large construction group told me that he had to remove one of his project managers and put him in a job where he didn't have to work with people. The fellow knew construction. He knew how to plan. But he constantly made people angry, and the director was spending far too much of his own time smoothing ruffled feathers.

As I said in Chapter 1, people skills are placed at the bottom of the pyramid representing a project management system simply because they are the foundation that holds up everything else. Nevertheless, these are undervalued by most organizations. Every year I teach about 40 three-day seminars in planning, scheduling, and control, and only about 4 in leading, managing, and facilitating project teams. It seems that companies still see no bottom-line relevance in these "soft skills," so they won't pay for their people to attend them.

Yet I don't believe I have ever seen a project fail because the project manager didn't know how to put together a PERT schedule. I *have* seen many projects get into serious trouble because of interpersonal issues. Perhaps one of these days managers will wake up and realize that people need training in this area, simply because the skills aren't being taught in schools.

PERSONAL CHARACTERISTICS OF PROJECT MANAGERS

Over the years I have asked members of project teams what they expect of their project managers. Here are the responses I received:

Good listener	Mutual ownership
Supportive	Buffer to rest of organization
Organized	Visible leadership
Clears roadblocks	Technical knowledge
Mutual respect	Fair
Team builder	Flexible
Knows own limitations	Open-minded
Sense of humor	Delegates
Gives feedback	Honest/trustworthy
Good decision maker	Understanding
Follows up	Challenges team to do well
Shares experience	Knows strengths/weaknesses of team members

Clearly, this list is a tall order for any one individual to fill. My suggestion is that you take stock. Be aware of the need to have other members of your team support you in the areas you feel are weaker than others.

Thinking Styles

No doubt, everyone has heard about left-brain, right-brain orientations in thinking. Left-brain thinkers are more analytical, logical, and sequential in their thinking than are right-brain thinkers. These folks are more parallel thinking, intuitive, and global.

In his studies of how people think, Ned Herrmann (1995) found that the left-right dichotomy did not go far enough to explain thinking differences, and he postulated another axis based on cerebral-limbic thinking. When this dimension is added, four quadrants emerge to yield four different thinking styles.

The instrument that measures these styles is the Herrmann Brain Dominance Instrument (HBDI), and the respondent receives a profile like the one shown in Figure 29.1. In this profile, scores range from 1 (most preferred) to 3 (least preferred). There is no such thing as a 0 score, since everyone uses all four styles to some degree. Note also that the instrument measures *preferences,* not skills or abilities. Herrmann believed that the preference for a way of thinking was based on brain chemistry or genetics. Whether this is true or not, the preferences are very real. To date, more than 1 million people have taken the HBDI, and most find that the measures represent them fairly well. Seldom does anyone say, "That's just not me!"

People with strong quadrant A preferences tend to be very logical, analytical, technical, mathematical, and problem solving in orientation. They are attracted to tasks and jobs that allow them to think in these ways. Engineers, financial analysts, and others tend to cluster in this quadrant.

The B quadrant involves thinking in organizational, administrative, conservative, controlled, and planning ways.

F I G U R E   29.1

HBDI Profile of Thinking Styles

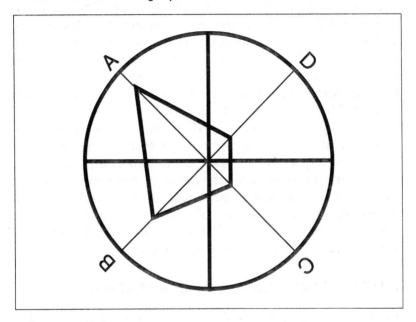

People who have a preference for this thinking style are often managers, administrative assistants, and so on.

C quadrant thinkers have an interpersonal, emotional, musical, spiritual, and talker orientation. Many of them become teachers, counselors, and other human services workers.

Finally, people who endorse the D quadrant prefer artistic, holistic, imaginative, synthesizing, and conceptualizing ways of thinking. This is clearly the quadrant for creative types—artists, sculptors, and so on. People who tend toward AB preferences see D quadrant thinkers as a bit "flaky," as not having their feet planted firmly on the ground.

Is there a *best* profile? No.

Is there a best profile for a specific job? Perhaps.

The HBDI is an excellent instrument for counseling individuals about career choices, and it is administered only under the guidance of a certified practitioner.[1] The profile is accompanied by a write-up on the meaning of the results, and is best reviewed with the practitioner by phone or in person. However, the Herrmann group stresses strongly that the HBDI was not designed as a selection instrument, and cautions against using it for that purpose unless the inventory is validated by a skilled psychometrician.

One application of the HBDI that is now well documented is its use in putting together teams. A team should collectively represent a "whole brain," meaning that if you overlay the profiles of all members of the team, they will form a composite profile that shows preferences in all four quadrants. If a team is "out of balance"—if it has a strong aversion to one of the quadrants—issues requiring thinking in that area may not be handled very well.

NONCREDIT TRAINING IN PROJECT MANAGEMENT

Many individuals, universities, and other organizations offer seminars and workshops in project management. These range from one-day to week-long sessions. The one-day programs are limited to an overview of project management, and most participants come away with only a conceptual understanding upon completion of the course. It takes at least three days to cover the fundamentals of planning, scheduling, and control in enough depth that students can apply what they have learned. Programs are best when they contain some group and individual exercises, which permit students to test their understanding of principles through application to a classroom problem. In addition, case studies are helpful for allowing group discussion and for testing the application of principles in hypothetical situations.

Many project management programs offer a certificate in project management. Following is the curriculum offered by the Lewis Institute, and it is representative of those provided by most schools. Contact the short-course or continuing-education department at your local university to find out if it offers such programs.

Project Management: Tools, Principles, Practices

This course provides the necessary skills to plan, schedule, and control projects of all kinds. Tools provided include work breakdown structures, critical path/PERT scheduling, earned-value analysis, and much more.

How to Lead, Manage, and Facilitate Project Teams

The missing area for many project managers, this program fills the gap, offering practical skills for dealing with the "people problems" that cause many projects to fail.

How to Manage Risks and Contracts

These are major sources of difficulties for project managers in all kinds of projects. This program provides guidance in how to handle all aspects of these two subject areas.

How to Communicate, Influence, and Negotiate Effectively

Project managers are universally faced with a basic problem—they have considerable responsibility and little authority. This program will enable managers to get things done even when they have no authority!

Project Simulation Workshop

This three-day workshop allows new and experienced project managers to practice their skills in a safe environment. The class is divided into four teams, each of which has to plan, schedule, and build part of a diorama. The instructors assist each team in scheduling its subproject with Microsoft Project software, and the construction phase is given over to tracking and progress reporting, so that actuals can be compared with estimates. This is the ideal way to learn by doing.

For people taking these courses over the Web, the simulation workshop is replaced with a capstone project, in which students manage a real project and submit their documentation to the instructor for review. This is, of course, the ultimate learn-by-doing approach.

FOREIGN LANGUAGE TRAINING

For project managers who are involved in international work, learning a second language may be necessary. There are basically two approaches: classroom and self-learning. Classroom programs usually involve intense "doses" of training over perhaps a one-month period. While they are effective, they are also expensive, typically costing in the thousands of dollars.

Self-learning programs rely on language tapes or records. A number of providers exist, and if you have the self-discipline, this method works. However, most programs rely on rote learning through "overlearning," as it is called, which means that you repeat, repeat, repeat, ad nauseam.

A much more effective approach was developed by Dr. Paul Pimsleur. He based his method on a principle from learning theory, which is that learning is more effective if a stimulus is presented to the learner at *unequal intervals*, rather than equal ones. Dr. Pimsleur developed his courses using this method, which he called *graduated interval recall*. As it turns out, the most effective approach is to present the stimulus in intervals of 2, 4, 8, 16, 256 time units. So, for example, if you were trying to learn how to say "potato" in German, you would be presented with the German word, which is *Kartoffel*. About two minutes later, the instructor would ask, "Do you remember how to say 'potato' in German?" You would be given a chance to respond, and regardless of whether you got it right, the native speaker would say the word *Kartoffel*, which would either verify your correct response or provide a memory jogger for you. Then about four minutes later, the same steps would be repeated. This would be done again in eight minutes, then sixteen, and again on a later tape, so that by the time you have had the stimulus word presented at least five times, in graduated intervals, it has gone from short-term memory to long-term memory. In other words, you know the word for potato now.

What this means is that the method makes learning virtually painless. You can work on the language in your car, on a plane, etc, because the instructions are given in your native language, making a book unnecessary. (In fact, a book is undesirable. A language is auditory, not visual, and it is far more effective to learn entirely through the ears than through the eyes. Once you can speak the language, reading and writing are easily mastered.) See the Pimsleur entry in the Resources.

PUTTING IT ALL TO WORK ON THE JOB

Developing one's skills and abilities is a lifelong process. The process is most effective when it is self-directed and proactive. Learning by simply behaving like a sponge is not the most effective strategy for an adult. Rather, an active, seeking-out method has been found to be the best.

There is one barrier to learning new behavioral skills: the reaction of your employees. If you start managing them differently, they are going to feel uncomfortable, because they can no longer predict you. To deal with their discomfort, they will try to pull you back into the old patterns.

In order to minimize the impact of your own subordinates on your new behavior, it helps to discuss with them the changes you want to make. This will keep them from experiencing such an abrupt change in your behavior. Ask for their support and suggest that they discuss their feelings with you when they notice new behavior on your part. One of the best ways to neutralize resistance is to talk about it!

As a method of developing your skills in project management, the following procedure will help you deal with ongoing self-development.

♦ Identify the skill(s) you wish to improve or acquire.

♦ Assess your current level of ability using the scale below—draw a *circle* around the number that represents your **present** level of skill:

Absent	Low	Moderate	High	Very High
0	1	2	3	4

♦ Decide what level you **want** the skill to be, and draw a *box* around the level on the scale above.

♦ List some of the resources available to help you improve your skills in the area identified.

♦ Engage in the learning experience you identified above.

♦ Reassess your skills to determine if the learning objective was met.

N O T E S

1. The HBDI is available on the Lewis Institute website at www.lewisinstitute.com. We are beginning a study at the institute to determine how various profiles affect performance in project management. Check our website for periodic updates on the results. If your organization would be interested in participating in the study, you can contact us at the website.

30
CHAPTER

Checklists for Managing Projects

PROJECT PLANNING

1. A problem statement has been written for the project.
2. The project mission has been communicated to all participants.
3. Risks have been identified and contingencies developed when possible.
4. Project strategy has been tested for P, C, T, S feasibility.
5. Force-field analysis is satisfactory.
6. Consequences have been analyzed and are acceptable.
7. The ultimate purpose of the project is understood by all team members.
8. At least one of the P, C, T, S variables is estimated, rather than all four being dictated.

9. Clear definition(s) of project performance requirements exist.

10. Adequate criteria exist for measuring achievement of performance targets.

11. The work breakdown structure has been developed to levels sufficient to permit estimates of cost, time, and resource requirements at desired accuracy.

12. The WBS has been reviewed with

   ♦ Client
   ♦ Contributors
   ♦ Senior management.

13. Schedule milestones have been established with planned reviews.

14. A task-level schedule has been developed against the WBS in network form.

15. The critical path has been identified.

16. The critical path allows the required end date to be met.

17. The critical path has been examined to determine if it is realistic.

18. A Gantt chart has been developed to be used as a working tool.

19. Resource allocation has been checked to ensure that no one is overloaded.

20. Resources are not allocated at more than 80% productivity.

21. Resource conflicts with other projects have been eliminated or resolved.

22. The control system has been designed.

23. Measures of progress have been established.

24. People who must implement the project plan participated in preparing it.

25. The plan is at the right level of detail (neither too much nor too little).

26. Estimates are based on recorded data for similar tasks when possible.

27. Padding of estimates has been done aboveboard.

28. Padding is acceptable to management.

29. The project plan has been reviewed in a sign-off meeting.

30. The project notebook has been signed off by all stakeholders.

31. Concerns raised in the sign-off meeting have been addressed to the satisfaction of everyone.

32. The plan contains the following:

    - Problem statement
    - Mission statement
    - Project strategy
    - Project objectives
    - QFD analysis or other means of identifying customer needs
    - SWOT analysis
    - Statement of project scope
    - List of deliverables and other contractual requirements
    - End-item specifications to be met
    - A work breakdown structure
    - Both milestone and task-level schedules
    - Resource requirements
    - Control system, including change control procedures
    - Major contributors in the form of a linear responsibility chart

- Risk analysis with contingencies
- Statements of work as required

33. Resource allocations include deductions for vacations, holidays, sick leave, and so on.

34. Cost estimates include travel and living expenses as required.

35. Costs for project security are included as appropriate.

36. Plans include time for reviews, meetings, approvals, and so on.

37. All physical facilities are expected to be available.

38. Testing facilities are adequate.

39. Steps have been taken to ensure availability of new hires as required.

40. All project team members are qualified for their work.

41. Any required training of team members has been budgeted and provided for.

42. Any political problems that could affect this project have been identified and can be handled.

43. Arrangements have been made to promote free and open communication among all members of the team.

44. Members have been collocated as necessary to facilitate communication. When physical collocation is not possible, *virtual* collocation has been arranged.

45. Vendors have been required to submit their own project plans to ensure that all deliveries can be met.

46. Boundaries have been preestablished for change control.

47. The system has provided that all project revisions be distributed to all appropriate individuals/departments/parties.

48. Chart-of-account numbers have been set up for all project work.

49. Schedules and charts of accounts are traceable to the work breakdown structure.

50. Unbudgeted project expenditures must be approved by the project manager.

51. Functional managers must inform the project manager before reassigning personnel to other jobs.

52. Critical ratios have been established to aid project monitoring.

53. A system is in place to revise the project budget both upward and downward when appropriate.

54. All team members have personal plans for conducting their part of the project work.

55. Variance limits have been established for all contributors.

56. Bonus/penalty arrangements have been applied to vendors as needed.

57. A vendor certification program is followed to ensure vendor capability.

58. Critical future events have been evaluated for project impact.

59. Resource usage has been smoothed as much as possible.

60. The initial plan does not require significant overtime to meet initial schedule dates.

61. All deliverables (schedules, reports, etc.) have been identified for each milestone.

62. Performance specs have been written and agreed upon by all stakeholders.

63. Government regulations (and others) have been identified and cited in the project plan.

64. For product design projects, representatives from manufacturing have been included on the team.

65. The *real* customer has been consulted in order to pin down requirements.

66. SWOT analysis is based on data, rather than strictly personal biases or other subjective factors.

67. Team members have been selected whose individual needs will be met through participation in the project (when possible).

68. A project termination procedure has been developed.

69. Team members have been convinced of the value of the project goals.

70. Controls are not so rigid that they stifle innovation.

71. Project planning has been based on reviews of previous records for similar programs.

72. Unique physical resources (such as test equipment) have been entered into the schedule so bottlenecks can be spotted.

73. Required resources that do not yet exist have been identified as risks to project success.

74. Roles and responsibilities of each team member have been clearly defined.

75. Procedures for doing work have been developed by participants and approved by managers.

76. No performance specifications greater than required have been asked for.

77. Tasks with durations greater than four to six weeks have been subdivided to avoid back-end loading.

78. Parallel critical paths have been eliminated when possible.

79. Network diagrams have been checked for logic violations.

80. Functional managers in matrix projects have resource-loading diagrams to support their ability to staff projects.

81. Projects that span long periods have been budgeted to account for inflation.

82. Exit criteria have been established to define completion of each project phase.

PROJECT EXECUTION

1. Meetings are scheduled on a regular basis to review progress.

2. An auditor has been assigned for all audits.

3. Estimates of progress on nonquantifiable work are checked by an independent party.

4. Estimates of work remaining are not just linear projections—unless those can be justified.

5. Causes of delays and other problems have been explained in progress reports and documented in the project notebook.

6. Impact of scope changes has been explained to stakeholders and approved.

7. Impact of unexpected resource shortages has been computed and explained.

8. All team members have been trained in earned-value analysis.

9. Meetings have been scheduled for the project team to look at improving its work processes.

10. Transfer or termination of a team member has been coordinated with his or her replacement.

11. When coordination is impossible, the predecessor has left written instructions for his or her successor.

12. Progress reports show "red flags" for situations that are expected to have serious impact on project performance.

13. Monitoring of outside vendors is periodic.

14. Progress payments to vendors are based on earned-value analysis.

15. Team reviews are facilitated by an independent party.

16. Action plans are in place to address the outcomes of team review meetings.

17. Action assignments have been made to follow up team meetings.

18. Time worked is logged daily by contributors to the project.

19. All hours worked on a project are tracked back to the project, including nonpaid overtime hours.

20. Competition is kept to a minimum within the project team.

21. When concurrent engineering or concurrent project management is applied, frequent coordination meetings are held to keep everyone informed.

22. Corrective action for off-target tasks has been developed and approved.

23. Progress reports are distributed in appropriate increments.

24. The expression "If it ain't broke, don't fix it" is repeatedly challenged.

25. There are no penalties for performance that is better than the plan.

26. A climate of open discussion and inquiry exists in the project team.

27. Team members are encouraged to provide "early warnings" about developing problems.

28. The project manager keeps *all* team members as fully informed as possible.

29. Decisions are made at the lowest possible level in the project.

30. Consensus decisions are made when appropriate, but not *every* time a decision is required.

31. A structured problem-solving approach is employed.

32. Taguchi methods are applied in design projects.

33. Functional managers are kept informed of changes that may impact them.

34. When the project is a disaster, the project manager has a current résumé ready.

35. When no contingency exists for a risky task, precautions are taken to minimize the risk.

36. Critical path activities are managed so that they complete *at least* on time, and earlier if possible.

37. Tasks with float are completed at the earliest times possible. Float is reserved to handle unforeseen problems.

38. Memos to team members require RSVP to ensure that they were received.

39. Deliverables are used as milestone measures.

40. Actual project costs compare well with planned costs.

41. Personnel problems (absenteeism, turnover, etc.) are addressed in a positive way, rather than being ignored.

42. Decisions made by the project manager are accepted without complaint.

43. Morale in the team seems to be good.

44. Change procedures are being followed.

45. The customer is involved and aware of project status.

46. Upper management is aware of project status.

SOFTWARE QUALITY

1. All next-in-line parties have been involved in planning the project to ensure that their needs will be met.

2. When appropriate, privacy, security, and audit matters have been taken into account in the design.

3. Adequate plans have been developed to ensure that the architecture of the system is correct.

4. Testing has been assigned to an independent test group for objectivity.

5. Technical standards (for design, coding, etc.) are being followed.

6. The documentation is complete, understandable, and accurate, as certified by an independent auditor.

7. Primary deliverables are of satisfactory quality.

8. Deliverables meet customer requirements, as certified by the customer.

PROJECT CHANGE PROCEDURE

1. There is a documented change procedure for the project.

2. Provision is made for handling requests for clarification and interpretation of existing documents.

3. Change requests are approved by the appropriate parties, with complete visibility by the project manager.

4. All change requests are evaluated for project impact, and stakeholders are informed of the impact before a change is approved.

5. Resources allocated to the project are changed as necessary to accommodate project changes.

6. All changes are documented and stored in the project notebook.

SOFTWARE INSTALLATION AND CONVERSION

1. Conversions are audited by an independent party to ensure quality.

2. An adequate recovery system exists in case data are lost during conversion.

3. Plans exist for maintenance of the new system.

4. Installation has been planned to have minimum impact on users.

5. New equipment and supplies required for the conversion have been identified and ordered.

6. Installation plans have been developed for new equipment.

7. A training program has been developed to ensure user capability with the new system.

8. A fall-back plan is in place in the event of conversion problems.

9. Arrangements have been made with outside service providers to ensure an on-time conversion.

WORKING CONDITIONS

1. Adequate work space has been provided for all team members.

2. Lighting, temperature control, noise level, privacy, and safety issues have been addressed.

3. Adequate storage space exists.

4. A conference facility exists for team meetings.

5. Clerical support has been provided at adequate levels.

6. Provision has been made to stock adequate supplies.

RESOURCES FOR
PROJECT MANAGERS

ASSOCIATIONS

Following is a listing of some of the professional associations that may be of interest to project managers. Contact information is provided. No endorsement is offered as to whether a source is worthwhile.

American Management Association
135 West 50th Street
New York, NY 10020
Tel: 212-586-8100

American Society for Training and Development
1630 Duke Street
Alexandria, VA 22313
Tel: 703-683-8100

Engineering Management Society of
Institute of Electrical and Electronic Engineers
345 East 47th Street
New York, NY 10017-2366
Tel: 212-705-7900

Internet
Secretariat
Internet/CRB Switzerland
Zentralstrasse 153
Zurick CH 8003 Switzerland

National Management Association
2210 Arbor Boulevard
Dayton, OH 45439-1580
Tel: 513-294-0421

Project Management Institute
Four Campus Boulevard
Newtown Square, PA 19073-3299
Tel: 610-356-4600
FAX: 610-356-4647
Internet: www.pmi.org

MAGAZINES AND JOURNALS

La Cible: Le Journal du management de projet
Association Francophone de Management de Projet
3, rue Françoise 75001 Paris
Tel: 42-36-36-37
FAX: 42-36-36-35

CrossTALK: The Journal of Defense Software Engineering
A free journal available at www.STSC.Hill.AF.Mil/

Finnish Project Management Journal
Editor-in-Chief, Associate Professor Karlos Artto
Helsinki University of Technology
P.O. Box 9500
02015 HUT, Finland
Tel: 358-9451-4751
FAX: 358-9451-3665
Internet: Karlos.Artto@hut.fi

International Journal of Project Management
Elsevier Science Ltd.
The Boulevard
Langford Lane Kidlington
Oxford OX5 1GB
Tel: 44 (0) 1865 843 010
e-mail: cdhelp@elsevier.co.uk

Project Management Journal
and PMNETwork
Project Management Institute Communications Office
323 West Main Street
Sylva, NC 28779 USA
Tel: 704-586-3715
e-mail: pmnetwork@aol.com

NEWSLETTERS

ALLPM Today!
Internet: www.ALPM.com
A free project management services vendor newsletter of
ALL project management, an Internet Project Management
resource center.

Project News
Balcombe Associates
Freepost (HR140)
Dilwyn, Herefordshire
Tel: 44 (0) 1544-388 848
FAX: 44 (0) 1544-388 400
e-mail: balcombe@pnews.kc3ltd.co.uk

Successful Project Management
Management Concepts
Internet: www.mgmtconcepts.com

WEBSITES OF INTEREST

Because the Web is growing exponentially, any listing is out of date almost before it reaches publication. These addresses should get you started, and provide links to other sites of interest. All Web addresses begin with http://www.

pmforum.org
lewisinstitute.com
pmi.org

OTHER ORGANIZATIONS

Following is a list of sources of information, books, and professional associations that may be helpful in managing projects. Not all are specifically aimed at project management, but you may find them helpful.

Air Academy Press, L.L.C.
Steve Schmidt
1155 Kelly Johnson Boulevard, Ste. 105
Colorado Springs, CO 80920
Tel: 719-531-0777 FAX: 719-531-0778
This group offers a *very practical* seminar on design of experiments, as well as training in statistical process control. The materials are first-class.

The Business Reader
P.O. Box 41268
Brecksville, OH 44141
Tel: 216-838-8653
FAX: 216-838-8104
A mail-order bookstore specializing in business books. If it's on business, the chances are it's here.

CRM Films
2215 Faraday Avenue
Carlsbad, CA 92008
Tel: 800-421-0833
A good source of films for training, including *Mining Group Gold, The Abilene Paradox,* and many others.

The Lewis Institute, Inc.
302 Chestnut Mountain Drive
Vinton, VA 24179
Tel: 540-345-7850
FAX: 540-345-7844
e-mail: jlewis@lewisinstitute.com
LII offers a certificate series in project management, together with courses for project team members. Related courses are also available.

MindWare
6142 Olson Memorial Highway
Golden Valley, MN 55422
Tel. 800-999-0398
FAX: 612-595-8852
The store for the other 90 percent of your brain, with an attractive catalog listing. A source of tools, books, and other materials to enhance learning and creativity in organizations.

Pegasus Communications
P.O. Box 943
Oxford, OH 45056-0943
Tel: 800-636-3796
FAX: 905-764-7983
Publishers of *The Systems Thinker,* a monthly newsletter, as well as videos by Russell Ackoff and Peter Senge, among others.

Pimsleur International
30 Monument Square
Concord, MA 01742
Tel: 800-658-8989
Producers of foreign language training tapes based on the
Pimsleur method.

FORMS FOR MANAGING PROJECTS

A number of forms for managing projects are available online
at www.lewisinstitute.com. These can be downloaded in pdf
format or in Word and WordPerfect format. Some spread-
sheets are also available.

G L O S S A R Y

A GLOSSARY OF PROJECT MANAGEMENT TERMS

activity   The work or effort needed to achieve a result. It consumes time and usually consumes resources.

activity description   A statement specifying what must be done to achieve a desired result.

activity-on-arrow   A network diagram showing sequence of activities, in which each activity is represented by an arrow, with a circle representing an **event** at each end.

activity-on-node   A network diagram showing sequence of activities, in which each activity is represented by a box or circle (that is, a **node**) interconnected with arrows to show precedence of work.

authority   The legitimate power given to a person in an organization to use resources to reach an objective and to exercise discipline.

backward pass calculation   Working backward through a network from the latest event to the beginning event to calculate event late times. Cf. **forward pass calculation**.

calendars   The arrangement of normal working days, together with nonworking days (holidays, vacations, etc.) and special work days (overtime periods), used to determine dates on which project work will be completed.

change order   A document that authorizes a change in some aspect of a project.

control   The practice of monitoring progress against a plan so that corrective steps can be taken when a deviation from plan occurs.

CPM   acronym for **critical path** method. A network diagraming method that shows the longest series of activities in a project, thereby determining the earliest completion time for the project.

crashing   An attempt to reduce activity or total project duration, usually by adding resources.

critical path   The longest sequential path of activities that are absolutely essential for completion of the project.

dependency   A relationship in which the next task or group of tasks cannot begin until preceding work has been completed.

deviation   Any variation from planned performance. The deviation can be in terms of schedule, cost, performance, or **scope** of work. Deviation analysis is the heart of exercising project control.

dummy activity   A zero-duration element in a network showing a logic linkage. A dummy does not consume time or resources, but simply indicates precedence.

duration   The time it takes to complete an activity.

earliest finish   The earliest time that an activity can be completed.

earliest start   The earliest time that an activity can be started.

estimate   A forecast or guess about how long an activity will take, how many resources will be required, or how much it will cost.

event   A point in time. cf. **activity.** An event is binary—either achieved or not—whereas an activity can be partially complete. An event can be the start or finish of an activity.

feedback   Information derived from observation of project activities that is used to analyze the status of the job and take corrective action if necessary.

float   A measure of how much an activity can be delayed before it begins to affect the project finish date.

forward pass calculation   Determining the **earliest start** time for each activity in a network diagram. cf. **Backward pass calculation.**

free float   The amount of time that an activity can be delayed without affecting succeeding activities.

Gantt chart   A bar chart that indicates the time required to complete each activity in a project. It is named for Henry L. Gantt, who developed a complete notational system for displaying progress with bar charts.

hammock activity   A single activity that actually represents a group of activities. It "hangs" between two events and is used to report progress on the composite that it represents. See also **activity; event.**

histogram   A vertical bar chart, typically showing **resource allocation** levels over time in a project.

i-j notation   A system of numbering each **node** in an **activity-on-arrow** network. The i-node is always the beginning of an activity, while the j-node is always the finish.

inexcusable delays   Project delays that are attributable to negligence on the part of the contractor and that may incur penalty payments.

latest finish   The latest time that an activity can be finished without extending the end date for a project.

latest start   The latest time that an activity can start without extending the end date for a project.

learning curve   The time it takes people to learn an activity well enough to achieve optimum performance. The learning curve must be factored into estimates of activity durations in order to achieve planned completion dates.

leveling   An attempt to smooth the use of resources, whether people, materials, or equipment, to avoid large peaks and valleys in their usage.

life cycle   The phases that a project goes through from concept to completion. The nature of the project changes during each phase.

matrix organization   A method of drawing people from functional departments within an organization for assignment to a project team, but without removing them from their physical location. The project manager in such a structure is said to have *dotted-line* **authority** over team members.

milestone   An event of special importance, usually representing the completion of a major phase of project work. Reviews are often scheduled at milestones.

most likely time   The most realistic time estimate for completing an activity under normal conditions.

negative float or slack   A condition in a network in which the *earliest time* for an event is actually later than its *latest time*. Also called *slack*. This happens when the project has a constrained end date, which is earlier than can be achieved, or when an activity uses up its float and is still delayed.

node   An **event** in a network.

PERT   Acronym for program evaluation and review technique. PERT makes use of network diagrams, as does **CPM**, but in addition applies statistics to activities to estimate the probabilities of completion of project work.

pessimistic time   Roughly speaking, the *worst-case* time to complete an activity. The term has a more precise meaning as defined in the **PERT** literature.

phase   A major component or segment of a project.

precedence diagram   See **activity-on-node**.

queue   Waiting time.

resource allocation   The assignment of people, equipment, facilities, or materials to a project. Unless adequate resources are provided, project work cannot be completed on schedule, and resource allocation is a significant component of project scheduling.

resource pool   A group of people who can generally do the same work, so that they can be chosen randomly for assignment to a project.

risk   The possibility that something can go wrong and interfere with the completion of project work.

scope   The magnitude of work that must be done to complete a project.

statement of work   A description of work to be performed.

subproject   A small project within a larger one.

time now   The current calendar date from which a network analysis, report, or update is being made.

time standard   The time allowed for the completion of a task.

variance   Any deviation of project work from what was planned. Variance can be around costs, time, performance, or project **scope**.

work breakdown structure   A method of subdividing work into smaller and smaller increments to permit accurate estimates of durations, resource requirements, and costs.

REFERENCES AND SUGGESTED READING

Argyris, Chris. *Overcoming Organizational Defenses: Facilitating Organizational Learning.* Boston: Allyn and Bacon, 1990.

Baker, Bruce, David Murphy, and Dalmar Fisher. *Factors Affecting Project Success.* In *Project Management Handbook,* Second Edition, Edited by David I., Cleland and William R. King, eds. New York: Van Nostrand Reinhold, 1988.

Baker, Bud, and Raj Menon. "Politics and Project Performance: The Fourth Dimension of Project Management." *PM Network,* November 1995, pp. 16–21.

Beer, Stafford. *Brain of the Firm,* Second Edition. Chichester, England: Wiley, 1981.

Bienvenu, M. J., Sr. An Interpersonal Communications Inventory. *The Journal of Communication,* 21, no. 4 (1971), pp. 381–388.

Brooks, F. P. *The Mythical Man-Month: Essays on Software Engineering.* Reading, MA: Addison-Wesley, 1975.

Buzan, Tony. *The Mind Map Book.* New York: NAL/Button, 1996.

Cartwright, Dorwin, and Alvin Zander. *Group Dynamics.* New York: Harper & Row, 1968.

Cialdini, Robert B. *Influence: The Power of Persuasion,* Revised Edition. New York: Quill, 1993.

Cleland, David. "Prudent and Reasonable Project Management." *Project Management Journal,* December 1985, pp. 90–97.

Cleland, David, and William King (Editors). *Project Management Handbook,* Second Edition. New York: Van Nostrand, 1988.

Couillard, Jean. "The Role of Project Risk in Determining Project Management Approach." *Project Management Journal,* December 1995, pp. 3–15.

Coxon, R. "How Strategy Can Make Major Projects Prosper." *Management Today.* April 1983.

de Bono, Edward. *New Think.* New York: Avon Books, 1971.

de Bono, Edward. *Serious Creativity.* New York: Harper, 1992.

Dimancescu, Dan. *The Seamless Enterprise: Making Cross-Functional Management Work.* New York: Harper, 1992.

El-Najdawi, Mohammad, and Matthew Liberatore. "Matrix Management Effectiveness: An Update for Research and Engineering Organizations." *Project Management Journal,* 28,1 (March 1997), pp. 25–31.

Farson, Richard. *Management of the Absurd: Paradoxes in Leadership.* New York: Simon & Schuster, 1996.

Fleming, Q. W. *Cost/Schedule Control Systems Criteria.* Chicago: Probus, 1988.

Fleming, Q. W., & Q. J. Fleming. *Subcontract Project Management: Progress Payments.* Chicago: Probus, 1992.

Fleming, Quentin, and Joel Koppelman. *Earned Value Project Management.* Upper Darby, PA: Project Management Institute, 1996.

Fortune, Joyce, and Geoff Peters. *Learning from Failure: The Systems Approach.* Chichester, England: John Wiley & Sons, 1995.

Gitlow, Howard, Shelly Gitlow, Alan Oppenheim, and Rosa Oppenheim. *Tools and Methods for the Improvement of Quality*. Burr Ridge, IL: Irwin, 1989.

Guinta, Lawrence R., and Nancy C. Praizler. *The QFD Book*. New York: AMACOM, 1993.

Hammond III, John S. "Better Decisions with Preference Theory." In *Harvard Business Review on Management*. New York: Harper & Row, 1975.

Harvey, Jerry. *The Abilene Paradox: And Other Meditations on Management*. San Diego: University Associates, 1988.

Herrmann, Ned. *The Creative Brain*. Lake Lure, NC: Brain Books, 1995.

Herrmann, Ned. *The Whole Brain Business Book*. New York: McGraw-Hill, 1996.

Janis, Irving, and Leon Mann. *Decision Making*. New York: The Free Press, 1977.

Juran, J. M. *Leadership for Quality*. New York: Free Press, 1989.

Juran, J. M., and Frank Gryna. *Quality Planning and Analysis*. New York: McGraw-Hill, 1980.

Kayser, Tom. *Mining Group Gold*. New York: McGraw-Hill, 1995.

Kelley, Robert, and Janet Caplan. "How Bell Labs Creates Star Performers." *Harvard Business Review*, July–August 1993, pp. 128–139.

Kepner, Charles H., and Benjamin B. Tregoe. *The Rational Manager*. Princeton, NJ: Kepner-Tregoe, Inc., 1965.

Kerzner, Harold. *In Search of Excellence in Project Management*. New York: Van Nostrand, 1998.

Kleese, Lee. *Lee Kleese Live* (Video). Chapel Hill, NC: Kleese Productions, 1996.

Koch, Richard. *The 80/20 Principle.* New York: Doubleday, 1998.

Levine, Harvey. "Risk Management for Dummies: Managing Schedule, Cost, and Technical Risk and Contingency." *PM Network,* October 1995, pp. 30–32.

Lewis, James. *Fundamentals of Project Management.* New York: AMACOM, 1993.

Lewis, James. *Mastering Project Management.* New York: McGraw-Hill, 1998.

Lewis, James. *Project Planning, Scheduling, and Control,* Revised Edition. New York: McGraw-Hill, 1995.

Lewis, James. *Team-Based Project Management.* New York: AMACOM, 1997.

Lock, Dennis, ed. *Gower Handbook of Project Management,* Second Edition. Hampshire, England: Gower, 1994.

McFarlan, Warren, and James McKenney. *Corporate Information Systems Management.* Homewood, IL: Irwin, 1983.

Meredith, Jack, and Samuel Mantel, Jr. *Project Management: A Managerial Approach.* New York: Wiley, 1985.

Might, R. J., and W.A. Fisher. "The Role of Structural Factors in Determining Project Management Success." *IEEE Transactions on Engineering Management,* EM-32: 2 (May 1985), pp. 71–77.

Miller, William C. *The Creative Edge: Fostering Innovation Where You Work.* Reading, MA: Addison-Wesley, 1986.

Mintzberg, Henry. *Mintzberg on Management.* New York: The Free Press, 1989.

Moder, Joseph J., Cecil R. Phillips, and Edward W. Davis. *Project Management with CPM, PERT, and Precedence Diagramming.* Third Edition. New York: Van Nostrand, 1983.

Murphy, David, Bruce Baker, and Dalmar Fisher. *Determinants of Project Success*. Springfield, VA: National Technical Information Services, Accession number: N-74-30392, September 15, 1974.

Nadler, Gerald, and Shozo Hibino. *Breakthrough Thinking*. Rocklin, CA: Prima Publishing & Communications, 1990.

Patterson, Marvin. *Accelerating Innovation: Improving the Processes of Product Development*. New York: Van Nostrand Reinhold, 1993.

Pinto, Jeffrey K. "Power and Politics: Managerial Implications." *PM Network*, August 1996, pp. 36–39.

Pinto, Jeffrey K. *Power and Politics in Project Management*. Upper Darby, PA: Project Management Institute, 1996.

Rickards, Tudor. *Problem Solving Through Creative Analysis*. Epping, Essex, England: Gower Press, 1975.

Saaty, Thomas L. *Decision Making for Leaders*. Pittsburgh, PA: RWS Publications, 1995.

Schmidt, Stephen, Mark Kiemele, and Ronald Berdine. *Knowledge Based Management*. Colorado Springs, CO: Air Academy Press, 1996.

Schultz, R. L., Dennis Slevin, and Jeffrey Pinto. "Strategy and Tactics in a Process Model of Project Implementation," *Interfaces*, May–June 1987, pp. 34–46.

Schuyler, John R. "Decision Analysis in Projects: Summary and Recommendations." *PM Network*, October 1995, pp. 23–28.

Senge, Peter. *The Fifth Discipline*. New York: Doubleday Currency, 1990.

Senge, Peter, Charlotte Roberts, Richard Ross, Bryan Smith, and Art Kleiner. *The Fifth Discipline Fieldbook*. New York: Doubleday Currency, 1994.

Smith, Preston, and Donald Reinertsen. *Developing Products in Half the Time.* New York: Van Nostrand Reinhold, 1995.

Thoms, Peg. "Creating a Shared Vision with a Project Team." *PM Network,* January 1997, pp. 33–35.

Trout, Jack, and Steve Rivkin. *The Power of Simplicity.* New York: McGraw-Hill, 1998.

Walpole, Ronald E. *Introduction to Statistics,* Second Edition. New York: Macmillan, 1974.

Watzlawick, Paul; Janet Beavin, and Don Jackson. *Pragmatics of Human Communication.* New York: Norton, 1967.

Weisbord, Marvin, and Sandra Janoff. *Future Search.* San Francisco: Berrett-Koehler, 1995.

Wheatley, Margaret. *Leadership and the New Science.* San Francisco: Berrett-Koehler, 1994.

Wheelwright, Steven, and Kim Clark. *Revolutionizing Product Development.* New York: The Free Press, 1992.

INDEX

ABOUT THE AUTHOR

James P. Lewis, Ph.D., is an experienced project manager, who now teaches seminars on the subject throughout the United States, England, and the Far East. His solid, no-nonsense approach is largely the result of the 15 years he spent in industry, working as an electrical engineer, engaged in the design and development of communication equipment. He held various positions, including Project Manager, Product Engineering Manager, and Chief Engineer, for Aerotron, Inc., and ITT Telecommunications, both of Raleigh, NC. He also was a Quality Manager for ITT Telecom, managing a department of 63 quality engineers, line inspectors, and test technicians.

While he was an engineering manager, he began working on a doctorate in organizational psychology, because of his conviction that a manager can succeed only by developing good interpersonal skills.

Since 1980, Dr. Lewis has trained over 20,000 supervisors and managers throughout the United States, Singapore, Malaysia, Indonesia, Thailand, India, and England. He has written articles for *Training and Development Journal, Apparel Industry Magazine,* and *Transportation and Distribution Magazine,* and is the author of *Project Planning, Scheduling and Control,* Revised Edition; *Mastering Project Management;* and *The Project Manager's Desk Reference,* published by McGraw-Hill, and *Fundamentals of Project Management, How To Build and Manage a Winning Project Team,* and *Team-Based Project Man-*

agement, published by the American Management Association. He has a B.S. in Electrical Engineering and a Ph.D. in Psychology, both from North Carolina State University in Raleigh. He is a member of several professional societies, including the Project Management Institute.

Jim is married to the former Lea Ann McDowell, and they live in Vinton, Virginia, in the Blue Ridge Mountains. Although they have no biological children, they have three exchange student daughters, Yukiko Bono of Japan, Katarina Sigerud of Sweden, and Susi Mraz of Austria.